1967

6G

ay be kept

The Range

OF

REASON

JACQUES MARITAIN

LONDON
GEOFFREY BLES
1953

Printed in Great Britain by
Lowe & Brydone (Printers) Ltd London
for Geoffrey Bles Ltd
52 Doughty Street London WC1

First published 1953

TO CHARLES JOURNET

ACKNOWLEDGMENTS

I wish to acknowledge with thanks the permission granted by the following for the use of material of mine which has appeared in English translations under their aegis:

The Commonweal for "The Ways of Faith" and "Blessed Are the Persecuted" reprinted from the issues of November 4, 1949 and October 11, 1946 respectively.

Fortune for "Christian Humanism" reprinted from the April, 1942 issue of *Fortune Magazine* by special permission of the Editors; Copyright Time Inc.

Jewish Frontier for "The Christian Teaching of the Story of the Crucifixion" reprinted from the issue of August, 1944.

Harper & Brothers for "A New Approach to God" reprinted by permission from *Our Emergent Civilization,* edited by Ruth Nanda Anschen, Harper & Brothers, New York, 1947.

Liturgical Arts Society, Inc., for "On Artistic Judgment" reprinted from the February, 1943 issue of *Liturgical Arts.*

The Modern Schoolman for "Philosophical Co-operation and Intellectual Justice" reprinted from the issue of November, 1944.

The Nation for "The Pluralist Principle in Democracy" reprinted from the issue of April, 1945 when it appeared under the title "The Foundations of Democracy," and for "A Faith to Live By" reprinted from the issue of May 17, 1947.

The Review of Metaphysics for "On Knowledge Through Connaturality" reprinted from the issue of June, 1951.

The Review of Politics for "The Meaning of Contemporary Atheism" reprinted from the July, 1949 *Review of Politics,* Notre Dame, Indiana, and for "The End of Machiavellism" reprinted from the issue of January, 1942.

Thought for "On Human Knowledge" reprinted from the issue of June, 1949.

J. M.

FOREWORD

THIS BOOK of seventeen chapters contains ten from *Raison et Raisons,* published in Paris by the Librairie Universelle de France, and some additional essays not contained in the French edition. I hope it has thus been possible to attain a more satisfactory degree of unity. I hesitated to insert the short essay which constitutes Chapter XII because it is only a first draft of some more completely developed pages in my book *Man and the State.* I have nevertheless kept it, for it seems to me to represent a logical step in the development of the views that I express in the second part of the present meditation on "The Range of Reason."

Some of the essays gathered together here were written in English, others in French. I am indebted to Mrs. Pierre Brodin who helped me in revising some of the former and in translating some of the latter. I wish to express my thanks for her cooperation and help.

J. M.

CONTENTS

PART I

HUMAN KNOWLEDGE
AND METAPHYSICS

CHAPTER ONE

ON HUMAN KNOWLEDGE

THE sorrows and hopes of our time undoubtedly stem from material causes, economic and technical factors which play an essential role in the course of human history, but even more profoundly they stem from the ideas, the drama in which the spirit is involved, the invisible forces which arise and develop in our minds and hearts. History is not a mechanical unfolding of events into the midst of which man is simply *placed* like a stranger. Human history is human in its very essence; it is the history of our own being, of that miserable flesh, subject to all the servitudes imposed by nature and by its own weakness, which is, however, inhabited and enlightened by the spirit and endowed with the dangerous privilege of freedom. Nothing is more important than the events which occur within that invisible universe which is the mind of man. And the light of that universe is knowledge. If we are concerned with the future of civilization we must be concerned primarily with a genuine understanding of what knowledge is, its value, its degrees, and how it can foster the inner unity of the human being.

I should like to discuss briefly two basic questions: the intrinsic diversity of human knowledge, and the inner value or the nature of knowledge—I mean knowledge which is rational and speculative, philosophical and scientific. Afterwards, it will be necessary to say a word about an entirely different type of knowledge, which is often neglected by the philosophers, but which plays an essential role in culture—poetic knowledge, the knowledge peculiar to the artist as such.

I. SCIENCE AND PHILOSOPHY

The first question deals with the dispute between science and philosophy. We are emerging from a positivistic period during which the science of phenomena was regarded as the only valid knowledge, the only one worthy of man. This was the upshot of a long history which began with Descartes' denial that theology could exist as a science, and continued with Kant's denial that metaphysics could exist as a science. We may say that, despite a number of remnants, or fossils, this positivistic period is over. Since the beginning of the century, philosophers like Bergson, or Whitehead, or the German phenomenologists, have set out to prove that besides scientific knowledge there is room for another field of knowledge, where philosophy, using its own instruments, is capable of grasping the innermost nature of reality, and the absolute.

On the other hand, the theorists of science and of its own particular logic—in France, especially Meyerson—have shown that the scientist, regardless of what his philosophical opinions or his prejudices and this theoretical allegiance to positivism might otherwise be, practices, in reality, if one observes not what he says but what he does, a logic which has nothing to do with the old classical positivistic framework.

Finally scientists themselves, especially since the time known as the crisis of modern physics—a crisis arising from growth—have been in a rather troubled and divided state of mind. Some cling to the idea that the only object capable of giving rise to an exact and demonstrable knowledge is that which is sense-perceivable and can be subjected to methods of experimental and mathematical analysis, and they continue to exclude philosophy or to regard it as a sort of mythology which is only fit to satisfy emotional needs. Other scientists, at the same time, led by their science itself to discover, in the *mysterious universe* of nature and man, problems which go beyond the mathematical analysis of sensory phenomena and to reject most decidedly both the mechanistic conception of the world and the prohibitions enacted by the positivistic discipline, have not hesitated to recognize the existence and the central importance of philosophical problems. I am thinking of physicists like Jeans, Eddington, Arthur Compton, Schrödinger, of mathematicians like Hermann Weyl or Gonseth, of biologists like Driesch, Vialleton, Buytendijck, Cuénot, Rémy Collin, W. R. Thompson, Lecomte du Noüy, Alberto-Carlo Blanc.

But it is not sufficient merely to get clear of the positivistic state of mind. Our intellect requires a constructive and genuinely philosophical solution. The task confronting us today is to find that solution. On the one hand, it is to be noted that Bergson, in conceiving of metaphysics as a sort of extension of science, or rather as a sort of probing into the intelligible universe of science itself, came ultimately to an irrational philosophy of pure movement. On the other hand, it can be said that most of the great contemporary physicists who turn to philosophical problems are still seeking a solution to these problems in a sort of extension or extrapolation of the very methods of their science without recognizing clearly that philosophy is concerned with an objectively distinct field of knowledge and constitutes a really autonomous discipline, possessing its own adequate means of exploring this field of knowledge. Thence arise many logical weaknesses, confusions or arbitrary assertions in the philosophical or rather philosophico-scientific investigations conducted by these inquirers. The problem before us is, therefore, to find a principle of differentiation clear enough to permit the justification of both scientific knowledge and philosophical knowledge, and to purify both at the same time by making each more perfectly conscious of *its* own truth.

The works of a school whose philosophical views are unfortunately very inadequate, but which has subjected the logic of science to a very scrupulous analysis, can help us in this quest. I allude here to the School of Vienna and to its "logical empiricism" or "logical positivism." The most important result of the works of the School of Vienna is, in my opinion, that it has shown in a decisive way that the assertions which *have meaning for the scientist* are not concerned with the substance of things, the nature or the essence of *what is,* but only with the connections that a good Dictionary or Syntax of Signs enables us to establish between the designations or symbols we elaborate, with regard to mathematically interpreted experience, from the data gathered by our senses and particularly by our instruments of observation and measurement. In this sense, science, in the modern acceptation of the word, deals only with the realm of what is sense-perceivable, that is, reached through our means of observation and measurement. And yet, because in physics, which is modern science in its purest form, all these data are translated into mathematical symbols; and because in microphysics such data escape the perception of our human sense organs; and because the world built by theoretical physics escapes all possible representation offered to our imagination, we may say, in another sense, that science goes beyond sense, and imagination. Its realm is a paradoxical realm of the supra-imaginable. For all that, it does not tend to *being* in itself, but to a symbolical meta-morphic or meta-sensory grasping of the observable and measurable. That is why I think

B

that a neologism like "empiriological" is the most appropriate word to designate this kind of knowledge.

A scientific definition does not tell us *what a thing is*, but only in what way we can agree on the observations and measurements we have taken from nature, so as to get a knowledge, not of the essence of that thing, but merely of the manner in which the signs which refer to its impact on experience and to the modes of verification grouped under its name, can give rise to a coherent language. If I say "matter," to the physicist this word does not denote a substance or a substantial principle whose nature he tried to reveal to us. It merely denotes a system of mathematical symbols built by microphysics upon an immense body of data of observation and measurement, which are furthermore subject to continual revision.

Let us note that it follows that a statement such as *I am*, or, *I love my country*, or, *Plato was a great philosopher*, or questions like *Is man endowed with free will?* or, *Does our intellect attain reality?* or, *Does the human being possess rights?* have no meaning for the scientist, because, to have a scientific meaning, a statement must express a stable relationship between designations which can ultimately be reduced to a certain class of sensory perceptions, and the terms contained in those statements are not such designations.

The crucial error of the School of Vienna has been to assume as self-evident that whatever has no meaning *for the scientist* has no meaning *at all*. In this respect logical positivism remains under the yoke of positivistic prejudices. But, as to science itself and its logical structure, and what has a meaning for the scientist *as such*, the analysis of the School of Vienna is, I believe, generally accurate and well-founded.

We are thus rid, at one stroke, of many forms of pseudometaphysics—materialism, mechanism, psychophysical parallelism, universal determinism—which were parasites of science while claiming to be part of it. The rigorous logical purification that the theorists of the School of Vienna impose upon our concept of science makes us aware of the noetic ideal to which science tends, and at the same time of the well-defined field in which science works and which is *not* that of the knowledge of being.

But is it possible that this other field of knowledge, the field of the knowledge of being, is beyond the reach of the human intellect and under no circumstances has any meaning for it? Is not the idea of *being* the matrix of all our ideas, the first and universal instrument of intelligence, so that even for strictly *deontologized* knowledge, such as scientific knowledge in its pure form, the signs and symbols it elaborates can only be grasped and manipulated by the intellect in the form of second-hand entities or second-hand beings —*entia rationis*—that scientific knowledge itself creates?

On the other hand—and this is what the School of Vienna does not see and what Meyerson saw admirably—science itself, even when it sets out to eliminate from its own structure the consideration of being and essences, is quickened by an unsatiated desire, by a thirst to attain the real and by an admirable eagerness always to be commanded by it. This happens in such a way that the inner being of things, situated outside of science's own sphere, remains for science a great and fertile unknown from which science draws the observations and measurements that it accumulates endlessly, and on which it bases the signs and symbols which serve to weave between these observations and measurements a coherent fabric of deductions, and thus to master nature.

Moreover, the reflective philosophy of the logicians of science, which deals with the work of knowledge achieved by our minds, disproves by its very existence the theory which claims that the meaning of a judgment, its intelligible content, never presents the mind with anything but the experimental procedures, the ways and means of observation and measurement by which that judgment is verified. While this theory holds true for the judgments of science, the judgments made by the *philosophy of science,* on the contrary, do not furnish the intelligence with the procedures of observation and measurement by which they are verified; they tell the mind *what* the nature of science *is* and *what* the ways of knowing *are.*

Finally, it is not possible that the intellect, which reflectively knows and judges itself as well as the nature of science, is unable to enter by its own power into the workings of knowledge, that is, *to see into* the nature of things. The intellect cannot be condemned always to remain *outside* of those workings, in the capacity of a mere witness and regulator of the senses, as occurs in the science of phenomena. There must be a science, a knowledge, where the intellect, with the exigencies peculiar to it, may engage *in the inside task, within* the workings of knowledge, and where it may develop freely its most profound aspirations, the aspirations of the intellect as intellect. Such a knowledge directly concerns the being of things intelligibly grasped, it is philosophical and metaphysical knowledge.

Thus we know how the correct division should be made between the scope of science and that of philosophy, and thus we have the

principle of differentiation that we were seeking. It is necessary to
recognize two essentially distinct ways of analyzing the world of
sense-perceivable reality and of building the concepts required for
this. The first way is by a *non-ontological* analysis, an "*empiriological*" analysis of the real. This is the scope of scientific knowledge. The second way is by an *ontological* analysis of the real. This
is the scope of philosophical knowledge. Let us say it is the scope
of that science which is also wisdom, for, in the last analysis, sapien-
tial knowledge, the knowledge that is wisdom, is that which in one
way or another reveals to us the very being of things. Wisdom is a
savory knowledge; phenomena have no savor, but being is for the
intellect a fruit whose taste captivates it. Science resolves its concepts and its definitions in the observable and the measurable as
such. Philosophy resolves its concepts and its definitions in the intelligible being.

This solution of the dispute between science and philosophy assumes that in order to master becoming and the flux of phenomena,
science works, so to speak, against the grain of the natural tendencies of the intellect, and uses, as its own instruments, explanatory
symbols which are ideal entities (*entia rationis*) *founded on reality,*
above all mathematical entities built on the observations and measurements collected by the senses. On this condition, the human mind
can scientifically dominate becoming and sense-perceivable phenomena, but, at the same time, it gives up any hope of grasping
the inner being of things.

And this same solution assumes that philosophy has its own instruments of intelligible perception and judgment which are provided by the abstractive intuition that is a property of the intellect.
If positivism, old and new, and Kantianism do not understand that
metaphysics and philosophy are authentically *sciences,* that is to
say, fields of knowledge capable of certitude which is demonstrable,
universal and necessary, it is because they do not understand that
the intellect *sees.* (For instance, the intellect sees the primary principles—principles of identity, of non-contradiction, of causality, etc.,
because the intellect brings out from sense experience intelligible
contents—first of all that intelligible object, Being—which exist in
things but are not perceived by the senses.) In the eyes of the
Kantians and Positivists, the senses alone are intuitive, the intellect
serving only to connect and to unify.

Therefore, they would do better to keep silent, for we cannot say
"I," or pronounce a noun in any language, without manifesting

that there are in things objects or centers of visibility, which our senses do not reach but which our intellect does reach. Doubtless, we do not have any *angelic* intellectual intuition, in the sense of Plato or Descartes—I mean intuition which does not require the instrumentality of the senses. Doubtless, there is nothing in the intellect which is not originally derived from sensory experience. But it is precisely the activity of the intellect which extricates from sense experience—and raises to the white heat of immaterial visibility *in actu*—objects which the senses cannot uncover in things and which the intellect sees: being and its properties, and the essential structures and the intelligible principles seizable in the light of being. That is the mystery of abstractive intuition. And in those objects that it sees, the intellect knows, without seeing them directly, the transcendental objects which are not contained in the world of sensory experience. That is the mystery of analogical intellection. The problem of metaphysics is thus reduced, in the last analysis, to the problem of intuitive abstraction and to the question whether, at the peak of abstraction, being itself, insofar as it is being— being which penetrates and imbues the world of sensory experience, but which also extends beyond this world in all directions—is or is not the object of such an intuition. It is this intuition which makes the metaphysician.

The tragedy of the philosophers who call themselves existentialists, whether they be Christian existentialists like Gabriel Marcel, or atheistic existentialists like the French disciples of Husserl and Heidegger, lies in their having the feeling or apperception of the primacy of being, or existence, while at the same time denying, under the pretext that it is abstract, that the notion of being has any value: so that they see in it only an empty word. If I, on the other hand, am a Thomist, it is in the last analysis because I have understood that the intellect sees, and that it is cut out to conquer being. In its most perfect function, which is not to manufacture ideas, but to judge, the intellect seizes upon existence exercised by things. And at the same time it forms the first of its concepts—the concept of being, which metaphysics will bring out, in its own light, at the highest degree of abstractive visualization.

Now, consequently, we can understand how the various typical categories of knowledge, distributed over different levels of intelligibility, are distinct from one another—inter-related, but essentially distinct. We can understand how the science of the phenomena of nature—with its "empiriological" analysis of the real—then mathematics, then the philosophy of nature, and finally metaphysics, constitute the natural degrees of speculative knowledge. These various disciplines of knowledge cannot be substituted for one another, nor can they compete with one another because they do not fish in the same waters, but apply their various insights to different objective fields; physics, chemistry, biology can progress indefinitely, each on its own level, in their knowledge of the human being, for example, without ever encountering the questions and answers peculiar to the philosophical knowledge of this same human being, which lie on a different level. If a biologist is led to ask these questions while reflecting about his science, he is then no longer just a biologist, but a philosopher as well, and he will have to resort to the tools of philosophy to answer them properly. We can advance endlessly in our knowledge of ocular apparatus and the nerve centers of vision, but the question, "What is sensation?," will always depend upon another order of knowledge. We can advance endlessly in our knowledge of the chemical constitution or the physiology of the human being, or even his psychology empirically considered and interpreted, but the question, "Has man a spiritual soul?," will always depend upon another order of knowledge.

In the last analysis, this consideration of the specific diversity and the organic hierarchy of the degrees of knowledge enables us to understand how science and wisdom can be reconciled, and how, because wisdom creates order in knowledge, man can regain his unity in a living peace of his intelligence which is one of the blessings that he most lacks today and to which he aspires most desperately often without even knowing it.

But in order to understand all these things, it is first necessary to put an end to the great error that Descartes introduced into modern thought with his theory of the essential and specific *unity* of science. No, human knowledge is not endowed with essential and perfect unity; human knowledge is not a single diamond radiating the unity of the spirit. It has unity only as an ensemble of typically differentiated parts. God's science, creative science, is perfectly one, because it is identical with the divine intellect and essence itself. But human science is an effect distinct from the mind from which it emanates, and it is a mendicant knowledge, depending upon things about which it is forced to take specifically diverse views, owing to specifically diverse intellectual virtues, which extricate from sensory experience an intelligible content with specifically diverse powers of abstraction.

In the history of human knowledge we see now one, now another of these intellectual virtues, now one, now another, of these types of knowledge, trying, with a sort of imperialism, to seize, at the expense of the others, the whole universe of knowledge. Thus, at the time of Plato and Aristotle, there was a period of philosophical and metaphysical imperialism; in the Middle Ages, at least before St. Thomas Aquinas, a period of theological imperialism; since Descartes, Kant and August Comte, a period of scientific imperialism which has progressively lowered the level of reason while at the same time securing a splendid technical domination of material nature.

It would be a great conquest if the human mind could end these attempts at spiritual imperialism which bring in their wake no less serious damage, to be sure, than that which results from political imperialism; it would be a great achievement if the human mind could establish on unshakable foundations the freedom and autonomy as well as the vital harmony and the mutual strengthening of the great disciplines of knowledge through which the intellect of man strives indefatigably toward truth.

II. THE VALUE OF KNOWLEDGE

Thus we come to the second part of this discussion, for Descartes' error concerning the absolute unity of human science is essentially linked to his idealistic conception of knowledge. Idealism or realism —that is the great dispute confronting us when we examine the nature and inner value of knowledge. I believe that the ancients —I mean especially Plato and Aristotle, then St. Thomas Aquinas and his great commentators of the sixteenth and seventeenth centuries—had more profound views on the subject than the moderns, although they did not think of formulating separately a special critical treatise on knowledge. It is these views of the ancients that I should like to summarize briefly.

Their primary concern was to keep intact the nature of knowledge, which is the highest mystery that philosophy can contemplate, without reducing it—as we are tempted to do at every moment—to one of the usual comparisons, borrowed from our vision of bodies, which lie dormant in our imagination. That is why they warn us,

when they discuss knowledge, to elevate our spirits to a higher
plane.

For St. Thomas, knowing consists neither in receiving an impression nor in producing an image; it is something much more intimate
and much more profound. To know is to *become;* to become the
non-I. Does this therefore mean to lose one's being and to be absorbed in things? That would perhaps be Bergsonian intuition
pushed to extremes. That is certainly not Thomistic intellection.
Furthermore, no type of material union or transformation can attain to the degree of union which exists between the knower and
the known. If I lost my being in something else, in order to be
united with it, I would not *become* that other being; it and I
together would make a composite, a *tertium quid,* instead of the
knower's becoming the known itself. The union of the knower and
the known is thus a true and genuine unity; they are *more one*
than matter and form joined together.

But to posit such a "transubstantiation" between two entities
which nevertheless retain their own being—for I remain what I
am and the thing remains what it is while I know it—amounts to
saying that the process involves an immaterial becoming, an immaterial identification, and that knowledge is a dependent variable
of immateriality. To know, therefore, consists of immaterially becoming another, insofar as it is another, *aliud in quantum aliud.*

Thus, from the outset, Thomas Aquinas makes knowledge *absolutely dependent* upon what is. To know, in fact, is essentially to
know *something,* and something which, as specifier of my act of
knowing, is not produced by my knowledge, but on the contrary
measures it and governs it, and thus possesses its own being, independent of my knowledge; for it would be absurd for the measuring
device as such to be dependent upon the thing measured. Far from
its being true that the object of knowledge is, as Kant put it, a
product manufactured by thought, and something other than *what
is,* it must, by its very nature of known object, be that which a thing
is—a thing other than myself and my subjective activity, a thing
precisely taken in its otherness, in what it has of itself and not of
me. The entire specification of my act of intelligence comes, therefore, from the object *as something other,* as free from me. In
knowing, I subordinate myself to a being independent of me; I
am conquered, convinced and subjugated by it. And the truth of
my mind lies in its conformity to *what is* outside of it and independent of it.

That is the fundamental realism and objectivism of Thomistic philosophy. St. Thomas teaches, moreover, that while the subjective inclinations of the appetite play an essential part in the practical knowledge which governs our behavior, and while they can also intervene, either for good or evil, in our speculative knowledge, the latter, when it attains its natural perfection—that is, when it becomes *science,* and provides us with unshakable rational truths— is in itself absolutely pure and independent of all consideration of what is good and advantageous for the human subject (or the State, or the nation, or the social class or the spiritual family to which it belongs); speculative knowledge is absolutely pure and independent of all contact with the preferences, proprieties and accommodations of feeling or action; here the object alone is master; and whatever conclusion is drawn, the intellect would be ashamed even to ask itself whether this conclusion pains or pleases it. The intellect contemplates the object; it is fixed on it; does it know indeed that the *I* exists and asks for something? If, despite more than a century of sentimentalism, we still have some idea of the adamantine objectivity of science, we owe it to the old Scholastic discipline.

But, for St. Thomas, science is not only the "empiriological" analysis of sensory detail, or even mathematics, which is on a level with us. It is above all metaphysics, which compels us to raise our heads. For if our intellect, insofar as it is human, has as its proportioned or "connatural" object the nature of sense-perceivable things, it tends, however, insofar as it is intellect, to the entire being and to the Supreme Being, and it rises, by the process of analogy, to a veritable science of spiritual realities and of God, known doubtless not through His essence, such as He is in Himself—known only through the effects of His causality, in the mirror of creatures, and in a piecemeal way, but known with certainty and truth.

Now here is the point which it is important to note carefully. If the Thomistic philosophy, while it leads us in this way to the conquest of the intelligible being, makes our knowledge dependent upon the thing known insofar as it is another, and subordinates our knowledge absolutely to the extra-mental being; if it thus requires our intellect to be, in a certain sense, *passive* with regard to the thing, nevertheless at the same time it states that to know is something essentially *active,* vital and spontaneous.

The passivity of our intelligence with respect to the thing fulfills a condition that is human, and it is a necessary condition; it is

necessary for us to receive from the object, in order to be specified
by it. But though it is thus passive in its cause, intellection, by its
very nature, proceeds like pure spontaneity—I mean *vital* or immanent activity, not transitive, and spontaneous because it is vital.
For I have said that to know is essentially to *become immaterially
the other;* and this immaterial bursting open of the intellectual
faculty in *the other* is something so purely immanent that it does
not even consist of the production of a fruit dwelling within it;
it is a purely qualitative consummation of the intellectual faculty
which perfects itself by causing itself to be the object. A concept
is, in fact, produced in the knowing intellect, but that is a (necessary) means, and not the very essence of intellection; the same act
of intellection which in its productive capacity winds up in the
concept, a thing produced within us, in its *knowing* capacity winds
up in the intelligible nature itself, which is seen intuitively in the
concept, and with which the intellect is immediately identified.

Hence, one understands how, in the act of intellection, de-
pendency with respect to the object is reconciled with active spontaneity, how in this act all the vitality comes from the faculty or
the subject, all the specification comes from the object, so that the
intellection proceeds entirely from the intellect and entirely from
the object, because, at the instant when it knows, the intellect is,
immaterially, the object itself; *the knower in the act of knowing
is the known itself in the act of being known;* before knowing, our
intellect is like a formless vitality, waiting to be shaped; as soon
as it has received from the senses, by means of its own abstractive
power, the intelligible impression of the object, the intellect becomes that object, while carrying it, through the concept it produces of it, to the ultimate degree of formation and intelligible
actuality, in order at the same time to raise to the supreme point
its own immaterial identification with the object.

Thus St. Thomas collected in advance all the truth that modern
idealism was to touch upon concerning the *activity* and the *spontaneity* of the spirit in knowledge. While Kant only affirmed activity
by ruining objectivity because he had in mind only a productive
activity, Thomism, because it aims at a truly immanent and truly
vital activity, makes the objectivity of knowledge the reason for
and the end of activity. Our intelligence lives by becoming all
things; and it is in order thus to exercise its perfect spontaneity—
as perfect as is possible in its human and created state—that it

entirely submits to being, asking to be fecundated by being so as to conceive fruits of truth.

Thomism also collects all the truth that modern idealism has been able to touch upon concerning the interiority of knowledge. For Descartes saw very well that our mind—and therein lies its greatness—reaches its object within itself, in a perfect interiority. But St. Thomas saw this better than he. According to the Thomistic theory, the intellect, in order to grasp its object, transfers it within itself, so that this object bathes in the intellect's own immaterial light; unlike the senses, which grasp the thing insofar as it is acting concretely outside of the mind, the intellect knows the thing insofar as it exists within the intellect, inside of it. Yet Descartes, with a great naïveté, and because he devoted only a few hours a year to metaphysics, believed that, as a result, our mind immediately grasps only its own ideas (which thus become things). On the contrary, the Thomists have seen that what the intellect thus grasps within itself is not its idea, but the thing itself by means of the idea, the thing stripped of its own existence and conveyed within the intellect, transferred into the intellect's own immateriality.

That is how the study and probing of the nature of knowledge show us its objective value and its essentially realistic character. If in man this basic realism of knowledge is subjected to many restrictions, if, as we have seen in the first part of this discussion, the knowledge which best succeeds in mastering nature and the detail of sense-perceivable phenomena—that is, science, in the modern sense of the word—is obliged, in order thus to succeed, to abandon the conquest of the very being of things, and to resort to symbols, to entities constructed by the mind, to a sort of mathematical idealization of observed and measured reality, it remains nevertheless that in its deepest dynamism knowledge tends to forms of knowing which, however imperfect they may be, grasp being itself, and which therefore are wisdom as well as science.

Knowledge! Wisdom! These words have fascinated man since the origin of the species. The great deviation that appeared in primitive times and which threatens to reappear in turbulent moments of our history is the confusion or identification of Knowledge with Power. That is the magic conception of wisdom or science. One of the barbaric traits of Germanic imperialism has been the revival of this confusion of Science with Power. We find the same confusion in Marxism. I wonder whether, to a lesser degree, all the modern world is not infected by it. There is, no doubt, a practical knowledge which tends toward action—not toward power—and the aim of which is either to create a well-constructed work, as in the case of art, or to accomplish good actions, as in the case of moral knowledge and the virtue of prudence. But, by its very nature, knowledge does not tend toward power, nor even toward action; it tends toward truth. And at all the degrees of knowledge, from the lowest to the highest, it is truth that liberates. The only authentic civilization is one where man has released the idea of knowledge in its objective purity, and kept and developed within himself the sense of truth. If civilization, which is profoundly shaken today, is to be reborn, one of the basic conditions for this rebirth must be, in the realm of human communications, that the function of language, which has been perverted by the procedures of the totalitarian states, be returned to its true nature, and, in the realm of the inner life of the spirit, that knowledge likewise be returned to its true nature; knowledge must cease being ordained to power or being confused with it; the intellect must recognize, at all degrees of the scale of knowing—whether we consider the most simple factual truths of daily experience, or truths by which science formulates, in terms of observation, the laws of phenomena, or truths by which philosophy grasps, in terms of intelligible perception, the structures of being and the universal principles of existence—the intellect must recognize in the whole expanse and diversity of its domain the *sacred* nature of truth.

III.   POETIC KNOWLEDGE

The preceding analyses were concerned with the knowledge of speculative reason, the knowledge peculiar to the philosopher and the scientist.

But we would have only a very incomplete picture of human knowledge if we did not take into account another type of knowledge, entirely different, which is not acquired through concepts and reasoning, but through *inclination,* as St. Thomas says, or through sympathy, congeniality or connaturality.

Such is the moral knowledge of the virtuous man, who may not know theoretically what justice or honor is, but who has these virtues in himself, and who has only to consult his own inner bent to know whether an act is or is not unjust and dishonorable.

Such is the mystical knowledge of the contemplative, who may never have learned philosophy or theology, but who lives divine things and who knows them by virtue of his love-union with God.

Such is finally the poetic knowledge of the artist, who may not know theoretically either psychology or sociology, cosmology, ethics or anything at all, but who, in order to reveal to himself his most secret being in a work that he produces, is given in his creative intuition or emotion, through the impact he receives from reality in the unconscious life of the spirit and the depths of subjectivity, a non-conceptual knowledge of the things of the world and their secrets.

I shall not discuss the problems which are related to this type of knowledge; I should simply like to note that the way in which art and poetry have become aware of themselves and of the knowledge which is peculiar to them—*poetic* knowledge—appears to me to be a great conquest of modern times; this movement of particularly intent reflective awareness began, I believe, with the German romanticists and Baudelaire.

The essential points to be made concerning poetic knowledge can, I believe, be expressed as follows:

The activity of art is not in itself an activity of knowledge, but of creation; art aspires to creating an object in accordance with that object's inner needs and its own good.

It is true that artistic activity presupposes and collects much previous knowledge; it requires, moreover, either a contemplative frame of mind, like that which the great Chinese painters stressed so much, or a kind of ceaseless rumination of everything that comes to the soul through the senses—in short, a spiritual awakening of the senses. But this amount of knowledge (in the ordinary sense of the word) is prior to the art activity itself. The art activity begins after that, and occurs in a separate, autonomous world, because it is a creative activity and because, by its very nature, it requires the mind not to be shaped by a thing to be known, but to shape a thing to be put into existence.

What interests us now is the fact that this creative activity itself implies in its essence a certain type of knowledge, the poetic knowledge of which I am speaking. How can we explain that?

An act of thought which by its very essence is creative, which shapes something in existence, instead of being shaped by things— what does such an act express and manifest when it produces the work if not the very being and substance of the one who creates?

But the substance of man is obscure to himself; it is only by receiving and suffering things, by awakening to the world, that our substance awakens to itself. The poet can only express his own substance in a work if things resound in him, and if, in him, at the same awakening, they and he emerge together from sleep. All that he discerns and divines in things is thus inseparable from himself and his emotion, and it is actually as a part of himself that he discerns and divines it, and in order to grasp obscurely his own being through a knowledge the end of which is to create. His intuition, the creative intuition or emotion, is an obscure grasping of himself and things together in a knowledge by union or connaturality, which only takes shape, bears fruit and finds expression in the work, and which, in all its vital weight, seeks to create and produce. This is a very different knowledge from what is generally called knowledge; a knowledge which cannot be expressed in notions and judgments, but which is experience rather than knowledge, and creative experience, because it wants to be expressed, and it can only be expressed in a work. This knowledge is not previous or presupposed to creative activity, but integrated in it, consubstantial with the movement toward the work, and this is precisely what I call poetic knowledge.

Poetic knowledge is the intrinsic moment of contemplation from which creation emanates. From it springs the melody that every work of art implies, and which is a meaning that animates a form. For art cannot be satisfied with the object, enclosed in a given category, to which it tends as a merely *productive* activity. As *intellectual* activity, art tends in a certain way—I mean a creative way—to Being, which transcends all categories. It is therefore necessary that the object that the artist is shaping, whether it be a vase of clay or a fishing boat, be significant of something other than itself; this object must be a sign as well as an object; a meaning must animate it, and make it say more than it is.

CHAPTER TWO

ON ARTISTIC JUDGMENT

OUR attitude before a work of art depends upon our natural taste and our artistic education, but it depends also, and more basically, on the very conception we entertain on the subject of art. If we believe that art is merely an exercise of skill intended to give pleasure or to distract us momentarily or to figure forth for us in easy and agreeable fashion some likeness of ideas which we already bear within ourselves, what we shall demand of a painting or of a symphony is that they confirm us in our own vision of things; what will interest us in them is the subject they treat, and we shall require that this subject be treated in such a way as to agree with the assortment of concepts previously formed in our minds, and which seem to us to express the truth about the subject. We shall judge the work of art as an article subject to our whim, an article the measure of which is our own bent of mind. Under such circumstances, to tell the truth, we do not judge the work of art; rather, it is we who are judged by it.

Everything changes the moment we think that art is a creative effort of which the wellsprings lie in the spirit, and which brings us at once the most intimate self of the artist and the secret concurrences which he has perceived in things by means of a vision or intuition all his own, and not to be expressed in ideas and in words—expressible only in the work of art. Then that work will appear to us as infused with the double mystery of the artist's personality and of the reality which has touched his heart. And what we shall demand of it is to make this mystery manifest to us, in that ever renewed joy produced by contact with beauty. We shall judge the work of art as the living vehicle of a hidden truth to which both the work and we ourselves are together subject, and which is the measure at once of the work and of our mind. Under such circumstances we truly judge because we do not set ourselves up as judges but strive to be obedient to that which the work may teach us.

19

The first condition necessary for such a judgment is a kind of prior consent to the artist's general intentions and to the creative perspective in which he has placed himself. For to judge a work of art is above all to have an understanding of another intellect; and before judging we must know—not only know but accept—the paths which the artist's intelligence has chosen to lead him into the secret heart of things and to express it. Then only can we perceive whether the artist really had something to say; which is the first and most indispensable step in artistic judgment. However skillful an artist may be, and however perfect his technique, if he unhappily has nothing to tell us, his work is valueless.

The great achievement of modern art and of modern poetry is that they have become, to a degree never before attained, conscious of themselves and of the spiritual mystery hidden within them. They have understood—and sometimes at a terrible cost—that the first duty of the artist and the poet is to be unshakeably faithful to their own truth, to the individual and incommunicable truth about themselves and about things, which is obscurely revealed to them and which must take shape in their work. An artist and a poet need much courage—a great artist and a great poet need heroism—if they are to remain faithful unto the end to that elusive spiritual element endowed with all the demands of an absolute and which does not forgive the least trespass. For, the more deep and trenchant is this truth, so personal with every artist, the more it risks at first seeming to his contemporaries something worthless or even foolish; for the artist has seen it and his contemporaries have not yet seen it. Later they will see it, thanks to him and to his suffering. By now we all know from what a heroic virtue of painting the work of a Cézanne sprang forth.

Of course, I am not unaware that, things being so, the artist runs every risk; I realize also that for a great and genuine creator to triumph in so strange a struggle with the Angel, many lesser men must fall shattered by the wayside. Be it noted, nevertheless, that if the latter have been truly faithful to their insight, even of limited compass, and to their love, however slight, for something greater than themselves, a tiny corner of heaven will have been reached by them. And even if they fall short and are shattered beyond repair, their efforts and their defeat itself deserve our respect. Respect for the effort of an artist, feeling for the spiritual mystery which pervades his creative work as a man grappling with beauty, are the prerequisites for every artistic judgment worthy of its object. The only artist who does not deserve respect is the one who works to please the public, for commercial success or for official success.

I make no plea here for indulgence for every work of art, even for every sincere work of art; much less do I plead for those which exploit the truths I have just tried to outline, in order to produce a sort of theatrical aping of the modern or of misunderstood genius. I do not ask for easy-going judgments. I think that the purer one's artistic judgment, the more it is demanding, nay, even pitiless. But what we have a right to require also is that this judgment be truly an artistic judgment: it must not set out to judge art from the mountain peaks of an incompetence which is sure of itself and yet knows nothing of the laws and the internal reality of the thing judged, it must itself be aware of the human and spiritual dignity of that special universe which is the universe of artistic creation, it must buttress itself by a genuine knowledge of the structure and principles of such a universe. As for everything else, in this case what is needed is a fitting intellectual training, based at once upon a deep-rooted study of the past and upon a wakeful interest in the searchings of the present.

The previous remarks are valid for sacred as well as for profane art. The arts of the liturgy are in their essence moored to a sacred tradition; but this is not the tradition of an artistic school, whatever it may be, and however great it may have been in the past. It is the sacred tradition of the dogma and the life of the Church which transcend every form of human art. This is why the Church has made her own, both in her buildings and in their adornment, the great forms of art which have succeeded each other through the centuries—Byzantine, Romanesque, Gothic, Renaissance, Baroque. It is a misfortune that the same statement cannot be made, as a rule, with respect to the great forms of modern and contemporary art. Yet certain invaluable, though still exceptional, instances show us that the time is coming when the thread of that genuine life of religious art will be taken up again.

The fact remains that, obviously, it is in the evolution of profane art that we find today most freely displayed the searchings, the anxieties, the conquests of our own time, and that we are able to study them most clearly.

c

CHAPTER THREE

ON KNOWLEDGE
THROUGH CONNATURALITY*

I.   ST. THOMAS AND THE NOTION OF KNOWLEDGE THROUGH CONNATURALITY

THE notion of knowledge through connaturality—that is, of a kind of knowledge which is produced in the intellect but not by virtue of conceptual connections and by way of demonstration —seems to me to be of particular importance, both because of the considerable part played by this kind of knowledge in human existence, and because it obliges us to realize in a deeper manner the *analogous* character of the concept of knowledge. Henri Bergson and William James, who were so much concerned, the one with intuition, and the other with experience, never did, I think, bring out and make use of the old notion of knowledge through connaturality. Had they done so, I assume that a number of things would have been clarified in their own teachings.

This notion of knowledge through connaturality is classical in the Thomist school. Thomas Aquinas refers in this connection to the Pseudo-Dionysius (*On Divine Names,* chapter II), and to the *Nicomachean Ethics,* Book x, chapter v, where Aristotle stages that the virtuous man is the rule and measure of human actions. I have no doubt that this notion, or equivalent notions, had, before Thomas Aquinas, a long history in human thought; an inquiry into this particular chapter in the history of ideas—which would perhaps have to take into account such philosophers as Ramanuja, and the Indian school of *bhatki*—would be of considerable interest. I did not embark on such historical research; the question for me was rather to test the validity of the notion of knowledge through connaturality, as elaborated in the Thomist school, and more sys-

*Paper read to the Conference of the *Society of Metaphysics,* February 24, 1951.

tematically to recognize the various domains to which it must be
extended.

To begin with, I shall refer to a basic distinction made by Thomas
Aquinas, when he explains* that there are two different ways to
judge of things pertaining to a moral virtue, fortitude for instance.
On the one hand, we can possess in our mind moral science, the conceptual and rational knowledge of virtues, which produces in us a
merely intellectual conformity with the truths involved. Then, if
we are asked a question about fortitude, we shall give the right
answer by merely looking at and consulting the intelligible objects
contained in our concepts. A moral philosopher may possibly not
be a virtuous man, and yet know everything about virtues.

On the other hand, we can possess the virtue in question in our
own powers of will and desire, have it embodied in ourselves, and
thus be in accordance with it, or co-natured with it, in our very
being. Then, if we are asked a question about fortitude, we shall
give the right answer, no longer through science, but through inclination, by looking at and consulting what we are and the inner
bents or propensities of our own being. A virtuous man may possibly be utterly ignorant in moral philosophy, and know as well—
probably better—everything about virtues, through connaturality.

In this knowledge through union or inclination, connaturality or
congeniality, the intellect is at play not alone, but together with
affective inclinations and the dispositions of the will, and is guided
and directed by them. It is not rational knowledge, knowledge
through the conceptual, logical and discursive exercise of Reason.
But it is really and genuinely knowledge, though obscure and perhaps incapable of giving account of itself, or of being translated
into words.

St. Thomas explains in this way the difference between the knowledge of divine reality acquired by theology and the knowledge of
divine reality acquired by mystical experience.† For the spiritual
man, he says, knows divine things through inclination or connaturality, not only because he has learned them, but, as the
Pseudo-Dionysius put it, because he suffers them.

As I said at the beginning, knowledge through connaturality plays
an immense part in human existence, especially in that knowing of
the singular which comes about in everyday life and in our relationship of person to person. Yet it is not with this everyday prac-

*Sum. theol., II–II, 45, 2.
†Sum. theol., I, 1, 6, ad 3.

tical experience that I shall be concerned here. For the sake of
brevity, I would like only to outline in a few words its role in some
particular typical fields of human knowledge.

II.   MYSTICAL EXPERIENCE

It is especially with respect to mystical experience, as witnessed
by Christian contemplatives, in whom alone, according to Bergson,
it came to full fruit, that the Schoolmen developed their theory of
knowledge through connaturality. I shall not dwell on this point,
which is more theological than philosophical. Suffice it to note that
they described mystical contemplation as grace-given or supernatural contemplation, because depending both on faith and charity,
and on a special inspiration from God who inhabits the soul. They
observed that obviously a fruitive experience of the deity cannot
be provided by our concepts or ideas, which, as true as they may be,
make us know divine things at a distance, and through the analogy
of creatures. Consequently, such supra-conceptual knowledge can
come about only through connaturality, through the connaturality
that love of charity, which is a participation in God's very love,
produces between man and God. The great gnoseological achievement of the best commentators of Thomas Aquinas, John of St.
Thomas for instance, was to show that in mystical experience this
love grows into an *objective means* of knowing, *transit in conditionem objecti,* and replaces the concept as intentional instrument
obscurely uniting the intellect with the thing known, in such a way
that man not only experiences his love, but, through his love, that
precisely which is still hidden in faith, the *still more* to be loved,
and to be tasted in love, which is the hidden substance of faith.
Then, as St. Thomas puts it, "at the summit of our knowledge we
know God as unknown," *tanquam ignotus cognoscitur,* that is, He
is known, through love, as infinitely transcending any human knowledge, or precisely as *God.*

*   *   *

There is, I think, another kind of mystical experience, which, in
contradistinction to the one I just mentioned, may be called natural
mystical experience; and an example of which we can find in Plo-
tinus and in the classical schools of Indian contemplation. I can
only state in a few words the conclusions of a certain amount of
research I did on the matter. Here again, to my mind, we have

to do with a particular type of knowledge both supra-conceptual and through connaturality. But the connaturality in question here is merely intellectual, and the essential part played by the will consists in forcing the intellect inwards, against the grain of nature, and in obliging it to empty itself of any particular representation. The reality to be experienced is the very Existence, the very *Esse* of the Self in its pure metaphysical actuality—Atman—and as proceeding from the One Self: and it is by means of a supreme effort of intellectual and voluntary concentration, sweeping away any possible image, recollection or idea, any passing phenomenon and any distinct consciousness, in other words, it is through the void that the intellect is co-natured to the unconceptualizable spiritual reality of the thing known.

III. POETIC KNOWLEDGE

Another typical instance of knowledge through connaturality appears in Poetic Knowledge. Since German Romanticism and since Baudelaire and Rimbaud, poetry has become self-aware to an unprecedented degree. Together with this self-awareness, the notion of poetic knowledge has come to the foreground.

The poet has realized that he has his own way, which is neither scientific nor philosophical, of knowing the world. Thus the fact of that peculiar kind of knowledge which is poetic knowledge has imposed itself upon philosophical reflection. And it would be no use to try to escape the problem by considering poetry a set of pseudo-statements—with no meaning—or a substitute for science intended for feeble-minded people. We must confront in a fair manner the fact of poetic experience and poetic intuition.

Poetic experience is distinct in nature from mystical experience. Because poetry emanates from the free creativity of the spirit, it is from the very start oriented toward expression, and terminates in a word proffered, it wants to speak; whereas mystical experience, because it emanates from the deepest longing of the spirit bent on knowing, tends of itself toward silence and internal fruition. Poetic experience is busy with the created world and the enigmatic and innumerable relations of existents with one another, not with the Principle of Being. In itself it has nothing to do either with the void of an intellectual concentration working against the grain of nature or with the union of charity with the subsisting Love.

Yet poetic experience also implies a typical kind of knowledge through connaturality. Poetic knowledge is non-conceptual and non-

rational knowledge; it is born in the preconscious life of the intellect, and it is essentially an obscure revelation both of the subjectivity of the poet and of some flash of reality coming together
out of sleep in one single awakening. This unconceptualizable
knowledge comes about, I think, through the instrumentality of
emotion, which, received in the preconscious life of the intellect,
becomes intentional and intuitive, and causes the intellect obscurely
to grasp some existential reality as *one* with the Self it has moved,
and by the same stroke all that which this reality, emotionally
grasped, calls forth in the manner of a sign: so as to have the self
known in the experience of the world and the world known in the
experience of the self, through an intuition which essentially tends
toward utterance and creation.

IV. MORAL EXPERIENCE

Finally moral experience offers to us the most wide-spread instance of knowledge through connaturality. As we have noticed,
it is in the experiential—not philosophical—knowledge of moral
virtues that Thomas Aquinas saw the first and main example of
knowledge through inclination or through connaturality. It is
through connaturality that moral consciousness attains a kind of
knowing—inexpressible in words and notions—of the deepest dispositions—longings, fears, hopes or despairs, primeval loves and options—involved in the night of the subjectivity. When a man makes
a free decision, he takes into account, not only all that he possesses
of moral science and factual information, and which is manifested
to him in concepts and notions, but also all the secret elements of
evaluation which depend on what he is, and which are known to
him through inclination, through his own actual propensities and
his own virtues, if he has any.

But the point on which I should like to lay stress deals with that
most controversial tenet in moral philosophy, Natural Law. I don't
intend to discuss Natural Law now, I shall only emphasize an
absolutely essential element, to my mind, in the concept of Natural
Law. The genuine concept of Natural Law is the concept of a law
which is natural not only insofar as it expresses the normality of
functioning of human nature, but also insofar as it is *naturally
known,* that is, known through inclination or through connaturality,
not through conceptual knowledge and by way of reasoning.

You will allow me to place myself in the perspective of a philosophy of Natural Law: I do so not in order to assume that you take such a philosophy for granted, but in order to clarify the very idea of Natural Law. My contention is that the judgments in which Natural Law is made manifest to practical Reason do not proceed from any conceptual, discursive, rational exercise of reason; they proceed from that *connaturality or congeniality* through which what is consonant with the essential inclinations of human nature is grasped by the intellect as good; what is dissonant, as bad.

Be it immediately added, to avoid any misunderstanding, first, that the inclinations in question, even if they deal with animal instincts, are essentially human, and therefore, reason-permeated inclinations; they are inclinations refracted through the crystal of reason in its unconscious or pre-conscious life. Second, that, man being an historical animal, these essential inclinations of human nature either developed or were released in the course of time: as a result, man's knowledge of Natural Law progressively developed, and continues to develop. And the very history of moral conscience has divided the truly essential inclinations of human nature from the accidental, warped or perverted ones. I would say that these genuinely essential inclinations have been responsible for the regulations which, recognized in the form of dynamic schemes from the time of the oldest social communities, have remained permanent in the human race, while taking forms more definite and more clearly determined.

But let us close this parenthesis. What are the consequences of the basic fact of Natural Law being known through inclination or connaturality, not through rational knowledge?

First: not only the prescriptions of positive law, established by human reason, but even those requirements of the normality of functioning of human nature which are known to men through a spontaneous or a philosophical exercise of conceptual and rational knowledge are not part of Natural Law. Natural Law, dealing only with regulations known through inclination, deals only with principles *immediately known* (that is known through inclination, without any conceptual and rational medium) of human morality.

Second: being known through inclination, the precepts of Natural Law are known in an *undemonstrable* manner. Thus it is that men (except when they make use of the reflective and critical disciplines of philosophy) are unable to give account of and rationally to justify their most fundamental moral beliefs: and this very fact is a token, not of the irrationality and intrinsic invalidity of these beliefs, but on the contrary, of their essential *naturality,* and therefore of their *greater* validity, and of their *more than human* rationality.

Third: this is so because no conceptual and rational exercise of human reason intervenes in its knowledge of Natural Law, so that human reason knows Natural Law, but has no part, either in causing it to *exist,* or even in causing it *to be known.* As a result, uncreated Reason, the Reason of the Principle of Nature, is the only reason at play not only in *establishing* Natural Law (by the very fact that it creates human nature), but in *making Natural Law known,* through the inclinations of this very nature, to which human reason listens when it knows Natural Law. And it is precisely because Natural Law depends *only* on Divine Reason that it is possessed of a character naturally sacred, and binds man in conscience, and is the prime foundation of human law, which is a free and contingent determination of what Natural Law leaves undetermined, and which obliges by virtue of Natural Law.

Philosophers and philosophical theories supervene in order to explain and justify, through concepts and reasoning, what, from the time of the cave-man, men have progressively known through inclination and connaturality. Moral philosophy is *reflective* knowledge, a sort of after-knowledge. It does not discover the moral law. The moral law was discovered by men before the existence of any moral philosophy. Moral philosophy has critically to analyze and rationally to elucidate moral standards and rules of conduct whose validity was previously discovered in an undemonstrable manner, and in a non-conceptual, non-rational way; it has also to clear them, as far as possible, from the adventitious outgrowths or deviations which may have developed by reason of the coarseness of our nature and the accidents of social evolution. Eighteenth-century rationalism assumed that Natural Law was either discovered in Nature or a priori deduced by conceptual and rational knowledge, and from there imposed upon human life by philosophers and by legislators in the manner of a code of geometrical propositions. No wonder that finally "eight or more new systems of natural law made their appearance at every Leipzig booksellers' fair" at the end of the eighteenth Century, and that Jean-Paul Richter might observe that "every fair and every war brings forth a new Natural Law."* I submit that all the theories of Natural Law which have been offered since Grotius (and including Grotius) were spoiled by the disregard

*Rommen *Natural Law,* St. Louis, Herder, 1948, p. 106.

of the fact that Natural Law is known through inclination or connaturality, not through conceptual and rational knowledge.

V.   METAPHYSICS AND KNOWLEDGE THROUGH CONNATURALITY

I think that the critique of knowledge is part of metaphysics,
and that the recognition and analysis of that kind of knowledge
which is knowledge through connaturality pertain to the object
of the critique of knowledge. But knowledge through connaturality
has nothing to do with metaphysics itself: metaphysics proceeds
purely by way of conceptual and rational knowledge. Like all rational knowledge it presupposes sense experience; and insofar as it
is metaphysics, it implies the intellectual intuition of being *qua* being. But neither in this intellectual intuition nor in sense-perception
is there the smallest element of knowledge through inclination. In
its rational development as in its primal intuitions metaphysics is
purely objective. If one confuses the planes and orders of things,
if poetic knowledge or mystical experience or moral feeling claim
to become philosophical knowledge, or if a philosophy which
despairs of reason tries to capture those kinds of knowledge through
connaturality, and to use them as an instrument—everyone loses his
head, knowledge through inclination and metaphysics are simul-
taneously spoiled.

CHAPTER FOUR

PHILOSOPHICAL
CO-OPERATION AND
INTELLECTUAL JUSTICE

A FEW years ago an American philosopher, Doctor Eilmon Sheldon, whose high ideals and vast erudition I particularly admire, published in *The Modern Schoolman** two articles entitled, "Can Philosophers Co-operate?" which raised interesting discussions. Doctor Sheldon would not put himself among the strictly orthodox Thomists, although he thinks of Thomism with congenial and comprehensive insight, and has long meditated on the hylomorphist doctrine† and the idea of substantial form. As he contemplates the tragic problems with which humanity is struggling today, he sees with sorrow that those who, specializing in philosophy, should lead men toward wisdom are separated by ever-increasing disagreement. In the two articles I have just mentioned he wonders whether this disagreement cannot be settled and whether it is truly impossible for philosophers to co-operate. And since the two currents of thought which seem particularly significant to him in the United States today are the pragmatist current, on the one hand, and the neo-Thomist current, on the other, he endeavors, with fine intellectual generosity and remarkably penetrating analyses, to show that those who represent these two currents of thought could discover, upon studying each other's systems more broad-mindedly, many points held in common, and the germs of agreement and joint progress. They would find these even when the systems seem, at first sight, absolutely opposed to each other as in the contrast,

---

*January and March, 1944.
†That is, the Aristotelian conception of material being as composed of *prime matter* (with absolutely no determination of its own) and *substantial form* or *entelechy*.

for example, between the rational *demonstration* dear to the Thomists and the experimental *verification* dear to the Pragmatists, or between the idea of *process* and that of *immutability,* or between the theory of *substantial forms* and the idea of *evolution.*

It seemed to me that an appeal as honest as that made by Doctor Sheldon deserved to be discussed in a manner just as honest and that a Thomist should really try to answer the question from his own point of view. Although in discussing Doctor Sheldon's suggestions we shall have to consider the case of pragmatism in particular, it is clear that analogous observations could and should be made (within the proper proportions, of course) concerning the other great currents of contemporary thought.

"Can philosophers co-operate?" The problem is eternal but particularly pressing today, and brings to mind one of the saddest conditions of our human, conceptual and discursive way of thinking.

To make my position clear, I would state that, in my opinion, co-operation between philosophers can only be a conquest of the intellect over itself and the very universe of thought it has created —a difficult and precarious conquest achieved by intellectual rigor and justice on the basis of irreducible and inevitably lasting antagonisms.

In the perspective of the *inner,* conceptual and logical structure of philosophical systems and, if I may put it thus, of *doctrinal exchanges,* each system can avail itself of the others for its own sake by dismembering them, and by feeding on and assimilating what it can take from them. That is co-operation indeed, but in quite a peculiar sense!

Yet from a deeper point of view, and in the perspective of the judgment which each one passes on the other, contemplating it as a whole, as an object situated in an *external* sphere, and trying to do it justice, a mutual understanding is possible which cannot indeed do away with basic antagonisms, but which may create a kind of real though imperfect co-operation, to the extent that each system succeeds (1) in recognizing for the other, in a certain sense, a right to exist; (2) in availing itself of the other, no longer by material *intussusception,* and by borrowing or digesting parts of the other, but by bringing, thanks to the other, its own specific life and principles to a higher degree of achievement and extension.

In the first part of this essay, I shall consider the question of co-operation between philosophers from the first of the two points of view I have indicated, that is from the point of view of the inner structure of the systems and their possible doctrinal exchanges.

In the second part, I shall treat of the same question from the other point of view, that of the intellectual grasp which various philosophical systems can have of each other, each being taken as a whole.

I. DOCTRINAL EXCHANGES

Human beings, whatever may be the error under which they labor, have a right to exist. But philosophical doctrines are not human beings; their internal truth is their only right to intelligible existence, recognized by the mind, in the immaterial realm of thought. Co-operation between philosophers as men, in the human field, takes place as a matter of course. But the issue we are discussing deals with co-operation between philosophers as philosophers, or between philosophies.

In the perspective of that tissue of elaborate concepts, assertions, and negations which constitutes the inner structure of a system, woe to the system which overlooks the many "valid insights, fresh though partial visions of the truth" (to quote Doctor Gerald Phelan) which the other systems bring forth or with which they are pregnant! Yet the system in question would not be a philosophical system if, in recognizing and taking care of these insights and visions, it did not, at the same time, endeavor to encompass them in its own way of conceptualizing reality—which naturally does not answer the purpose of the systems involved.

Rational Proof and Pragmatic Verification

For example, when we base ourselves on sound Thomistic doctrine, what are we to think of the Pragmatist tenet that the knowledge of the existence of God requires *experimental verification?* (For the Pragmatist this is not only required but should take the place of a *rational demonstration.*) Can we allow, if not the pragmatist tenet itself, then at least the idea of an experimental verification of the proofs of the existence of God?

Scholasticism can assuredly admit that "experimental verification" of the philosophical proofs of God's existence is "indispensable." But in what sense? First, it seems to me, in the sense that the philosophical knowledge of God must tend to that higher knowledge in which divine reality is "known as unknown" and more experienced than known, and which is peculiar to contemplative or "mystical "wisdom (here we are far removed from Pragmatic verification). And secondly (here we come nearer to Pragmatic verification), in the sense that either the testimony of the great mystics and the religious experience of mankind (such as examined by Henri Bergson or William James) or the deepest requirements of human action and the psychological and moral attitudes proper to a balanced and integrated personality—once we have become aware of them—pave the way for the rational demonstration of God's existence, remove obstacles, and also strengthen, not, to be sure, the internal validity of the proof, but the inner unity, harmony, and security, and consequently the power of adhesion of the whole man grasping the intellectual demonstration.

But the Scholastic will immediately insist that all this process of "Pragmatic verification" is but an external preparation for, or an external confirmation of, the philosophical task itself. It involves the intellect *and* the will, as Doctor Sheldon rightly points out, whereas metaphysics is a merely speculative and intellectual knowledge, and whereas its purity, rigor and mobility require that no interference of the will and the affective powers should cast the slightest shadow of subjectivity over the intelligible necessities with which the metaphysical insight deals. Thus the Scholastic will use the Pragmatist's discoveries in order to compensate for and remedy the negligence which, through routine, laziness or lack of attention, he had evinced toward a certain set of experimental truths; but in so doing he will completely recast the meaning which the Pragmatist has given to these truths; for he will put them outside the field with which speculative philosophy is concerned—that is, in the case of our philosophical knowledge of God's existence, outside the field of metaphysics; and, on the other hand, he will still feel that, when the intellectual instrument and the habit of reason are denied the power or possibility of grasping the existence of the Cause of being, both God and the Intellect are offended.

Process and Immutability

Likewise, when it is a question of the idea of *process,* which the Pragmatist deems co-existential with that of reality, whereas the Scholastic sees divine reality as immutable, the Scholastic gladly welcomes the subtle and profound analysis through which a metaphysician like Doctor Sheldon emphasizes the instantaneous character of the act of understanding (which is the *terminus* of a time process) to make us realize the notion of the timeless and immutable, and perceive the supremely active and life-filled character of the immutability of God. He is even prepared to describe, in our human words, divine eternity as an *instant which lasts,* and to say that God is *an intellectual flash eternally subsisting.* And he will, for that very reason, definitely reject the word "static," a quite inappropriate term to designate the timeless, which in his opinion has an eminently dynamic density.

But when it comes to the inner and essential meaning of concepts, he will consider that any definition of the timeless as a time process infinitely swift, and of eternity as a time infinitely concentrated, is perhaps a helpful and somewhat illuminating but metaphoric or equivocal expression, and therefore a pseudo-definition for the passage "into a higher dimension" which Doctor Sheldor correctly mentions here, means, in reality, that between the immutable and the mutable, particularly between eternity and time, there is an insuperable difference of nature or essence; so that the notion of "process" is, like that of "duration," an essentially analogical notion. This notion of process could perhaps be applied to the infinite perfection and aseity of God, Who is Life subsisting, Intellection subsisting and Love subsisting (do not the theologians use the word "procession" with regard to the divine Trinity?); but the notion of process could be so applied only in an analogical sense and on condition that it lose any connotation of time, and designate only act, and pure act. Similarly, time is a kind of duration—the duration of the mutable; and eternity is a kind of duration—the duration of the immutable; but not a shadow of univocal community, only an analogical community of meaning is here involved.

This point is not denied, nor is it emphasized, in Doctor Sheldon's reflections on the matter. I am aware that these reflections, which are to my mind an especially remarkable piece of philosophy, may have a persuasive appeal for many modern thinkers—both the experiential-minded and the lovers of metaphysics. Bergson would have been delighted with them. I remember a conversation I had with him a long time ago, long before he wrote *Les Deux Sources.* He made clear to me the difficulties that he met with in the traditional—so-called "static"—concept of divine immutability; and the solution he outlined at that time was exactly of the nature of the one suggested by Doctor Sheldon. Later on, however, he was not to insist upon this solution. Moreover, as a matter of fact, he had nothing of the Pragmatist. Taking into account the observations offered above, I am honestly afraid that, were a Pragmatist philosopher able to agree with Doctor Sheldon's views without fear of risking what Professor John Dewey's disciples so amiably term* a "failure of nerve," his agreement would, in the last analysis, rest upon an involuntary equivocation.

Substantial Forms and Evolution

With regard to the third specific issue—substantial forms and finality—we may wonder whether any vindication of substance, substantial form and finality, however persuasive in itself it may be, can really convince a Pragmatist thinker. For the latter is indeed disposed to admit that we have *signposts* "telling us what behavior we may expect of things" and "enabling us to adjust successfully to the things that behave." But precisely the "behavior" that substance and substantial form lead us to expect and enable us to adjust ourselves to, is, if I may say so, the intelligible behavior, the very intelligibility of things insofar as their reality is analyzed in terms of being and resolved into the root intelligibility of being; whereas the behavior to which the Pragmatist philosopher is eager to adjust himself is the sense-perceivable behavior of things analyzed in terms of becoming and inter-activity, and resolved in the observability and measurability of "scientific" phenomena.

In the same way, finality, as Doctor Sheldon rightly observes, is the primary reason for becoming, and the deepest stimulus in the drama of the universal process, but I doubt whether we can realize this if we philosophize on the level of the empirico-mathematical explanation of phenomena and not on the level of metaphysics' abstractive intuition. And finality implies that the process tends toward an "end," toward a point where there is no longer any motion, but only repose and possession, so that the universal process and dynamism which permeates the cosmos and which carries along, so to speak, each agent beyond its own particular ends, making creation groan after its accomplishment, has its ultimate reason in the transcendent finality by virtue of which He Who is the self-subsisting Being is desired and loved by every being more than itself. Would such a view be acceptable to Pragmatist philosophy?

On the other hand, whereas I believe that it is perfectly right to emphasize the need for Thomistic philosophy, in the various

*"A New Failure of Nerves." *Partisan Review*, January and February, 1943 (concerning the renewed interest in Thomism in the United States).

phases of its conceptualization, to give greater scope to the general idea of dynamism and evolution—the real conquest of modern thought—and to deepen in this connection the traditional notion of substantial form, I think, nevertheless, that such statements should be further developed in order to remain true.

Substance is not a static inert substratum; it is the first root of a thing's activities and, while remaining the same as to its substantial being, it ceaselessly acts and changes—through its accidents, which are an expansion of itself into another, non-substantial, dimension of being. But *as* substance it does not change. As long as a material substance is not "corrupted" and transformed into another, it is immutable in its metaphysical—merely intelligible and non-experiential—reality of substance. Man's nature, while keeping its fixed specific determination, owing to a substantial form which is spiritual and subsisting, is, of course, capable of an endless increase of knowledge and intellectual achievement—this is the privilege of reason. But the root power and natural strength of the human intellect are not able to go beyond the capacities of reason and to pass into the degree of intellectuality of the least of the angels.

I am convinced that the hylomorphic theory involves no incompatibility with the discoveries of modern physics; and the suggestion that "the Scholastic should lay more stress on recent physics and less on chemistry" seems to me highly commendable. Surely, as Doctor Sheldon writes, "it would present his Thomistic cosmology in a fairer light, bringing out its power of adaptation and progressive character." Nevertheless, I should like to point out that it would be illusory to seek a verification of the hylomorphic theory in modern physics, for the one and the other are at work on different levels of thought, and the entities constructed by the physicomathematical explanation of matter involve a great deal of symbolization: they sound like *entia rationis* grounded in the nature of things rather than like ontological realities.

Finally, as concerns evolution, I believe that the evolutive process of nature and the notion of substantial form can and must be reconciled. Yet Doctor Sheldon put his finger on the crucial point when he wrote: "The difficulty is to see how, if a substantial form is fixed and definite, it can contain a principle that allows for its own transformation, not merely into another substantial form, but into a greater one." This difficulty is a logical impossibility indeed; no substantial form can be transformed into another; when a substantial change occurs, the new substantial form is drawn out ("educed") from the potentiality of matter according to the ultimate root dispositions introduced in matter by the physical agents which modify atomic structure and cause the transmutation of an element, or, in the case of compounds, by the activities of the very substances which are in the process of "corruption," and which will cease to exist at the instant in which the new substance comes into being.

The new substance can be more "perfect"—imply a higher degree of integration and individuality—in the ontological scale of physical nature, not only because matter (prime matter) "aspires" to the full actualization of all the forms it contains potentially, but because the new "more perfect" substance results from an atomic redistribution which, in its capacity of an "ultimate disposition," requires the "eduction" of a higher form, or because, in the case of compounds, this new "more perfect" substance is the integration, in a new formal and subsisting unity, of the activities brought about in matter by the antecedent substances which "generate" it at the instant when they destroy each other (and whose forms remain *virtually* in the new substantial form then educed). This also presupposes that the entire cosmos and the interaction of all its energies co-operate in the production of the new substance, that is, in the "eduction" of the new substantial form.

Now, when it comes to the biological realm, a new problem arises; the new living organism has of necessity the same specific substantial form as the organism or organisms from which it proceeds. How, then, is biological evolution to be conceived in terms of substantial forms? I think there are two possible ways of explaining it. First of all, species (the ontological species, not the taxonomic species dealt with in botany, zoology or genetics) could be understood in a more dynamic as well as in a more extensive manner. When I say "a more extensive manner," I mean that such large groups as those which classification terms families, orders, etc., should perhaps be considered as belonging to one and the same ontological species. When I say "a more dynamic manner," I mean that the substantial form, in the realm of life, could be considered as protruding, in its virtualities, beyond the capacities of the matter it informs in given conditions, like, for example, an architectural style or poetic idea which we might imagine as thrown into matter and working it by itself. In short the substantial form would then be viewed as an ontological impulse realizing itself in various patterns along the line of a certain phylum. Yet such evolution could,

D

of course, only take place within the limits of the phylum or the ontological species in question.

Secondly, concerning the hypothetical origin of the various phylums themselves, if now we take into account the transcendent action of the First Cause, we may obviously conceive that (particularly in those formative ages when the world was in the state of its greatest plasticity, and when the divine influx was penetrating nature and completing the work of creation) that existence-giving influx of God, passing through created beings and using them as instrumental causes, was able—and is still able—to heighten the vital energies which proceed from the form in the organism it animates, so as to produce within matter, I mean within the germ-cells, dispositions beyond the limits of that organism's specificity. As a result, at the moment of generation a new substantial form, specifically "greater" or more elevated in being, would be educed from the potentiality of matter thus more perfectly disposed.

These much-too-summary considerations may give perhaps some idea of the manner in which the fact of evolution (leaving aside what concerns the origin of man which entails quite different problems)* is to be integrated into Scholastic philosophy. Would such a way of thinking have a meaning from the Pragmatist point of view? That is another question.

Pragmatism and Thomism

I have tried to stress the difficulties a Thomist may find in any effort, however fine its inspiration, toward a conciliation with Pragmatism based on a kind of mutual adjustment and exchange of ideas. I am not qualified to represent the Pragmatist outlook. I am, however, inclined to surmise that a Pragmatist would probably have similar difficulties to point out from his own perspective.

In the last analysis we are confronted here with a metaphysical opposition which is more basic and more comprehensive than any partial agreement. At the root of Thomistic philosophy lies the affirmation of the primacy of being over becoming. At the root of

*The profound ontological break in continuity introduced, beneath the apparent continuity with which science deals, by the advent of a spiritual soul which can come to exist only as immediately created by God, presupposes not only the above-mentioned action of the creative influx, the principal agent of evolution, passing through nature, but also a special intervention of God to create a spirit, a soul "in His own image," which is the entelechy of a new living species, and by virtue of which the body of the first human being also represents, metaphysically speaking, an absolute beginning, and has God alone as its engendering cause and Father, even if the body in question resulted from the infusion of a human soul into a pre-ordained animal cell—which, by the very fact of the infusion, was changed in its very essence, to the point of being contra-distinguished to the whole animal realm.

Pragmatist philosophy (as of Hegelian philosophy—despite the historic struggle of Pragmatism against Hegelianism, they have some common grounds, particularly perceivable in John Dewey's Pragmatism) lies the affirmation of the primacy of becoming over being. We could express this opposition in another way, by stating that the crucial place which is occupied in Thomism by *truth*, is occupied in Pragmatism by *verification*.

I am not forgetting, of course, that the Pragmatist makes use of the notion of truth—particularly in the usual sense of everyday life—and so does the Thomist with the notion of verification. But as a primarily significant philosophical concept, Truth is for the one, Verification for the other, that concept on which all the rest depends. In the eyes of the Thomist, verification is only a way and a means of grasping truth. And when the intellect has made itself true, the truth thus attained possesses objective consistency because it is the vital conformity of the intellect with what exists (actually or possibly) independently of the mind; and, however humble it may be, this truth is an end in which the intellect comes to fruition and has its perfection, rest, and joy. Every truth, even dealing with the most fleeting event, has something of the immutable (a butterfly touches a rose and then flies away—at least it will remain eternally true that it touched the flower at that given moment); and the truths which deal with the inner necessities of essences are immutable by their very object. To enjoy truth, without further ado, is the very life of the intellect *qua* intellect, and the aim of science *qua* science as well as that of metaphysical wisdom. Whereas the Thomist emphasizes in this way the contemplative import of knowledge, the Pragmatist distrusts it as a "static" illusion, opposed to the reality of intellectual life which is only becoming and laboring. This quarrel between Being and Becoming, and between Truth and Verification, reveals a deep-seated antagonism that the best efforts cannot overcome. That is why, however praiseworthy may be the attempts toward conciliation on this or that particular point, one cannot escape feeling that "co-operation" as a whole is in an extremely precarious position.

II. THE MUTUAL INTELLIGIBLE ENVELOPMENT OF PHILOSOPHIES

I come now to the second part of this inquiry. I should like to consider the problem of philosophical co-operation from a more profound point of view.

And first let us remark that, if we were able to realize, in a higher light, that most often our mutually opposed affirmations do not bear on the same parts of aspects of the real and that they are of greater value than our mutual negations, then we should come nearer the first prerequisite of a genuinely philosophical understanding; that is, we should become better able to transcend and conquer our own system of signs and conceptual language, and to take on for a moment, in a provisional and tentative manner, the thought and approach of the other so as to come back, with this intelligible booty, to our own philosophical conceptualization and to our own system of reference.

Following this line of thought and endeavoring to satisfy the demands of intellectual justice up to the very end, we come upon a new and deeper aspect of the problem: "Can philosophers cooperate?" Then, we are no longer concerned with analyzing or *sorting* the set of assertions peculiar to various systems in spreading them out, so to speak, on a single surface or level in order to examine what conciliation or exchange of ideas they may mutually allow in their inner structure. But we are concerned with taking into account a third dimension, in order to examine the manner in which each system, considered as a specific whole, can, according to its own frame of reference, do justice to the other in taking a view of it and seeking to penetrate it as an object situated on the outside—in another sphere of thought.

From this new standpoint, two considerations would appear all-important: the one is the consideration of the central *intuition* which lies at the core of each great philosophical doctrine; the other is the consideration of the *place* which each system could, according to its own frame of reference, grant the other system as the legitimate place the latter is cut out to occupy in the universe of thought.

Actually, each great philosophical doctrine lives on a central intuition which can be wrongly conceptualized and translated into a system of assertions and negations seriously deficient or erroneous as such, but which, insofar as it is intellectual intuition, truly gets hold of some aspect of the real. And, consequently, each great philosophical doctrine, once it has been grasped in its central intuition, and then re-interpreted in the frame of reference of another doctrine (in a manner that it would surely not accept), should be granted from the point of view of this other doctrine some place considered as legitimately occupied, be it in some imaginary space.

If we try to do justice to the philosophical systems against which we take our most determined stand, we shall seek to discover both that intuition which they involve and that place we must grant them from our own point of view. And then we shall benefit from them, not by borrowing from them or exchanging with them certain particular views and ideas, but by seeing, thanks to them, more profoundly into our own doctrine, by enriching it from within and extending its principles to new fields of inquiry which have been brought more forcefully to our attention, but which we shall make all the more vitally and powerfully informed by these principles.

Pragmatism as Viewed and Re-interpreted By a Thomist

What is the view that a Thomist, under these circumstances, might take of Pragmatism? If I may summarize in a few brief statements some considerations which would require further development, I would say tentatively that in my opinion the central intuition which lies at the core of Pragmatism is the intuition of the reality of time and becoming as immanent to experience and to the human conditioning of the effort of the understanding. And as regards the place in which, according to the Thomistic system of reference, both the inspiration and the specific principles of Pragmatist philosophy would receive, once duly transposed, a legitimate meaning, I would suggest that for a Thomist, Pragmatist philosophy is to be placed neither at the level of metaphysics nor at the level of the philosophy of nature, but at the level of ethics and moral philosophy. I do not mean that in doing so we would consider Pragmatism as offering us a particular system of morality which would be true in the Thomistic perspective—I am far from thinking that. I mean that Pragmatism embraces the whole extent of the philosophical subject matter, and especially the process of knowledge, from the practical outlook which is peculiar to ethics, the knowledge of human acts.

Here we have the conditions under which in the Thomistic perspective the Pragmatist notion of truth and verification might have its case; for according to the views of Scholasticism, at the final point of the practical or moral order, truth (which then pertains no longer to "science," but to the virtue of "prudence") is deprived of all speculative and contemplative import and becomes thoroughly experiential, not theoretical; in other words, truth is now the adjustment to what is to be done, to fully integrate action; it implies the joint activity of the will and the intellect, and is to be looked at, not as the conformity of the mind with what exists, but as the conformity of the mind with the right tendency to action, "with the right appetite," as Cajetan put it.

Similarly, and to take another example, there is in the ethical field an approach to God which is not theoretical but practical, and does not deal with the proofs of reason, but is immersed in moral experience, if it be true that a man really chooses God as his ultimate end when in an occasion where his act of free will is deep enough to have the value of a first beginning in his moral life, he chooses to do a certain good action because it is good and for the sake of the good alone, and thus makes his whole moral activity appendent to *bonum honestum*.

At that moment, although this man can have no thought of God in a conceptual manner, he nevertheless knows God in a merely practical manner, by virtue of the implications involved in the dynamism of the moral act. And such a strictly moral and vital knowledge of the supreme Good is, so to speak, an elemental, re- mote and implicit experience, which, by meeting, and being en- lightened by, the illuminations of reason and faith, may develop into higher experiential knowledge—the peak of which is the genuine, grace-given and supernatural experience of divine life, such as is attained in mystical contemplation. I realize that these considera- tions would need deeper and more explicit discussion; I propose them only to suggest how the Thomist, in his own thoroughly non- Pragmatist manner, might satisfy, in transferring them to their right place, the inspiration and basic views which the Pragmatist holds dear.

By the same token, he might himself become more aware of the potentialities of his own doctrine as well as of the improvements and wider scope he could afford for the application of his own principles. He might, for instance, feel attracted to exploring more completely the field of moral philosophy regarding those implica- tions of the dynamism of the moral act, which I just pointed out. Or else, by considering the Pragmatist's epistemological analysis and the impact of the historical and social environment and the human practical concerns upon the formation of our philosophical notions, the Thomist might endeavor more carefully and sys- tematically to rid his speculative concepts, especially the primary metaphysical concepts, of the extraneous elements which are part of the complex human heritage carried along by language, and to make these concepts more perfectly free of any streak of subjectivity or relativity, by establishing them in a more criticallv elaborated manner.

Thomism as Viewed and Re-interpreted by a Pragmatist

Should I now try to play the part of a Pragmatist philosopher? I feel neither authorized to do so, nor hopeful of success. Let us attempt, nevertheless, to imagine how a Pragmatist, supposing he accepted the methodological approach we are now examining, would take a view of Thomism according to his own frame of reference and in order—to the best of his abilities—to do intellectual justice to Thomism. As a Thomist I feel that I may, without appearing presumptuous, safely say that I have some idea of the central intuition which is at the core of Thomistic philosophy and on which it lives. It is the intuition of the basic intelligible reality of being, as analogically permeating everything knowable; and especially the intuition of existence, as the act of every act and the perfection of every perfection. This intuition has no place in the Pragmatist's universe of thought (which is, I daresay, less hospitable than the Thomist's). If, however, the Pragmatist tries to recognize the value of this intuition, or rather to find in his own perspective something equivalent to it, I imagine he would say, more or less in the following terms, that for him the central intuition of Thomistic philosophy is that of the architectural power, inner coherence and all-pervading logical rigor of reason. That would in any case be more fair than seeking in Thomism, as do certain Pragmatists I have known, the ghost of authoritarianism and the Inquisition.

And as regards the place in which, according to the Pragmatist frame of reference, both the inspiration and the specific principles of Thomistic philosophy would receive, even duly transposed, a legitimate meaning, I am aware that such a place does not exist in the Pragmatist's universe of thought. But it might exist for him outside this universe, in an imaginary space, after the fashion of an *as if,* or of the intelligible world of Reason in Kant's philosophy. I would therefore imagine that, just as the Thomist tells the Pragmatist: "Your philosophy is not a philosophy, but a philosophy viewed in the distorting mirror of a merely ethical outlook," so the Pragmatist—in no less gracious terms—would tell the Thomist: "Your philosophy is not a philosophy, but a system of Plato-like intelligible myths, a mythology of reason which transposes reality into terms of rationally organized patterns. These would have a legitimate meaning in an imaginary world, *if* the abstractive power of the human mind were also an intuitive power; and *if* the intellect were able to perceive essences, nature and ontological structures in and through the data of sense-experience."

Yet the very possibility of such a system of rational myths (to use the language he would probably use) raises, it seems to me, many problems for the Pragmatist from his own point of view. For this system of rational myths is coherent in itself, and by means of its own lexicon of signs it is able to propose a synthesis in which all degrees of human knowledge, and especially modern physics and experimental knowledge of nature, find a justification, and many apperceptions dear to the Pragmatist are saved, though interpreted according to another frame of reference. How is this possible? And would not some deeper inquiry as to the instrumental value of abstraction and reason appear here as suitable? By trying to take a real view of Thomistic philosophy and to do it justice from his own point of view, the Pragmatist would certainly enlarge the boundaries of his own system, enrich it from within, and discover new potentialities in his own principles, by striving to find, in particular, how he could better interpret and save the function and power of abstract thought.

I have tried to indicate what I consider to be the inner difficulties, the limitations and also the least ambiguous possibilities of philosophical co-operation.

Perhaps, in the last analysis, we shall have an idea that this word "co-operation" is perhaps a bit too ambitious. All that can be said on the question can be summed up in the philosophical duty of understanding another's thought in a genuine and fair manner, and of dealing with it with intellectual justice. This already is difficult—and is sufficient, if only we are aware that there cannot be intellectual justice without the assistance of intellectual charity. If we do not love the thought and intellect of another as intellect and thought, how shall we take pains to discover what truths are conveyed by it while it seems to us defective or misguided, and at the same time to free these truths from the errors which prey upon them and to reinstate them in an entirely true systematization? For intellectual justice is due to our fellow-philosophers, but first of all to truth.

In other words, what essentially matters is to have respect for the intellect, even if, in its endeavors, it appears to us as missing the point, and to be attentive to disentangling and setting free every seed of truth, wherever it may be. Thus, philosophers should be capable, if not of co-operating, at least of understanding each other and practicing justice toward each other in the field of philosophy itself.

The Hegelian Dialectics

Since these reflections were occasioned by Doctor Sheldon's attempt to reconcile Pragmatism and Thomism, I have referred to Pragmatism as a typical example when I discussed, from my viewpoint as a Thomist, the questions relative to philosophical co-operation and the effort at intellectual justice which must be accomplished among philosophers. It is clear that the same considerations would apply in the case of other systems.

For instance, what about the Hegelian dialectics? We shall not try to re-invent history, philosophy or religion in the perspective and through the procedures of the Hegelian dialectics. We prefer to leave such exercises to minds, I shall not say bolder or more flexible, but rather to minds more timid and more naïve.

But we shall ask ourselves from what central intuition the Hegelian dialectic derives its life. And we shall not be far wrong, it seems to me, if we answer that this central intuition is that of *reality as history;* for history as such, which, like time, cannot complete its being without the mind and the memory, offers to our consideration the development of ideas or *logical loads* incarnate in time; and it is true, as a matter of fact, that each of these "historical" ideas, which is a form immanent in time, can only reach its own final accomplishment—in time—by provoking its contrary and denying itself, because its very triumph exhausts the potentialities which summoned it and by the same stroke unmasks and provokes, in the abyss of the real, the contrary potentialities.

But reality is not *only* nor *primarily* history. Before the Hegelian "idea" or the idea as form of the historical development (which is an accidental or secondary form), there is the Aristotelian "idea," the act, the substantial or primary form of reality as being. The error has been to mistake the form which is immersed in time as an immanent germ loaded with potentialities of historical development, for the form through which the reality of things is con-

stituted; and, to tell the truth, it is in the hylomorphic doctrine
that the interpretation and conceptualization of the intuition of
which we are speaking should have been sought.

We shall also ask ourselves in what place Hegelianism, duly
transposed and re-interpreted, should be situated, according to the
Thomistic frame of reference, in order to be given a legitimate
significance. It is obvious that the philosophy of history, not metaphysics, will then appear to us the natural locus of Hegelian thought.

Existentialism

To take another example, shall we consider what is today called
Existentialism? I believe that the central intuition on which the
Existentialism of Kierkegaard lived was, in the last analysis, the
very same which is at the core of Thomism: the intuition of the
absolutely unique value and primacy of existence, *existentia ut
exercita;* but then this intuition arose in the midst of an anguished
faith, stripped of its intelligible or super-intelligible organism, a
faith which desperately awaited miracle and refused the mystical
possession after which it thirsted, and was born of a radically irrationalist thought which, rejecting and sacrificing essences, fell back
upon the night of subjectivity. And I believe that the central intuition on which contemporary Existentialism lives, or dies, is the
negative aspect of that Kirkegaardian intuition, henceforth emptied
of the faith which once animated it—I mean the intuition of the
absolute Nothingness of the creature, henceforth without a Creator,
and the radical absurdity of existence uprooted from God.

Is there a place or situation where these two kinds of Existentialism can find a legitimate significance? Doubtless there is. For
the first it would be the mystical experience of apophatic theology
in which God is known as unknown and which Existentialist philosophy misconstrues, pilfering it all the while from the saints. For
the second kind of Existentialism it would be the mystical knowledge of Hell.

To be thorough, we should finally ask ourselves what kind of an
idea a Hegelian philosopher and an Existentialist philosopher, if
they, for their part, made a like effort to be intellectually just,
could form of the central intuition of Thomism, and in what place,
according to their own frame of reference, they would put Thomism in order to give it a legitimate significance. But the question
would be naïve, for it seems to be of the essence of Hegelian and
Existentialist thought to be unconcerned, with regard to other

forms of thought, with any attempt at intellectual justice but simply to consider outgrown and invalidated by time any endeavor of the human mind which, being born in time, claims nevertheless to rise above time.

III. THE PURIFICATION OF THE SUBJECTIVE POWERS

If I were to follow my line of thought to its last end, I should say, and not without a certain feeling of melancholy, that only two disciplines of knowledge are truly and actually capable of intellectual justice, namely, either *mere history of ideas* (because it is not a philosophy and has no doctrine), or *Thomist realism* (because it is a doctrine which is possessed both of love and zeal for being and of the sense of analogy). That is why it is sad to contemplate on the one hand, the behavior of those Christians who deem that they must turn away from this philosophy and ignore or despise it in order to do justice to modern philosophical systems; and, on the other hand, the behavior of those among the disciples of this philosophy who wrong its infinite capacity for understanding and use the formulas they have been taught in order to save themselves from regarding the thought of others, and to criticize it all the more peremptorily because they expect it to display only error. The universe of intelligible objects, to which first and foremost we owe our loyalty, is not that universe of verbal conclusions which serve all too often as material blinders which keep a man from gazing into the eyes of other men. It is the universe of reality itself, made intelligible in act and objectivized before the mind, and that universe is transparent, not opaque. From the perceived object, and through the perceived object, it leads to that other reality which is the thought that also seeks to grasp it, albeit perhaps clumsily, and which must in its turn be made intelligible in act and objectivized before the mind, and respected in its depths.

If the notion of objectivity is thus taken in its real meaning, as including existing reality and even that of the subjects which seek to grasp it, it must be said that the more a philosophy possesses objective value and derives its life from the object, the more it has the sense of intellectual justice. And the more a philosophy discards the object in order to seek itself in the folds of subjectivity—a subjectivity entrenched within the individuality of the ego, instead of being spiritualized and universalized by its communication with objective being—the more it loses the sense of intellectual justice.

Today all intellectual objectivity seems to be concentrated in the realm of science where, moreover, an admirable co-operation of minds can be seen. But in the realm of philosophy contemporary thought is most often, and increasingly, subjective and introverted.

And yet we may observe that rarely has so much intellectual talent been spent, rarely have so many truths—not only so many errors, but also so many truths—been circulated. Truths are running rampant. We meet them in every corner of our daily newspapers and weekly magazines, and in the speeches of our politicians. People are even beginning to notice that the world is perishable, and that science without wisdom is of no use to men. But the ordinary intellect hardly profits from this swarm of truths; it takes them in one on top of the other, along with the mass of errors which are also running rampant—a blotter soaking up everything without discrimination.

This means that setting forth and elaborating philosophically even the best-established truths is to little purpose if intellects are not purified, but instead remain intoxicated by the poisons which afflict the world. How can clear vision be expected of ailing eyes? How can a debilitated organism be expected to sort out the queer mixture it receives as food, and to assimilate what is healthy and burn what is poisoned?

As to the work of Christian thought, it thus happens that to many contemporary minds the meat furnished by the philosophy in which that thought reaches its highest fulfillment and greatest vigor, I mean Thomistic philosophy, appears as too strong a food. One solution consists in diluting or more or less adulterating the food itself, and in discarding articulate knowledge and its too rigorous disciplines. An argument in favor of this solution is the pressing need we feel to go to our neighbor's help. But in reality, I am afraid, this solution would serve both to weaken and diminish the verities, and to prolong or aggravate the attack of pernicious anemia which the powers of the subject are now undergoing.

The true solution would require that one succeed in strengthening these powers from within, in restoring the taste for truth within the minds of men, and in purifying and refreshing the sight of their eyes. Finally, in order to achieve these ends—and this is the point I want to make—there is only one remedy: to re-awaken in the world a sense of, and esteem for, contemplation. The world is prey to a great thirst, an immense mystical yearning which does not even know itself and which, because it remains without objective, turns to despair or neurosis. The prognosis is hardly favorable if we refuse to have recourse to what was recently described as "the only method which has proved its worth when it is a question of transforming man." This was written by Aldous Huxley, who does not understand much about Catholic dogma, but whose testimony is important and significant.

For my part, after having travelled along the ways of the world and after coming to know many countries, I am persuaded that if the *perennial philosophy* is to act again upon culture and humanity and to bear fruit in civilization, instead of becoming enclosed within the limits of a school where it would be content merely to transmit to a few rare minds the heritage of a wisdom grown perforce esoteric, the essential condition required for this change is that the environment within which this philosophy labors be itself purified by a rising of the contemplative life-force.

I do not only mean that those who are nourished on the doctrine of the Angelic Doctor should follow his example and quicken intellectual study by love for contemplative wisdom. I also mean that there should be established everywhere, on a larger scale, centers of spiritual life where the practical science of the contemplative ways and the lessons taught by the saints could be studied (in themselves and also in their relation to poetry and knowledge, to works of culture and to everyday morality). There this multitude of thinking beings of every background and every denomination (including also philosophers and those who read their writings) whose hearts are troubled by a secret aspiration could be helped to rise above the life of the senses and to receive a spark of that fire which used to consume the heroes of the spirit. It is a fact that great contemplatives are rare. But, from the viewpoint of what might be termed the sociology of the intellect, the important thing for the health of the world as well as for the health of philosophy (which of itself pertains to the world), is above all that the authentic scale of values be recognized, and that, even at the price of much "trial and error," the average level of man's spiritual experience be sufficiently raised.

Then the intellect would be able to cast off many of the toxins which today dim its sight. I am well aware that the subject's good dispositions are not enough, and that purity of vision is not enough to make men discern truth: it is also necessary for the object to be set forth in its true light. But, at least truth would be loved, words would no longer be perverted, and a minimum of common language would once more be possible.

And, to get back to the subject of this essay, the sense of intellectual justice would grow stronger among the philosophers; and, in the very midst of doctrinal conflicts, it would be possible to see the development of a certain philosophical co-operation like that which I have tried to describe, instead of the deaf-men's quarrels in which philosophical discussions consist today.

> The immortality of the soul is a matter which concerns us so strongly, which touches us so closely, that a man must have lost all feeling not to care to know about it.
>
> PASCAL

CHAPTER FIVE

THE IMMORTALITY OF

THE SOUL

I. THE VIEWS OF THEODOR FECHNER

BEFORE writing these lines,* I re-read the little book in which Gustav Theodor Fechner, the founder of Psychophysics, presented his thoughts on *Life After Death*. This book was published in 1836; an American edition appeared in 1904 with an Introduction by William James, and was reprinted some years ago with a Prefatory Note by John Erskine.†

We do not find any specific demonstration in Fechner's book, but rather a large conception of the world in which scientific concepts are subjected to philosophical extrapolation. In my opinion, this conception of the world is marred by a kind of idealist and panpsychist metaphysics; yet the views of such a great thinker on immortality are especially stimulating, and we cannot look without emotion upon this philosophical effort and personal testimony, which bear witness to the natural belief of man in immortality, and which are permeated by Christian elements transposed into a secular frame of mind. I do not believe that Mr. Erskine is right when he states that never does "Fechner make of immortality a moral problem." Rather does Fechner admit a sort of law of Karma; according to him, life after death is hampered or exalted, made unhappy, at least for a time, or happy, in accordance with our evil or good deeds.‡ But the fact remains that, in Fechner's views, man, in his

---

*This essay is complementary to the essay *The Immortality of Man,* Chapter II in *Man's Destiny in Eternity,* A Symposium (The Garvin lectures), Beacon Press, Boston, 1949.

†Pantheon Books, New York, 1943.

‡"According as the man has been good or bad, has behaved nobly or basely, was industrious or idle, will he find himself possessed of an organism, healthy or sick, beautiful or hateful, strong or weak, in the world to come, and his free activity in this world will determine his relation to other souls, his destiny, his capacity and talents for further progress in that world." *Op. cit.,* pp. 33-34.

third life (which succeeds death just as his second life—in his own body—succeeds birth, which is death with regard to uterine life), man in his life after death survives in other men by virtue of the spiritual waves he has produced in humanity and acquires a new organism in the whole universe: which supposes a strange and precarious idea of the self, and assumes that man is but a dwelling-place in which other spirits unite and intersect. I would say that Fechner, who at the same time admitted the reality of free will, self-determination, consciousness and reason, had a poor metaphysical concept of the soul as well as of God.

The Scholastics, on the contrary, were always concerned with demonstrative, apodictic rational proofs. In the late and decadent Middle Ages, they became skeptical with regard to the philosophical establishment of the soul's immortality, and considered immortality a mere datum of faith, unattainable by the natural forces of reason, precisely because they sought a perfectly demonstrable proof, and had become unable to realize it. But in the great age of Scholasticism, at the time of Thomas Aquinas, they were able to work out, understand and provide us with such a proof. Fechner's theory, compared with their logical and scientifically philosophical requirements, would have appeared to the great Scholastics as a set of harmonious metaphorical insights, a kind of Platonic myth.

II. "SUBJECTIVE" IMMORTALITY

I am very far, nevertheless, from despising that kind of survival which consists in living in men's minds and hearts. Auguste Comte called it subjective immortality, and Fechner speaks of it in a much more profound manner, all the while mingling with it, and trying to superimpose upon it, a theory of genuine or "objective" immortality. To endure in human minds, and in the movement of human history is something momentous, in which each human person is interested by a deep-seated and more or less obscure aspiration.

At this point a great problem arises, one which is far from being solved—the problem of the universal intersolidarity. We have a feeling that there is a mysterious unity of the world, that the whole of mankind suffers from the iniquities which each one undergoes and is helped by the generosity and love which each one displays in his individual life. Somehow this feeling must be true.

Yet it does not mean that there exists a soul of the world, in a Stoic or Spinozistic sense. We live in time; each man is a spiritual unit engaged in the world of matter and change; it is by some ex-

ternal expression in this world, by some utterance, that the inner
achievements or disasters of these spiritual units may exert influence, and that this influence may worm its way into human history
and endure in it. Otherwise, why should each of us so ardently
yearn to express or manifest what fills his mind and his heart, and
to be heard by other spirits? "A Goethe, a Schiller, a Napoleon, a
Luther, still live among us," as Fechner puts it—yes, but because
they were able to make their thoughts or deeds resound loudly
throughout the world.

What is true is that the energy of the spirit is so great, and its
pressure on the material structures of life is so powerful, that it
passes through the smallest interstices, it makes use of every possible
means of communication, so as to penetrate into men's existence
and human history by hidden, invisible channels.

It is in this way that the feeling I mentioned a moment ago, the
feeling of the lasting, immaterial and secret progression of our
deeds and thoughts, long after the death of each one of us, in the
mysterious texture of the world, corresponds to reality. But such a
survival remains precarious and exceedingly far from including the
whole of what we bear in ourselves.

In the case of men whose life is immersed in time, their actions
are born in time and die in time; but because they are men, their
actions always involve and express something of the spirit abiding
in them; this dynamic spiritual charge may be taken on by other
minds; thus part—a small part indeed—of their spiritual efforts or
trials may possibly survive in a more or less fragile way, especially
in the memories of their descendants. In the case of men whose
life is lived chiefly in the spirit and above time, their actions are
able to conquer time; they can claim to survive for generations to
come, but always on condition that certain external means of communication—however humble, poor, or humanly weak—be provided
for them. And when they do survive, it is always in a terribly vul-
nerable, and often a terribly disappointing, manner. In any case,
an immense part of the sufferings and ordeals, of the spiritual
flame, love or heroism of the inner life of men, is irreparably lost,
so far as their influence in the world and their survival in time and
history are concerned.

When thousands of human beings are tortured and driven to
despair in prisons and concentration camps, and die without their
cries falling on any human ear or being heard by any star in
the heavens, doubtless some slight waves of their agony find their

E

way through cracks in the walls, and come to stir up or disturb the dreams of the world. Yet the frightful mass of their individual sufferings, heroic deeds or despairing deaths will simply fall into the gulf of forgetfulness, without exerting upon human history any influence comparable to what they have undergone and done. It is only through the justice of God, as Supreme Ruler of this universe, that they may hope that their silent sacrifice will be useful to their brothers, or to the human cause they wanted to serve.

What I mean is that it would be a supreme delusion to seek in time, and in history, and in the results of our deeds here below, to seek, that is, in subjective immortality, any adequate fulfilment of that irrepressible aspiration to survival which inhabits the depths of our substances.

It is true that death is but a second birth, and that our life on earth is a kind of uterine life, in the obscure womb of the griefs and dreams and passing images of this enigmatic world. "Life is changed, life is not taken away." That is why, in the liturgy of the Catholic Church, the feasts of the saints are celebrated on the anniversary of their death, that is, of their real and definite birth. But this is so only because the soul of man is an individual substance, existing by and unto itself as a perfectly defined unit; because it is destined to objective immortality, genuine personal immortality, not in time and history, but in eternity.

III. PERSONAL IMMORTALITY

The Existence of the Soul

It is of this immortality, and of the way in which the Scholastics established its rational certainty, that I should now like to speak.

We must of course realize that we have a soul before we can discuss whether it is immortal. How does St. Thomas Aquinas proceed in this matter?

He observes first that man has an activity, the activity of the intellect, which is in itself immaterial. The activity of the intellect is immaterial because the proportionate or "connatural" object of the human intellect is not, like the object of the senses, a particular and limited category of things, or rather a particular and limited category of the qualitative properties of things. The proportionate or "connatural" object of the intellect is the nature of the sense-perceivable things considered in an all-embracing manner, whatever the sense concerned may be. It is not only—as for sight—color or the colored thing (which absorbs and reflects such or such rays of light) nor—as for hearing—sound or the sound-source; it is the whole universe and texture of sense-perceivable reality which can be known by the intellect, because the intellect does not stop at qualities, but pierces beyond, and proceeds to look at essence (that which a thing *is*). This very fact is a proof of the spirituality, or complete immateriality of our intellect; for every activity in which matter plays an intrinsic part is limited to a given category of material objects, as is the case for the senses, which perceive only those properties which are able to act upon their physical organs.

There is already, in fact, a certain immateriality in sense-knowledge; knowledge, as such, is an immaterial activity, because when I am in the act of knowing, I become, or am, the very thing that I know, a thing other than myself, insofar as it is other than myself. And how can I be, or become, other than myself, if it is not in a supra-subjective or immaterial manner? Sense-knowledge is a very poor kind of knowledge; insofar as it is knowledge, it is immaterial, but it is an immaterial activity intrinsically conditioned by, and dependent upon, the material functioning of the sense-organs. Sense-knowledge is the immaterial achievement, the immaterial actuation and product of a living bodily organ; and its very object is also something half material, half immaterial, I mean a physical quality *intentionally* or immaterially present in the medium by which it acts on the sense-organ (something comparable to the manner in which a painter's idea is immaterially present in his paint-brush).

But with intellectual knowledge we have to do with an activity which is in itself completely immaterial. The human intellect is able to know whatever participates in being and truth; the whole universe can be inscribed in it; this means that, in order to be known, the object known by the intellect has been stripped of any existential condition of materiality. This rose, which I see, has contours; but Being, of which I am thinking, is more spacious than space. The object of the intellect is universal, for instance that universal or de-individualized object which is apprehended in the idea of man, of animal, of atom; the object of the intellect is a universal which remains what it is while being identified with an infinity of individuals. And this is only possible because things, in order to become objects of the mind, have been entirely separated from their material existence. To this it must be added that the operation of our intellect does not stop at the knowledge of the nature of sense-perceivable things; it goes further; it knows by analogy the spiritual natures; it extends to the realm of merely possible things; its field has infinite magnitude.

Thus, the objects known by the human intellect, taken not as things existing in themselves, but precisely as objects determining the intellect and united with it, are purely immaterial.

Furthermore, just as the condition of the *object* is immaterial, so is the condition of the *act* which bears upon it, and is determined or specified by it. The object of the human intellect is, as such, purely immaterial; the act of the human intellect is also purely immaterial.

And, moreover, if the act of the intellectual power is purely immaterial, that *power* itself is also purely immaterial. In man, this thinking animal, the intellect is a purely spiritual power. Doubtless it depends upon the body, upon the conditions of the brain. Its activity can be disturbed or hindered by a physical disorder, by an outburst of anger, by a drink or a narcotic. But this dependence is an *extrinsic* one. It exists because our intelligence cannot act without the joint activity of the memory and the imagination, of the internal senses and external senses, all of which are organic powers residing in some material organ, in some special part of the body. As for the intellect itself, it is not *intrinsically* dependent upon the body since its activity is immaterial; the human intellect does not reside in any special part of the body. It is not contained by the body, but rather contains it. It uses the brain, since the organs of the internal senses are in the brain; yet the brain is not an organ of the intelligence; there is no part of the organism whose act is intellectual operation. The intellect has no organ.

Finally, since intellectual power is spiritual, or purely immaterial in itself, its *first substantial root,* the subsisting principle from which this power proceeds and which acts through its instrumentality, is also spiritual.

So much for the spirituality of the intellect. Now, thought or the operation of the intellect is an act and emanation of man as a unit; and when I think, it is not only my intellect which thinks: it is *I,* my own self. And my own self is a bodily self; it involves matter; it is not a spiritual or purely immaterial subject. The body is an essential part of man. The intellect is not the whole man.

Therefore the intellect, or rather the substantial root of the intellect, which must be as immaterial as the intellect, is only a part, albeit an essential part, of man's substance.

But man is not an aggregate, a juxtaposition of two substances; man is a natural whole, a single being, a single substance.

Consequently, we must conclude that the essence or substance of man is single, but that this single substance itself is a compound, the components of which are the body and the spiritual intellect: or rather matter, of which the body is made, and the spiritual principle, one of the powers of which is the intellect. Matter—in the Aristotelian sense of prime matter, or of that root potentiality which is the common stuff of all corporeal substance—matter, substantially united with the spiritual principle of the intellect, is ontologically molded, shaped from within and in the innermost depths of being, by this spiritual principle as by a substantial and vital impulse, in order to constitute that body of ours. In this sense, Saint Thomas, after Aristotle, says that the intellect is the form, the substantial form of the human body.

That is the Scholastic notion of the human soul. The human soul, which is the root principle of the intellectual power, is the first principle of life of the human body, and the substantial form, the *entelechy,* or that body. And the human soul is not only a substantial form or entelechy, as are the souls of plants and animals according to the biological philosophy of Aristotle; the human soul is also a spirit, a spiritual substance able to exist apart from matter, since the human soul is the root principle of a spiritual power, the act of which is intrinsically independent of matter. The human soul is both a soul and a spirit, and it is its very substantiality, subsistence and existence, which are communicated to the whole human substance, in order to make human substance be what it is, and to make it subsist and exist. Each element of the human body is human, and exists as such, by virtue of the immaterial existence of the human soul. Our body, our hands, our eyes exist by virtue of the existence of our soul.

The immaterial soul is the first substantial root not only of the intellect, but of all that which, in us, is spiritual activity; and it is also the first substantial root of all our other living activities. It would be inconceivable that a non-spiritual soul, that kind of soul which is not a spirit and cannot exist without informing matter— namely, the souls of plants or animals in Aristotelian biology—

should possess a power or faculty *superior* to its own degree in being, that is, immaterial, or act through a supra-material instrumentality independent of any corporeal organ and physical structure. But when it is a question of a spirit which is a soul, or of a *spiritual soul*, as the human soul is, then it is perfectly conceivable that such a soul should have, aside from immaterial or spiritual faculties, other powers and activities which are organic and material, and which, relating to the union between soul and body, pertain to a level of being *inferior* to that of the spirit.

The Spirituality of the Human Soul

Thus, the very way in which the Scholastics arrived at the existence of the human soul also established its spirituality. Just as the intellect is spiritual, that is to say intrinsically independent of matter in its operation and in its nature, so also, and for the same reason, the human soul, the substantial root of the intellect, is spiritual, that is, intrinsically independent of matter in its nature and in its existence; it does not live by the body, the body lives by it. The human soul is a spiritual substance which, by its substantial union with matter, gives existence and countenance to the body.

That is my second point. As we have seen, the Scholastics demonstrated it by a metaphysical analysis of the intellect's operation, carefully distinguished from the operation of the senses. They adduced, of course, much other evidence in support of their demonstration. In their consideration of the intellect, they observed, for instance, that the latter is capable of *perfect reflection*, that is, of coming back entirely upon itself—not in the manner of a sheet of paper, half of which can be folded on the other half, but in a complete manner, so that it can grasp its whole operation and penetrate it by knowledge, and can contain itself and its own principle, the existing self, in its own knowing activity, a perfect reflection or self-containing of which any material agent, extended in space and time, is essentially incapable. Here we are confronted with that phenomenon of self-knowledge, of *prise de conscience* or becoming aware of oneself, which is a privilege of the spirit, as Hegel (after St. Augustine) was to emphasize, and which plays so tremendous a part in the history of humanity and the development of its spiritual energies.

In the same way it is possible to show that the human will, which is rooted in the intellect, and which is able to determine itself, or to master the very motive or judgment which determines it and is made efficacious by the will itself, is spiritual in its operation and nature. Every material agent is subject to the universal determinism. Free will is the privilege, the glorious and weighty privilege, of an agent endowed with immaterial power.

We are responsible for ourselves; we choose for ourselves and decide' on our own ends and our own destinies. We are capable of spiritual, supra-sensuous love, and desire and joy, which are naturally intermingled with our organic and sensuous emotions, but which are in themselves affections of the spiritual will, and are awakened through the immaterial light of intellectual insight. We delight in beauty, we desire perfection and justice, we love truth, we love God, we love all men—not only the members of our social group, or our family, our class or nation—but all men because they are human beings, and children of God. The saints, those men who are called everywhere spiritual men, experience a contemplation which establishes their souls in a peace superior to and stronger than the whole world, and they go through inner trials, crucifixions and deaths which only a life superior to and stronger than biological existence can suffer and go through—and still remain alive. And we ourselves know that we can deliberate about ourselves, judge our own actions, cling to what is good because it is good and for no other reason; all of us know more or less obscurely that we are persons, that we have rights and duties, that we preserve human dignity within ourselves. Each one of us can, at certain moments in his existence, descend into the innermost depths of the Ego, to make there some eternal pledge or gift of himself, or face some irrefutable judgment of his conscience; and each one of us, on such occasions, alone with himself, feels that he is a universe unto himself, immersed in, but not dominated by, the great star-studded universe.

Through all these convergent ways, we may realize and experience in a certain measure, and in a concrete fashion, that living reality of our spiritual roots, or of what is above time in us, which the philosophical proofs make intellectually certain, but in the abstract manner of scientific knowledge.

The Immortality of the Human Soul

The third point follows immediately from the second. The immortality of the human soul is an immediate corollary of its spirituality. A soul which is spiritual in itself, intrinsically independent of matter in its nature and existence, cannot cease existing. A spirit

—that is, a "form" which needs nothing other than itself (save the influx of the Prime Cause) to exercise existence—once existing cannot cease existing. A spiritual soul cannot be corrupted, since it possesses no matter; it cannot be disintegrated, since it has no substantial parts; it cannot lose its individual unity, since it is self-subsisting, nor its internal energy, since it contains within itself all the sources of its energies. The human soul cannot die. Once it exists, it cannot disappear; it will necessarily exist forever, endure without end.

Thus, philosophic reason, put to work by a great metaphysician like Thomas Aquinas, is able to prove the immortality of the human soul in a demonstrative manner. Of course, this demonstration implies a vast and articulate network of metaphysical insights, notions and principles (relating to essence and nature, substance, act and potency, matter and form, operation, etc.) the validity of which is necessarily presupposed. We can appreciate fully the strength of the Scholastic demonstration only if we realize the significance and full validity of the metaphysical notions involved. If modern times feel at a loss in the face of metaphysical knowledge, I fancy that it is not metaphysical knowledge which is to blame, but rather modern times and the weakening of reason they have experienced.

It is not surprising, on the other hand, that the philosophical demonstration I have just summarized is an abstract and a difficult one. The great and fundamental truths which are spontaneously grasped by the natural instinct of the human mind are always the most arduous for philosophic reason to establish. With regard to the immortality of the human soul, philosophic reason must use the very refined and elaborate concept of immateriality, a concept remote from the natural understanding, not only of primitive men, but of everyone who thinks with his imagination rather than with his intellect. Were not certain monks of Asia Minor, in the early Christian centuries, indignant at the idea that God is an Immaterial Being? They did not use the English language, yet they were convinced that to be *immaterial,* or deprived of matter, actually meant to be something immaterial, or nothing at all. They surely believed in the immortality of the soul, but it is doubtful whether they would have understood the strength of the argument we have used.

Primitive men did not philosophize; but, for all that, they had their own way, an instinctive, non-conceptual way, of believing in the soul's immortality. It was a belief rooted in an obscure experience of the self, and in the natural aspirations of the spirit in us to overcome death. We need not embark on an analysis of this natural and instinctive, non-philosophical belief in immortality. I should like merely to quote a passage from a book by the late scientist Pierre Lecomte du Noüy. Speaking of prehistoric man, he said: "Not only did the Neanderthal Man, who lived in Paleolithic times, bury his dead, but sometimes he buried them in a common ground. An example of this is the Grotte des Enfants near Mentone. Because of this respect he had for his dead, we have reached an anatomical knowledge of the Neanderthal Man that is more perfect than that which we have of certain races which have recently become extinct, or which still exist, such as the Tasmanians. This is no longer a question of instinct. We are dealing already with the dawn of human thought, which reveals itself in a kind of revolt against death. And revolt against death implies love for those who have gone as well as the hope that their disappearance is not final. We see these *ideas,* the first perhaps, develop progressively alongside the first artistic feelings. Flat rocks in the shape of dolmens are placed so as to protect the faces and heads of those who are buried. Later, ornaments, weapons, food, and the colors which serve to adorn the body, are placed in the tombs. The idea of finality is unbearable. The dead man will awaken, he will be hungry, he will have to defend himself, he will want to adorn himself."*

The same author goes on to observe that because the primordial notions, like those of good and evil, or of immortality, were spontaneously born in the most primitive human beings, those notions would deserve for that very reason to be examined and scrutinized as possessing absolute value.

I think that these views expressed by Lecomte du Noüy are true and thought-provoking. *A priori* it is probable that the great and basic ideas, the prime ideas, which are contained in the myths of primitive man, and are handed down in the common heritage of mankind, are more sound than illusory, and deserve respect more than contempt. At the same time, we are free to prefer a genuine philosophical demonstration.

The Condition and Destiny of the Immortal Soul

What can philosophy tell us about the natural condition of the immortal soul after the death of its body? That is my fourth and last point. Philosophy can tell us very little indeed on this subject. Let us try to summarize the few indications there are. All the or-

*L'Avenir de l'Esprit, Gallimard, Paris, 1941, p. 188.

ganic and sensuous powers of the human soul remain dormant in
a separated soul, for they cannot be brought into play without the
body. The separated soul is itself engulfed in a complete sleep
with regard to the material world; the external senses and their
perceptions have vanished; the images of memory and imagination, the impulses of instinct and passion have vanished. But this
sleep is not like the sleep we know, obscure and filled with dreams;
it is lucid and intelligent, alive to spiritual realities. For now light
shines from within. The intellect and the spiritual powers are awake
and active. From the very fact of its separation from the body,
the soul now knows itself through itself; its very substance has become transparent to its intellect; it is intellectually penetrated to
its innermost depths. The soul knows itself in an intuitive manner;
it is dazzled by its own beauty, the beauty of a spiritual substance,
and it knows other things through its own substance already known,
in the measure in which other things resemble it. It knows God
through that image of God which the soul itself is. And in accordance with its state of incorporeal existence, it receives from
God, the sun of the spirits, certain ideas and inspirations which
directly enlighten it, and help the natural light of the human intellect, of that intellect which is, as Saint Thomas Aquinas phrased
it, the lowest in the hierarchy of spirits.

Saint Thomas teaches also that all that is of the intellect and the
spirit, and especially the intellectual memory, which is but one with
the intellect, keeps alive, in the separated soul, the whole treasure
of knowledge acquired during our bodily life. The intellectual
knowledge, the intellectual virtues acquired here below subsist in
the separated soul. Whereas the images of the sense-memory, which
had its seat in the brain, disappear, that which has penetrated into
the intellectual memory is preserved. Thus, in an intellectual and
spiritual manner, the separated soul ever knows those whom it loved.
And it loves them spiritually. And it is able to converse with other
spirits by opening to them what abides in its inner thoughts and
is taken hold of by its free will.

We may thus imagine that, at the moment when it leaves the
body, the soul is suddenly immersed into itself as into a shining abyss,
where all that was buried within it, all its dead, rise up again in
full light, insofar as all this was encompassed in the subconscious
or supraconscious depths of the spiritual life of its intellect and
will. Then all that is true and good in the soul becomes a blessing
for it at the touch of this all-pervading revelatory light; all that

is warped and evil becomes a torment for it under the effect of
the very same light.

I do not believe that natural reason can go further in its understanding of the natural condition of the separated soul. What would
be the life and happiness of souls if their state after death were
a purely natural state? Their supreme good would consist in wisdom, untrammeled spiritual life, mutual friendship, and first and
foremost in advancing constantly in their natural knowledge and
love of God, Whom they would, however, never see face to face. It
would be happiness in motion, never absolutely fulfilled—what
Leibniz called *un chemin par des plaisirs,* "a road amidst spiritual
pleasures."

But if we wish to know more, can we not go beyond philosophy?
Philosophy itself will then entrust us to the guidance of a knowledge
whose sources are superior to its own. Christians know that man
does not live in a state of pure nature. They know that he was
created in a state of grace, and that, after the first sin which
wounded our race, he has been living in a state of fallen and redeemed nature; they know that he is made for supernatural blessedness. In answer to the question of the separated soul's destiny, the
Scholastic doctors spoke not as philosophers, but as theologians
whose knowledge rests on the data of Revelation.

Insofar as man participates in the metaphysical privileges of spirit
and personality, he has aspirations which transcend human nature
and its possibilities, and which consequently may be called trans-
natural aspirations: the longing for a state in which he would know
things completely and without error, in which he would enjoy perfect communion with spirits, in which he would be free without
being able to fail or to sin, in which he would inhabit a realm
of unfading justice, in which he would have the intuitive knowledge
of the First Cause of being.

Such a longing cannot be fulfilled by nature. It can be fulfilled
by grace. The immortal soul is involved and engaged in the great
drama of the Redemption. If, at the moment of its separation from
the body, at the moment when its choice is immutably fixed forever, the immortal soul prefers its own will and self-love to the
will and gift of God, if it prefers misery with pride to the blessing
of grace, then it is granted what it has wished for. It has it, and
it will never cease wanting and preferring it, for a free choice made
in the condition of a *pure* spirit is an eternal choice. If the soul
opens itself to the will and gift of God, Whom it loves more than its

own existence, then it is granted what it has loved, it enters forever into the joy of the uncreated Being, it sees God face to face and knows Him as it is known by Him, intuitively. Thus, it becomes God by participation, as Saint John of the Cross phrased it, and, through grace, it attains that communion in divine life, that blessedness for the sake of which all things have been created. And the degree of its blessedness itself, the degree of its vision, will correspond to the degree of the inner impetus which projects it into God, in other words, to the degree of love to which it has attained in its life on earth. In the last analysis, therefore, we must say with Saint John of the Cross: It is upon our love that we shall be judged. In its state of blessedness the immortal soul will know creation in the Creator, by that kind of knowledge which Saint Augustine called "matutinal" knowledge, because it is produced in the eternal morning of Creative Ideas; the immortal soul will be equal to the angels, and will communicate freely with the whole realm of spirits; it will love God, henceforth clearly seen, with a sovereign necessity; and it will exert free will with regard to all its actions concerning creatures, but its free will shall no longer be liable to failure and sin; the soul will inhabit the realm of unfading justice, that of the three divine Persons and of the blessed spirits; it will grasp and possess the divine Essence which, infinitely clearer and more intelligible than any of our ideas, will illumine the human intellect from within and will itself be the intelligible medium, the actuating form through which it will be known. According to a line of the Psalms which Saint Thomas loved and often quoted: "In Thy light shall we see light."

Such are the teachings of Saint Thomas, both as a philosopher and as a theologian, about the condition and destiny of the human soul. Immortality is not a more or less precarious, successful or unsuccessful survival in other men, or in the ideal waves of the universe. Immortality is a nature-given, inalienable property of the human soul as a spiritual substance. And grace makes eternal life possible to all, to the most destitute as well as to the most gifted. The eternal life of the immortal soul is its transforming union with God and His intimate life, a union which is to be accomplished inchoatively here below, by love and contemplation and, after the body's death, in a definite and perfect manner, by the beatific vision. For eternal life begins here upon earth, and the soul of man lives and breathes where it loves; and love, in living faith, has strength enough to make the soul of man experience unity with

God—"two natures in a single spirit and love, *dos naturalezas en un espiritu y amor de Dios.*"

I do not believe that a philosopher can discuss the immortality of the soul without taking into consideration the complementary notions which religious thought adds to the true and inadequate answers which reason and philosophy can furnish by themselves.

CHAPTER SIX

THE IMMANENT DIALECTIC

OF THE FIRST ACT

OF FREEDOM

I. THE FIRST ACT OF FREEDOM

I AM considering any *first or primal* free act, any free act through which a new basic direction is imposed on my life. Such an act goes down to the sources of my moral life; through it I take hold of myself so as to project myself in a spray of ulterior actions which may be indefinite. Nevertheless, I am not necessarily aware of the profundity of what is happening; the available evidence may be but a very slight impact, a mere ripple on the surface of the waters.

This act may have been preceded by many others; yet it is, in a moral sense, an absolute beginning. (Such is the kind of act with which is concerned what theologians call the *gratia operans;* or, in philosophical terms, an activation coming from God and through which the will does not make an act proceed from another, but causes a primal act to surge from its own depths.)

For the sake of simplicity, I am considering the first or primal act of freedom exercised by a child when, for the first time, he ponders or "deliberates about himself."* He deliberates! He does not go in for any discursive deliberation; he takes himself in hand; he frees or delivers his own self from the deterministic crust under which he has lived until that moment; he ushers himself into the universe of moral life by freely deciding about the direction of his

---

*He has already accomplished many acts in which freedom was not lacking; but the part played by freedom, hitherto, was inchoate and superficial. We had only attempts of freedom broaching on the basic determination of nature, and through which the child was not yet introduced into the realm of personal activity and moral life. Thus, the expression "first act of freedom" is not taken, in this essay, as meaning "first act in which freedom plays a part"; it refers to a deep-seated determination—a root-act—in which the person freely commits himself and which impresses a definite direction upon his life as a person.

life. At the root of such an act there is a reflection upon oneself which takes place in the intellect and answers the question: "What do you live for?" Yet this reflection is not explicitly signified to the mind, and the question which it answers is not formulated in clear concepts. This question, on the contrary, is altogether engaged and involved in a choice whose immediate object may be a bit of straw, a trifle, but which is pregnant with a spiritual vitality, a decisive earnestness, a commitment, a gift of oneself the plenitude of which will not be experienced by adult age except in rare and miraculous occasions. *Puerile decus.* Children are told not to play with fire; they play with God.

Here is a child who refrains from telling a lie, under circumstances which, in themselves, are trivial. On a certain day he refrains from lying not because he is likely to be punished if he is caught, or because he has been told not to lie and is afraid of grown-ups, or because he does not want to grieve his mother. He refrains from telling a lie, because lying is wrong. It would not be right to tell a lie. That would not be *good.* Doubtless, he has already known of all sorts of little things labeled good or evil by his parents and his teachers; social custom has tamed him into doing the former and not doing the latter. But this time it is no longer a question of a kind of conditioned reflex. When he thinks: "It would not be *good* to do this," what is confusedly revealed to him, in a flash of understanding, is the moral good, with the whole mystery of its demands. He is face to face with this mystery, and he is all alone.

And it is the first time that he himself governs his own practical behavior, as a human being, according to this standard: the moral good, consciously perceived in an idea whose representative content is doubtless meager and confused, at the level of a child's intellect, but whose intuitive intensity and intentional value may be singularly powerful. *Bonum honestum; kalokagathon.* At this moment and all at once—but *in actu exercito,* not *in actu signato,* in a merely lived, not signified, manner—he has reflected upon himself or "deliberated about himself," and come to a decision about the direction of his life;* he has answered the question "What do you live for?" He will not remember this event any more than the day when, from the midst of images, the life of reason and of universal ideas awakened in him. For what took place was not a philosophical dis-

---

*He has decided about the direction of his life insofar as an act of the human will, exercised in time, can bind the future: that is to say in a fragile way. He is not forever confirmed in his decision; throughout his life he will be able to change his decision concerning his last end and the direction of his life, but by just as deep an act of freedom and of deliberation about himself.

covery of his ego, but a spontaneous reflection involved in a practical process whose object was not, by any means, extraordinary
or exceptional; and it is toward the object, not the event which
goes on within himself, that the attention of the child is always
turned. Moreover, the act then elicited, though conscious and deliberate, sprang from the unconscious depths where the spirit has
its sources.

Yet, in some rare cases, the first act of freedom will never be
forgotten, especially if the choice—however insignificant its object—
through which the soul was introduced into moral life occurred
rather late. In other cases there is a remembrance of some childish
remorse, whose occasion was unimportant but whose intensity, out
of proportion with its object, upset the soul and awakened its moral
sense. Let us think, finally, of the dreams in which the adolescent
sees himself as a hero or a knight, or as a man blessed with fortune
or pleasure; let us think of the chance statements in which, during
the course of his daily conversation, he unwittingly drops the first
hints of a philosophy of life. These dreams and rationalizations
are but the outward projection of the decisive act performed at
the moment when moral life was awakened, and of which no trace
was kept by memory.

II.   THE IMPLICATIONS OF THE FIRST ACT OF FREEDOM

What does such an act imply? What is the immanent dialectic,
the secret dynamism of the primal act of freedom? Let us unfold
and make explicit, in terms of speculative knowledge and philosophical discourse, what is contained in the indivisible vitality,
both volitional and intellectual, of this act.

The soul, in this first moral choice, turns away from an evil action
because it is evil. Thus, the intellect is aware of the distinction
between good and evil, and knows that the good ought to be done
because it is good. We are confronted, here, with a formal motive
which transcends the whole order of empirical convenience and
desire. This is the primary implication of the first act of freedom
when it is good.

But, because the value with which the moral object and the moral
act are permeated surpasses anything given in empirical existence
and concerns that which *ought to be,* the notion of a good action
to be done for the sake of the good necessarily implies that there
is an ideal and indefectible order of proper consonance between
our activity and our essence, a *law* of human acts transcending

all facts. This is the second implication of the first act of freedom when it is good.

Let us reflect upon this law. It transcends the whole empirical order; the act that I bring into existence must conform to it, if it is to be a good act; and the first precept of this law demands of me that my act be good. Such a law carries in the world of actual existence the requirements of an order that depends on a reality superior to everything and which is Goodness itself—good by virtue of its very being, not by virtue of conformity with anything distinct from itself. Such a law manifests the existence of a Separate Good transcending all empirical existence and subsisting *per se,* and subsists primarily in this Separate Good. But how could I, in an act of total commitment, strive to achieve conformity with this transcendental law unless, by the same token and on a still more profound level, I strive toward this Separate Good and direct my life toward it because it is both *the* Good and *my* Good? The initial act which determines the direction of life and which—when it is good—chooses the good for the sake of the good, proceeds from a natural élan which is also, undividedly, an élan by which this very same act tends all at once, beyond its immediate object, toward God as the Separate Good in which the human person in the process of acting, whether he is aware of it or not, places his happiness and his end. Here we have an ordainment which is actual and formal, not virtual—but in merely lived act (*in actu exercito*), not in signified act—to God as ultimate end of human life. This is the third implication of the act of which I am speaking.

These implications are not disclosed to the intellect of the child. They are contained in the act by which, at the term of his first deliberation about himself, he brings himself to do a good act for the sake of the moral good, of the *bonum honestum* of which he has an explicit idea, no matter how confused.

III. A NON-CONSCIOUS KNOWLEDGE OF GOD

In his first act in freedom—(at least, I say, if we analyze it from the standpoint peculiar to moral philosophy)—in his first act of freedom—supposedly good—which is his first act as a man, the child does not think explicitly of God, or of his ultimate end. He thinks of what is good and of what is evil. But by the same token he knows God, without being aware of it. He knows God because, by virtue of the internal dynamism of his choice of the good for

F

the sake of the good, he wills and loves the Separate Good as ultimate end of his existence. Thus, his intellect has of God a vital
and non-conceptual knowledge which is involved both in the practical notion (confusedly and intuitively grasped, but with its full
intentional energy), of the moral good as formal motive of his
first act of freedom, and in the movement of his will toward this
good and, all at once, toward the Good. The intellect may already
have the idea of God and it may not yet have it. The non-conceptual knowledge which I am describing takes place independently
of any use possibly made or not made of the idea of God, and independently of the actualization of any explicit and conscious knowledge of man's true last End.

In other words, the will, hiddenly, secretly, obscurely moving
(when no extrinsic factor stops or deviates the process) down to
the term of the immanent dialectic of the first act of freedom,
goes *beyond* the immediate object of conscious and explicit knowledge (the moral good as such); and it carries with itself, down
to that *beyond,* the intellect, which at this point no longer enjoys
the use of its regular instruments, and, as a result, is only actualized
below the threshold of reflective consciousness, in a night without
concept and without utterable knowledge. The conformity of the
intellect with this transcendent object: the Separate Good (attain-
able only by means of analogy) is then effected by the will, the
rectitude of which is, in the practical order, the measure of the
truth of the intellect. God is thus naturally known, without any
conscious judgment, in and by the impulse of the will striving
toward the Separate Good, whose existence is implicitly involved
in the practical value acknowledged to the moral good. No speculative knowledge of God is achieved. This is a purely practical
cognition of God, produced in and by the movement of the appetite
toward the moral good precisely considered as good. The metaphysical content with which it is pregnant is not grasped as a
metaphysical content, it is not released. It is a purely practical, non-
conceptual and non-conscious knowledge of God, which can co-exist
with a theoretical ignorance of God.

Thus, by virtue of a primal free act having the moral good,
bonum honestum, as its object, a man can tend toward God as
the end of his life without knowing God—that is, he then knows
God (unconsciously) without knowing Him (consciously).

Such is the typical case which moral philosophy must consider,
because moral philosophy sees things in the perspective of nature

and of the most natural and most spontaneous development of moral life within us.

IV. NATURE AND GRACE

The natural process I have just described constitutes—because it is a natural process—the fundamental and primordial fabric of the first act of freedom. But it takes shape in existence and bears fruit only if grace perfects and heals nature. For the natural movement through which the will tends toward God and ordains itself to Him as the ultimate end of life can be fulfilled in a real and decisive manner only if God is loved efficaciously above all things; and all I have said really amounts to asserting that in his first act of freedom, when it is good, man loves God efficaciously above all things. But this presupposes that grace and charity are operating within the soul.*

It would be possible for nature achieving a first act of freedom to turn toward God, efficaciously loved above all things, in that state which is called "the state of pure nature," and in which, as a matter of fact, man has never been established. Nature was able to do so in that state which is called the state of (grace-given) "integrity of nature," or of "original justice"—the general motion of God which activates all nature and without which nothing would act, being presupposed in any case. But through faith we know that, because both of original sin and the blood of Christ, mankind is in fact in the state of fallen nature which is either urged or healed and vivified by the grace of Christ and the supernatural gifts of the Redemption. And theology teaches us that, in the state of fallen nature, man is not capable by his own natural forces of loving God efficaciously above all things. Hence in his first act of freedom he is unable through his merely natural capacities to set the moral good as such for the formal object of his choice, to make his life appendent to the moral good, or the good seen by reason, and to settle on this formal motive his deliberation about himself.

We are confronted at this point with the deepest gash in our nature wounded by the first sin. Human nature has been forced

*Grace has a twofold action: it heals nature which original sin had prevented from loving God efficaciously above all things; and it grafts in nature a supernatural life which is an actual participation in the very life of God. Insofar as it is sanctifying grace, and the very principle of supernatural life, it enables man to love God with the supernatural love of charity, and to ordain himself to the only true end existentially given of human life, i.e., God as ultimate supernatural end. Insofar as it is *gratia sanans,* grace restores to nature its ability to love God above all things as the creator of the universe—natural love virtually contained in the supernatural love of charity—and to ordain itself to God as its natural end, an ordainment virtually contained in the ordainment to God as ultimate supernatural end.

out of joint.* By withdrawing his reason from the order of God, Adam also withdrew the life of the senses and desires from the order of reason, and henceforth our free will, while not destroyed, has become weakened and naturally invalid in the face of what appeals to self-love. Through its own natural capacities, a weak practical reason can accomplish its first act only in a weak manner. No *habitus* or natural virtue has yet developed within it. When taking his first step, a child will fall if his mother does not steady him. When, for the first time, an inexperienced man, and with an infirm hand, is suddenly called to drive the team of his desires, this disabled man cannot fail to upset the chariot. In his first step of freedom the child, if he has only his natural capacities, is bound to fall; he does not choose the rational good, but follows the attraction of the ego's desire for assertion, the "private good" which slakes his thirst for individual realization. He solves his "deliberation about himself" with the choice of a good which is not the good.

In that very act he is responsible and free; and this because, in consideration of the essential structure of the human soul, he is able (*in sensu diviso*), from the very moment when the idea of good and the life of reason awaken within him, to do good and to order his life toward the good and to love God above all things in his first act of freedom. Yet because of a sin which he has not himself committed but in which he nevertheless participates as a member of Adam, he is unable (*in sensu composito*) to exercise this power and royal privilege in his first decisive act. His free fault, which is that of a fallen king—an act at the same time free and inevitably defective†—committed in the weakness of a fault he did not commit, is as it were the excrescence or completion within him of the sin of the father of the human race.

I am well aware that this description concerns only a purely

---

*St. Thomas Aquinas used the word "corrupt," not as meaning that nature was vitiated in its very essence, but to signify that, where the use of its freedom is concerned, its internal order has been put out of order and its inclination toward the good weakened. In this respect man has become an "invalid."

In his commentary on the article (*Sum. theol.* I–II, 109, 3) in which St. Thomas teaches that in the state of integrity of nature man was able, through his natural capacities alone, to love God above all things, but that, in the state of fallen nature, "homo ab hoc deficit secundum appetitum voluntatis rationalis, quae propter corruptionem naturae sequitur bonum privatum, nisi sanetur per gratiam Dei" and that consequently "in statu naturae corruptae indiget homo etiam ad hoc (ad diligendum Deum naturaliter super omnia) auxilio gratiae naturam sanantis," Cajetan writes: "Medium ad secundam partem conclusionis seu ad secundam conclusionem, est *pronitas voluntatis ad privatum bonum. Haec enim, perdito vigore*, in nobis adeo viget, ut oporteat in malum aliquod cadere, ut ex dictis patet."

†The notion of an act which can be free and at the same time inevitably defective, is not self-contradictory, any more than is that of an act which is at the same time free and inevitably good, a notion which theologians use concerning the impeccability of Christ and of the blessed spirits.

theoretical hypothesis assuming that the existential condition of fallen nature is deprived of any other resources than merely natural resources. In actual fact if grace has left the house, it nevertheless keeps on knocking at the door. The sin of one who has not been healed by *gratia sanans* and therefore turns away from the good in his first act of freedom is not a free act which is inevitably defective—because grace offered to him made it avoidable; it is because he refused this grace that he was not healed by it.

God does not leave man to the weakness of his fallen nature (a nature thus fallen, and wounded as a result, because it has disrupted the superior balance, produced by grace, in which it had been created); grace, before healing and vivifying man anew, is still present to envelop and attract him, to call him and incite him in anticipation. Our fallen nature is exposed to grace as our tired bodies are to the rays of the sun. In the years before his first act of freedom, the child had his own span of history, during the course of which his moral life was being prepared as in a morning twilight—nor was he left to the sole influence of his fallen nature; even if he was not baptized he was spurred by actual grace on various occasions and guises as diverse as the contingencies of human life and the by-ways of divine generosity; in his first motions within that incipient freedom which could be his, he was able to accept or refuse these incitations of grace; thus he has been more or less well prepared to meet the test, a test out of all proportion to the preparation for it and which occurs when, for the first time, he is called upon to decide on the direction of his life. In any case, at that decisive moment when he enters upon his life as a person (and later at the other crucial moments that may occur until his last day) grace will still call to him, while being entangled with more or less strength amidst the more or less good tendencies and the more or less great obstacles which derive from nature, heredity and environment. As a result, if he does not decide upon the good, it means that he has slipped away from the help which would have given fallen nature in him the power to choose good for the sake of good and to direct itself toward man's true end, by "healing" that nature and raising it to participation in the divine life.

The fact remains, however, that, as we have already noted, fallen nature when it makes use of free will, is not able to choose the good for the sake of the good through its own natural forces alone. It remains also true that in the first act of freedom, if it is evil, that refusal to accept the proffered grace is by the same token a voluntary surrender to Adam's weakness and to that old primal sin which dwells in us so long as *gratia sanans* did not supervene; it is the surrender to the lure which nothingness holds out to what springs from nothingness, and which, in the case of fallen nature, has already bitten into the powers of the soul and set them at variance.

Essentially, then, the human person is a member, a member of Adam or a member of Christ. The grace which makes him a member of Christ cuts him off from the body of Adam, to which he only remains attached through concupiscence, but without the human person acting henceforth in the virtue (or rather the failing) of original sin and Adam's weakness.

Each of us carries Adam's weakness within himself, but in the case of a righteous man it is a wound inflicted by another, whereas in the case of the sinner it is a weakness born of his own substance and origin, a weakness of the body of which he is a part, a wound upon which he feeds and lives.

God does not refuse His grace to one who acts to the best of his own ability; but it is under the action of grace that man prepares to receive grace. If the child decides upon the good in his first act of freedom, he is set free from original sin and receives sanctifying grace; but this is because, in order for him to decide upon the good in his first act of freedom, grace, insofar as it heals nature, was vouchsafed him. If by acting to the best of one's own ability is meant choosing the moral good in one's first act of freedom, then man acts to the best of his own ability only if he does not take an initiative born of nothingness to render sterile the divine influx, only if he does not slip away from the proffered grace, and thus is healed by grace. *Causae ad invicem sunt causae.*

The first act of deliberate will, the first act of the moral life as such, bathes therefore in the mystery of grace and of original sin. Whatever may be the land of his birth, whatever may be the tradition handed down to him, whether or not he knows Christ, a child born of woman can initiate his moral life rightly only in the grace of Jesus Christ. And without that grace, as Saint Thomas taught, his primal act of freedom can only be a sin which turns him away from his ultimate End.

The indigence of a moral philosophy which sets itself up as a real system of ethics in actual existence without paying attention to the principles of faith and the data of theology is here apparent. According to such a moral philosophy, the first act of freedom would depend on the capacities of nature only, and nature alone would be responsible for having that first act initiate the life of a human being in moral rectitude. Such a philosophy would deceive man as he is in actual fact, or would be speaking to a non-existent man. It is apparent at the same time that, from its very origins, the moral life of man is indissolubly tied to the hidden realities which are at the source of religious life and whose knowledge develops in us through religious life.

V. HOW FAITH PLAYS ITS PART IN THE PROCESS

A child who has received religious education and has been taught the word of God, and who knows and loves God before accomplishing the first act of freedom in which he deliberates about himself, is helped in that first decisive act, as is normal, by the religious traditions of the human family. And he accomplishes his first act of freedom, if this act is good, by virtue of divine charity received in baptism together with grace; then he begins with the End, that is to say, he directs his heart more or less consciously toward his true ultimate End before deciding and in the very act of deciding upon the moral good.

In the opposite case, if a child who has received an a-religious or anti-religious education chooses the moral good in his first act of freedom, the immanent dialectic of that act carries him along in a practical and vital manner, but then, without knowing it, he is at odds with the set of speculative concepts which have been inculcated in him.

Nevertheless, as we have already noted, if we are to consider things from the point of view of philosophy or of nature and its most spontaneous developments, it is suitable to leave out of consideration any particularity pertaining to the social order, and therefore the religious or irreligious education that a child may have received. We are considering a child, any child, one brought up in a pagan or in a Christian, religious or irreligious environment, and we are considering him from the sole point of view of the inner dynamics of his first moral act. If his first act of freedom is to choose the good for the sake of good, that child receives divine grace (supposing he has not already received it by baptism); nor can he choose the good for the sake of good without this grace which heals nature.

Here I should like to digress and say a few words about a question which concerns a purely theological problem. When theologians discuss the salvation of infidels* and the question of implicit faith, they refer to the words of Saint Paul:† "Without faith it is impossible to please God; for he that approacheth unto God must believe that He doth exist, and is rewarder to those who seek Him." This shows that implicit faith in the other truths of Christian revelation presupposes explicit faith in the first truth which contains and envelops them all (the existence of the Savior Who proffers Himself to those who seek Him). Furthermore, grace is not bestowed without supernatural faith. Therefore, the first act of freedom, if it is morally good, must be brought about in faith as well as in grace. If then we consider a child who knows nothing of God, or, more generally speaking, if we consider only the inner dynamics and immanent dialectic of the first act of freedom—leaving out of consideration the transmission of the truths of faith by the preaching of the Gospel and religious education—how can we account for the presence of faith in the soul of the child in question at the moment when, deliberating about himself, he decides upon the moral good?

To say that the faith by which the soul adheres to the first truth is itself an implicit faith would be contrary to the teaching of Saint Paul and contrary to common sense, since it is necessary to believe explicitly in a first truth before one can believe implicitly in certain other truths it contains. On the other hand, it is impossible to say that in the case we are considering there is explicit faith, since our very analysis deals precisely with a child who does not make use of any concept relating to his ultimate end and who does not even know that he believes in God.

At this point I should like to observe that terms such as implicit and explicit are applicable to knowledge in the most usual and obvious sense—conscious knowledge, which is achieved by means of concepts. Only there do the notions of implicit and explicit have meaning. Now not only is it true that it is possible for the intellect not to be conscious even of something it rationally knows because it then attains through aberrant conceptual forms an object the true name of which escapes it; but the particular form of knowledge whose natural workings I have analyzed reaches its object within the unconscious recesses of the spirit's activity and is a merely practical and volitional knowledge of God. Such a knowl-

*Better to say, "of pre-Christians" (since having implicit faith, those of them who have grace are not really infidels). See Charles Journet, "Un problème de terminologie," *Nova et Vetera*, Janvier-Avril, 1948.
†Ep. to the Hebrews, 11, 6. Westminster Version. (Cf. *The Living Thoughts of St. Paul*, presented by Jacques Maritain, 1941, p. 93.)

edge is neither implicit nor explicit, but, although inexpressible, is a knowledge actual and formal, through which the intellect knows in a practical manner the Separate Good *per conformitatem ad appetitum rectum* and as the actual terminus of the will's movement. At the source of this natural non-conceptual knowledge of God there is an explicit concept which in its simplicity is accessible —*in confuso*—to the child's intellect as soon as it awakens to the life of reason; this concept is that of the moral good. In some given set of circumstances a child, having deliberated about himself, decides upon a certain good act *because it is good*—this he knows consciously and explicitly. If he does not then intellectually bring out the notion of the Separate Good implicitly contained in that concept, at least his will, passing on beyond its immediate object attains the Separate Good formally and actually, through a lived act (*in actu exercito*); and, in a fashion at once merely practical and inexpressible, the intellect knows in this way the Separate Good formally and actually—*in actu exercito*.

Well, let us now suppose that divine grace intervenes in that natural process; let us suppose that by the same token the moral good, through the influx of God, appears to the intellect not only as what is in order, not only as what it is right to do, but as *the good by means of which "I shall be saved,"* the good by means of which some mysteriously precious part of me will escape misfortune and find its way home. (And this is an inevitably defective attempt to express a flash of intuition in discursive terms.) Then it is *the Separate Good as a refuge and salvation,* through Whom my most precious being will be safe if I seek Him, it is God *as Savior,* that is the goal of the movement of my will, and adhered to by my intellect, by means of the volitional and inexpressible knowledge I have described. This knowledge is no longer merely practical since it no longer reaches only God as the Separate Good aimed at by the élan of the will, but now reaches God as Savior: an element of a speculative type therefore is present, one which concerns divine reality attained in one of the essential attributes of its supernatural transcendence.

And although this knowledge is still produced *per conformitatem ad appetitum rectum,* it must be said that under the light of faith, the right appetite then passes *in conditionem objecti* (into the sphere of objective actualization) and becomes, in the stead of any concept, the means of a knowledge which is speculative though escaping formulation and reflective consciousness, and in which it is the movement of the will which, in its own way, actualizes the analogical values contained in the intuition and more or less confused concept of the moral good "by which I shall be saved." It is the movement of the will which, reaching beyond this good to the mysterious Existent it implies, makes this Existent become an object of the speculative intellect. Such knowledge, however, remains pre-conscious, or else hardly reaches the most obscure limits of consciousness, because, for one thing, it possesses no conceptual sign, and, for another, the movement of the will which brings it about is itself neither felt nor experienced, nor illumined and highly conscious as is love in the exercise of the gift of wisdom.

This is how, to my mind, one can understand that supernatural faith penetrates into the inner dynamics of the first act of freedom at the same time as grace, so that a child, at the moment when he chooses and in order that he may choose the moral good, receives the grace which heals nature and which sanctifies, and knows God, without realizing it himself, through the knowledge of faith, and loves God above all things with a love which is charity.

VI. THEOLOGICAL PARENTHESIS

Perhaps opening a parenthesis destined for a theological incursion may help to clarify the meaning of the above reflections. John of Saint-Thomas* distinguishes between two different instants in the first act of freedom. In the first instant the child, if he acts rightly, turns toward God without yet having supernatural faith. That is what I have described in my analysis as being the natural process by which, in virtue of the dialectic implied in the first act of freedom, the child, when he decides upon the moral good, desires and loves the Separate Good as the ultimate end of his existence, and thus knows God with a non-conceptual and merely practical knowledge.† In point of fact, this same natural process (which is of the utmost interest for the philosopher from his own point of view) presupposes the assistance and prodding of grace, present from the very first instant to help nature produce an act which nature cannot do alone because of the wound of original sin. According to John of Saint-Thomas, the child, when he turns toward God by accepting in practice the moral law, is secretly stimulated by a great and superior motive (*aliquo superiori et grandi motivo*) which makes implicitly present some element of the supernatural

---

**Cursus theol.*, ed. Solesm, I q. 22–24, disput. 30, a. 3. n., 40, t. III, p. 567.
†Cf. above Sections II and III.

order pertaining to the object of faith and which envelops a *pius affectus ad credulitatem,* a God-given inclination to believe. But if, on the contrary, at that first instant, the child refusing the proffered grace does not decide upon the moral good and does not turn toward God, then he remains under the domination of original sin, yet he does not commit a sin of infidelity because the object of faith (the first *credibilia* mentioned by Saint Paul) has not yet been brought out before his mind in such a way that he can accept it on the testimony of God or else refuse it.

At the second instant which John of Saint-Thomas mentions, it is through supernatural faith that the child, provided he has not refused the proffered grace, adheres to God; and it is through charity that he ordains his life to God. Then by a genuine act of faith, he believes in the first two *credibilia: quia Deus est, et remunerator est* (that God exists, and is a rewarder). That is what has been described in the second stage of my analysis: the adherence to God *as Savior.*

But for John of Saint-Thomas this adherence to the first two *credibilia* is only possible if God sends an Angel or a preacher to instruct the child. "Et tales accipient notitiam eorum mysteriorum, quae requiritur ad justificationem et salutem, sive per Angelum, sive par praedicatorem." The reason for this is that the great seventeenth-century theologian was, like all the scholastic doctors, interested in analyzing the objective requisites of the act of faith in themselves and in theologically elucidated terms rather than in looking for the psychological modalities in which they are realized in the experience of the subject. He consequently limited his study to the sphere of conscious thought and of conceptual or notionally expressed knowledge. Hence, since it is clear for the reasons we have shown* that there can be no question of *implicit* faith in the first two *credibilia,* it must necessarily have been a question of an *explicit* faith, that is, a faith whose object is presented to the mind in explicit notions and accepted or "agreed to" by an explicit conceptual judgment. And how could these explicit notions be furnished without the intervention of an Angel or a preacher?

It is our belief that the only way out of this difficulty is to consider the innermost recesses of mental functioning and to use, as a prerequisite philosophical equipment of ours, those more complex and deeper views on knowledge which are not new to the experience of the experts in the human heart's mysteries, but which have been

---

*Cf. above pp. 76–77.

given scientific consistency through the progress of psychological research with regard to the unconscious or pre-conscious life of the mind. Thus, one can understand in what way the "inner inspiration revealing the things that are necessary for the act of faith"* comes into play—that inner inspiration which Saint Thomas considers capable of replacing, in the "child brought up in forests" (at least, I mean, with respect to the first two *credibilia*) the outer presentation—which is normal in itself—of the object of faith.

If our analysis is correct, it must be said that at the moment when the concept of moral good is transfigured into that of the good *by means of which I shall be saved,* a mysterious reality pertaining to the supernatural order is actually revealed—under the influence of divine inspiration—in and through the idea of salvation sprung from the depths of moral conscience and transvaluated by grace. A new objective content is thus presented to the mind which by the same token reaches the *Savior-God,* by means of a volitional and inexpressible knowledge rooted in the concept of "the good by means of which I shall be saved"—a knowledge in which the appetite "passes on into the sphere of objective actualization," as John of Saint-Thomas said with reference to mystical knowledge. As a result, far beyond the "God-given inclination to believe" (pius affectus ad credulitatem), it is through a genuine act of faith (though brought about in abnormal conditions), through a supernatural act of faith (expressed not in concepts or in a rationally formulated assertion, but rather in a lived *I believe*) that the intellect adheres, on the inner testimony of God, to the divine reality thus revealed to it. Under the light of faith the Savior-God toward Whom the élan of the will moves has become the object of a nonconceptual speculative knowledge which comes about through the instrumentality of this very élan of the will.

In contrast with any implicit or virtual knowledge, we might term "explicit" both the way in which, according to this analysis, the first two *credibilia* are presented to the mind (not in notions but in a volitional knowledge of faith rooted in the concept of the good by means of which I shall be saved) and the way in which the mind adheres to these first two *credibilia* (by virtue of the same knowledge which, although it does not proceed by means of concepts, reaches a goal that has been brought out as an object in the preconscious life—formed with no possible formulation—of the in-

---

*"Si enim aliquis taliter nutritus ductum naturalis rationis sequeretur in appetitu boni et fuga mali, certissime est tenendum, quod ei Deus *vel per internam inspirationem revelaret ea quae sunt ad credendum necessaria,* vel aliqua fidei praedicatorem dirigeret, sicut misit Petrum ad Cornelium. St. Thomas, *De Veritate,* 14, 11, ad 1.

tellect). But, in my opinion, this would strain the meaning of words since, like the word "implicit," the word "explicit" refers essentially to a conceptual type of knowledge, a knowledge which is conscious and notionally expressed. That is why I have preferred to say that it is not a question of explicit (conceptual) knowledge, nor of implicit (conceptual) knowledge, but of knowledge which is *formal and actual* although it is pre-conscious. It is certainly this double character John of Saint-Thomas deemed important when he considered, and rightly, that faith in the two first *credibilia* cannot be a merely implicit faith, but came to the conclusion—a conclusion true only on the plane of conceptual and conscious knowledge—that it must consequently be explicit faith, that is, faith expressed in explicit *concepts* and bearing upon *concepts* explicitly presented.

But let us return to our philosophical considerations.

VII.   ABOUT THE KNOWLEDGE OF GOD INVOLVED IN THE CHOICE OF THE MORAL GOOD

It is important for the philosopher to be attentive to the existence of that volitional and existential knowledge of God which is involved in the first act of freedom when it is good—a knowledge which is natural and merely practical insofar as it comes to the existence of God as the Separate Good, but supernatural or derived from the grace of faith, and therefore enriched with speculative content, insofar as it comes to the existence of the Savior-God. When the right will tends to its specifying object, the moral good (*bonum honestum*) perceived *in confuso,* at the same time it passes on beyond that object, goes to the Separate Good the existence of which is implied by that of the moral good; and the intellect borne along by the will (for intellect and will enclose each other) knows God existentially through conformity with the right will, and in the "dark mirror" of the moral good, but without any concept of God disengaged from that basic concept; the intellect knows God as the Separate Good, insofar as He is the actual terminus of the movement of the will, and it knows God as Savior insofar as, under the light of faith, the will tends toward Him as the mysterious Agent presupposed by the good "by means of which I shall be saved." Thus, the intellect knows Him without realizing it. Such knowledge (a *co-naissance* as Claudel puts it) having neither conceptual sign nor affective experience of its object, remains below the threshold of consciousness, or crosses that threshold only in remaining inexpressible to reflective consciousness. This knowledge is real, however, and enmeshed in the vital depths of the mind. We can reveal its existence only through the analysis of the inner dynamics of the first act of freedom, and not by any direct apperception.

But once this existence is recognized, it is but normal to think that it plays a definite part, though a hidden one, in the infrastructure of human knowledge. This unconscious and existential knowledge of God, in the first act of freedom when it is good, obviously cannot serve as a basis for the conceptual elaborations of the philosopher in his quest for divine existence. It is nevertheless important for the philosopher to take into account the inner disposition it creates within the soul. *He that doeth the truth cometh to the light.** The presence of that kind of preconscious knowledge doubtless explains why, under normal circumstances, the man who has decided upon the moral good finds himself instinctively and unconsciously prepared to recognize (as soon as the natural and spontaneous activity of his reason deals with the sight of visible things, and before any philosophical demonstration) the existence of that invisible Good, that Separate Good Which he already knows, without realizing it, by virtue of the right choice he made when he deliberated about himself in his first act of freedom.

The volitional knowledge in question is in no way mystical knowledge. For it is not a fruitional experience of the absolute, and through it the soul does not rest in God consciously known and experienced through and in the "ray of darkness," obscure because too transparent, of love enlightened by the gifts of the Spirit. In this volitional knowledge there is neither experience nor contemplation. It is a knowledge which does not proceed by the formal instrumentality of concepts, but it is a knowledge which plunges into darkness as soon as it sets forth from the intuition and more or less confused concept of the moral and salutary good; it is a knowledge in which the soul does not even know that it knows, which is a thing quite different from enjoying supreme knowledge through the cloud of unknowing.

The fact still remains, however, that this primitive existential knowledge of God is within us an obscure preparation for and a secret call to the natural religious experiences which may come about in very different ways during the course of development of the moral life; and when the life of faith and of the gifts of the Spirit takes hold of the soul, this same existential knowledge ap-

*John 3, 21.

pears as an obscure preparation for and call to that experimental knowledge of God which is supernatural in its very *mode* of operation, and which reaches its highest degree in mystical contemplation.

VIII. ABOUT PSEUDO-ATHEISM AND REAL ATHEISM

A final question arises. It concerns the relation between the conscious and the unconscious knowledge of God. The foregoing analyses dealt with the first act of freedom as it appears in the child who for the first time deliberates about himself. As I noted at the very beginning, that same deep-rooted act in which the person engages the whole weight of his being and his will, decides upon the meaning of his life, and takes his stand both for or against the moral good and for or against God as the ultimate end of his existence, that same root act can be reiterated in the adult, however infrequent this may be, when, by means of a decisive act of free will, he changes the essential direction of his moral life. Then, under the action of *gratia operans*, or on the contrary, of some overmastering alluring lust, he recovers something of the absolute beginnings of childhood.

Now let us consider the case of a child brought up in atheism, or the case of an atheistic adult. Can he, in such an act of freedom, decide upon the good, direct his life to the moral good and to moral righteousness?

There are two kinds of atheists: those who think they are atheists, and those who are atheists. It is not easy indeed to be a real atheist. We see this through the example of men like Proudhon who only half succeeded, or Nietzsche who may have succeeded, but at what a price! What, then, shall we say about the pseudo-atheist and the real atheist? The *pseudo-atheist*, when he denies the existence of God, denies the existence of an *ens rationis*, an imaginary entity which he calls God, but which is not God. He denies God because he confuses God with that imaginary entity which seems to him either to be impossible of existence or to entail revolting consequences with regard to nature or humanity. On the contrary, the *real atheist*, when he denies the existence of God, really denies the existence of that very God Who is the authentic object of reason and of faith and Whose authentic idea his mind misuses—through an intellectual act which demands to transform his whole table of values and to descend into the depths of his being.

To anyone who is in the least familiar with human psychology

it is clear, moreover, that between the conscious and the unconscious, between the world of conceptual assertions in which conscious reason is engaged, and the secret dynamics of the pre-conscious life of the mind, there can be all sort of cleavages and
discords, schisms and secessions and contradictions unknown to the
subject himself. Let us therefore suppose a *pseudo-atheist*, say a
child permeated with the formulas of an atheistic education but
who has not been able to realize the content of atheism, or else a
man who is not really an atheist but who sincerely believes he is—
because he was brought up in an atheistic social environment, or
because his own peculiar religious social environment has shocked
and wounded him, or because he has deceived himself by sophisms
and disordered reasonings. He may be ready to lay down his life
for the cause of atheism. Yet it is not impossible that in a first act
of freedom, he may decide upon the moral good and by the same
token turn his life toward the Separate Good, toward the true God
Whom he knows in a certain manner without knowing it. In the
mysterious secret of the spirit's unconscious, such a pseudo-atheist
then knows with a natural, volitional and merely practical knowledge that same God Whom he denies in his words and explicit,
formulated thoughts. And what is more, without knowing it, he has
faith, a merely vital and unformulated faith; and without knowing it, he has charity. (But there is within him schism and division,
and therefore a particular frailty.)

The case of *true atheism* is totally different. If a man really
denies in his heart the existence of God, not because he confuses
Him with a figment of his imagination, but because he refuses to
allow the existence of that same God Who is the object of faith
and of right reason and Whose authentic idea he grasps, and misuses, then, through an act of his intellect in which he commits his
own person explicitly and consciously, that man makes it impossible
for himself to take God as the end of his existence and his action.
Doubtless he loves God ontologically, as does every creature, however sinful, since every effort and every operation tends to some
good (even though the operation is itself sinful) and therefore to
God to the same extent.* But the real atheist cannot, even unconsciously, choose God as the end of his life, and love Him above all
things efficaciously.

The act of true atheism performed in the soul is indeed a lethal
obstacle to the inner dynamics and immanent dialectic of the first

*Cf. Saint Thomas Aquinas, *Sum. theol.* I, 103, 8 et ad 1.

act of freedom in its process of choosing the good; this act stops or turns aside the impulse by which the will, in tending toward the moral good (*bonum honestum*), tends indivisibly toward the separate Good. When he deliberates about himself such a real atheist is able to ordain his action and his existence toward the moral good, but then either he receives the grace of conversion and will cease to be an atheist, or else he ordains his life toward a concept which he believes to be that of the moral good but which is not really that, being a pseudo-moral-good, *bonum honestum taken as excluding God,* and thus it is toward a corpse or an idol of moral good that he is ordaining his life. He has killed the moral good by shattering and destroying the relationship with the Separate Good which it essentially implies. Moral good, duty, virtue inevitably become demands of his own perfection viewed as an absolute center, or a desolate rite of his own grandeur—or a total submission of himself to the sweet will of deified Becoming; and thus moral good, duty, virtue lose their true nature.

The fact remains that God knows infinitely better than he does, God alone fully and truly knows whether that man is really an atheist, just as He alone knows fully and truly whether a man really has faith and charity.*

*This essay is connected to two very important texts of the *Sum. theol.* I–II, 109, 3 and I–II, 89, 6. See also Cajetan's commentary on this latter article.

G

CHAPTER SEVEN

A NEW APPROACH

TO GOD

I. THE RATIONAL PRE-PHILOSOPHICAL KNOWLEDGE OF GOD'S EXISTENCE

A Rediscovery of Being

IF civilization is to survive, the coming age must be an age of spiritual as well as social integration.

Today the human mind is torn and divided between Positivism and Irrationalism. Pragmatism succeeded in obliging philosophers to take certain basic aspects of reality into consideration, and in developing what might be called the sociology of knowledge; as a universal system of knowledge and life—as a philosophy—however, Pragmatism has been a failure. The same can be said of Idealism's attempt at a supreme synthesis, an attempt which at times had unquestionable grandeur, but which wound up in a dream of dialectical reason, because it was centered solely upon the human mind.

What is essentially needed is a renewal of metaphysics. The conceptions of modern science—the unification of matter and energy, physical indeterminism, the notion of space-time, the new reality vouchsafed both to quality and duration, the concept of a cosmos of stars and electrons in which the stars are the heavenly laboratories of elements, and which is subjected everywhere to genesis and transmutation, a universe finite but whose limits cannot be attained because of the curvature of space, a world which dynamically evolves in a definite direction, namely, both toward the highest forms of individuation and concentration and toward a simultaneous degradation of the quality of its total energy—all this is, no doubt, external description and scientific imagery rather than ontological insight, and cannot directly serve the purpose of any

86

philosophical or metaphysical extrapolations; yet all this constitutes at the same time a basic representation of the world incomparably more favorable to the edification of a philosophy of nature and more open to the deepening labor of metaphysical reason than the old Newtonian physics. The opportunity is now given for that reconciliation between science and wisdom for which the human mind thirsts. What is needed first and foremost is a rediscovery of Being, and by the same token a rediscovery of love.

This means, axiomatically, a rediscovery of God. The *existential* philosophies which are today in fashion are but a sign of a certain deep want and desire to find again the sense of Being. This want is now unfulfilled, for these philosophies are still enslaved by Irrationalism and seek for the revelation of existence, for ontological ecstasy, in the breaking of reason, in the experience of Despair and Nothingness. True existentialism is the work of reason. The act by virtue of which I exist and things exist, transcends concepts and ideas; it is a mystery for the intellect. But the intellect lives on this mystery. It does so in its most natural activity, which is as ordinary, daily and vulgar as eating or drinking: for the act of existing is indeed the very object of every achieved act of the intellect, that is, of every judgment. It is perceived by that intellectual intuition, immersed in sense-experience, which is the common treasure (all the more precious as it is natural and imbues the depths of our thought) of all our assertions, of all this mysterious activity by means of which we declare either *ita est* or *fiat!* in the face of the world or at the moment of making a decision. Now, when the intellect passes the threshold of philosophy, it does so by becoming aware of this intellectual intuition, freeing its genuine power, and making it the peculiar weapon of a knowledge whose subject-matter is Being itself. I do not here refer to Platonic essences. I refer to the act of existing insofar as it grounds and centers the intelligible structure of reality, as it expands into activity in every being, and as, in its supreme, uncreated plenitude, it activates and attracts to itself the entire dynamism of nature. At their ontological peak, in the transcendence of the Pure Act and the Absolute, Being and Reason are one and the same reality. In the created realm Reason confronts Being and labors to conquer it, both to transfer Being into its own immaterial life and immaterially to be or become Being. In perceiving Being Reason knows God—the self-subsisting Act of being—in an enigmatic but inescapable manner.

Yet my thesis does not deal only with philosophers and philosophy, but with the mental behavior of the common man. Werner Sombart used to say that modern man was *neither "ontological" nor "erotic,"* had lost the sense of Being and the sense of Love. Torture and death as Europe has beheld them have made us aware of the meaning of that very existence they themselves scorned. Hate has awakened an awareness of the meaning of that very love it derided. Let us emerge from sleep, cease to live in the dream of magic of images and formulas, well-systematized words, practical symbols and world-bursting kabbala! Once a man is awakened to the reality of existence and the true life of Reason, to the intelligible value of Being, once he has really perceived this tremendous fact, sometimes exhilarating, sometimes disgusting and maddening: *I exist,* he is henceforth taken hold of by the intuition of Being and the implications it involves.

A Rediscovery of God

Precisely speaking, this prime intuition is both the intuition of *my* existence and of the existence *of things;* but first and foremost of the existence of things. When it takes place, I suddenly realize that a given entity, man, mountain, or tree, exists and exercises that sovereign activity *to be* in its own way, in an independence from *me* which is total, totally self-assertive and totally implacable. And at the same time, I realize that I also exist, but as thrown back into my loneliness and frailty by such affirmation of existence in which I have positively no part, to which I am exactly as naught. So the prime intuition of Being is the intuition of the solidity and inexorability of existence; and, secondly, of the death and nothingness to which *my* existence is liable. And thirdly, in the same flash of intuition, which is but my becoming aware of the intelligible value of Being, I realize that the solid and inexorable existence perceived in anything whatsoever implies—I don't know yet in what way, perhaps in things themselves, perhaps separately from them—some absolute, irrefragable existence, completely free from nothingness and death. These three intellective leaps—to actual existence as asserting itself independently from me; from this sheer objective existence to my own threatened existence; and from my existence spoiled with nothingness to absolute existence—are achieved within that same and unique intuition, which philosophers would explain as the intuitive perception of the essentially analogical content of the first concept, the concept of Being.

Then a quick, spontaneous reasoning, as natural as this intuition (and, as a matter of fact, more or less involved in it) immediately springs forth, as the necessary fruit of such primordial apperception and as enforced by and under its light. That is a wordless process of reasoning, which cannot be expressed in articulate fashion without sacrificing its vital concentration and the rapidity with which it takes place. I see that my Being, first, is liable to death; and, second, that it depends on the totality of nature, on the universal whole whose part I am. I see that Being-with-nothingness, as my own being is, implies, in order to be, Being-without nothingness—that absolute existence which I confusedly perceived as involved in my primordial intuition of existence. And I see that the universal whole, whose part I am, is Being-with-nothingness, from the very fact that I am part of it; so that finally, since the universal whole does not exist by itself, there is another Whole, a separate one, another Being, transcendent and self-sufficient and unknown in itself and activating all beings, which is Being-without-nothingness, that is, self-subsisting Being, Being existing through itself.

Thus, the inner dynamism of the intuition of existence or of the intelligible value of Being, causes me to see that absolute existence or Being-without-nothingness transcends the totality of nature—and makes me face the existence of God.

This is not a new approach to God. It is the eternal approach of man's reason to God. What is new is the manner in which the modern mind has become aware of the simplicity and liberating power, the natural and somehow intuitive characteristics of this eternal approach. The science of the ancients was steeped in philosophy. Their scientific imagery was a pseudo-ontological imagery. Consequently there was a kind of continuum between their knowledge of the physical world and their knowledge of God; the latter appeared as the summit of the former, a summit which was to be climbed through the manifold paths of the causal connections at play in the sublunar world and the celestial spheres; and the sense of Being that ruled their universal thought was for them a too usual atmosphere to be felt as a surprising gift. At the same time the natural intuition of existence was so strong in them that their proofs of God could take the form of the most conceptualized and rationalized scientific demonstrations, and be offered as skillful unfolding of logical necessities, without losing the inner energy of that intuition. Such logical machinery was quickened unawares by the basic intuition of Being.

We are in a quite different position now. In order enigmatically to reach physical reality and to conquer the world of phenomena, our science has become a kind of *Maya*—a Maya which succeeds and makes us masters of nature. But the sense of Being is absent from it. Thus, when we happen to experience the impact of Being upon our mind, it appears to us as a kind of intellectual revelation, and we realize clearly both its liberating and its awakening power and the fact that it involves a knowledge which is separated from that sphere of knowledge peculiar to our science. At the same time we realize that the knowledge of God, before being developed into logical and perfectly conceptualized demonstrations, is first and foremost a natural fruit of the intuition of existence, and forces itself upon our mind in the imperative virtue of this intuition.

In other words, we have become aware of the fact that human reason's approach to God in its primordial vitality is neither a mere intuition, which would be suprahuman, nor is it that art-like philosophical reasoning by which it is expressed in its achieved form, each step of which is pregnant with involved issues and problems. Human reason's approach to God in its primordial vitality is a *natural* reasoning, that is, intuitive-like or irresistibly vitalized by and maintained within the intellectual flash of the intuition of existence. In this natural reasoning it is the very intuition of existence which, grasping in some existing reality Being-with-nothingness, makes the mind grasp by the same stroke the necessity of Being-without-nothingness. And nowhere is there any problem involved, because the illumining power of this intuition takes hold of the mind and obliges it to see: so that the mind then naturally proceeds, within a primary intuitive flash, from imperative certainty to imperative certainty. I believe that from Descartes to Kierkegaard, the effort of modern thought—to the extent that it has not completely repudiated metaphysics, and if it is cleansed of the irrationalism which has gradually corrupted it—tends to such an awareness of the specific *naturality* of man's knowledge of God, definitely deeper than any logical process scientifically developed, and of the primordial and simple intuitivity in which this knowledge originates. Availing itself of any true progress achieved by the critique of knowledge, and realizing its own existential requirements, philosophy must now assimilate explicitly this new awareness and make clear in this way the manner in which the eternal approach of man, of the common man, to God proceeds.

On the other hand, becoming heedful of the subconscious life of the spirit, and considering not only our theoretical but also our practical approach to God, philosophy will have to lay stress on the following fact. When a man experiences, in a primary act of freedom, the impact of the moral good and is thus awakened to moral life, and directs his life toward the good for the sake of good, then he directs his life, even without knowing it, toward the absolute Good, and in this way knows God vitally, though unawares, by virtue of the inner dynamism of his choice of the good—even if he does not know God in any conscious fashion and by means of any conceptual knowledge.* Thus, Conscience, with its practical intuition of the moral good, in reference to a practical and preconscious knowledge of the supreme existing Good, has its own approach to God, just as Reason has its own approach with its speculative intuition of existence and in reference to the theoretical and conscious knowledge of the supreme existing Being.

A Rediscovery of Love

Finally, the rediscovery of the value of existence not only means the rediscovery of God, it also means the rediscovery of Love. For when the intuition of Being and Existence takes place in me, it normally carries along with itself another intuition, the intuition of my own existence or my Self, the intuition of Subjectivity as Subjectivity. Now Subjectivity, insofar as it is Subjectivity, is not an object presented to thought, but rather the very wellspring of thought—a deep, unknown and living center which superabounds in knowledge and superabounds in love, attaining only through love its supreme level of existence, existence as giving itself.

This is what I mean: Self-knowledge as a mere psychological analysis of more or less superficial phenomena, a wandering through images and memories, is but an egotistic awareness, however valuable it may be. But when it becomes ontological, then knowledge of the Self is transfigured, implying the intuition of Being and the discovery of the actual abyss of Subjectivity.† At the same time, it is the discovery of the basic generosity of existence. Subjectivity, this essentially dynamic, living and open center, both receives and gives. It receives through the intellect, by superexisting in knowledge. It gives through the will, by superexisting in love; that is, by having within itself other beings as inner attractions toward them and toward giving oneself to them, and by spiritually existing in

*See Chapter VI.
†Cf. *Existence and the Existent,* 1948, chapter III.

the manner of a gift. And "it is better to give than to receive." Spiritual existence as peculiar to love is the supreme revelation of existence for the Self. The Self, being not only a material individual but also a spiritual personality, possesses itself and holds itself in hand insofar as it is spiritual and insofar as it is free. And to what purpose does it possess itself and dispose of itself, if not for what *is better* in actual existence and absolutely speaking, namely, to give itself? Thus it is that when a man has been really awakened to the sense of Being or Existence, and grasps intuitively the obscure, living depth of the Self and Subjectivity, he experiences, by virtue of the inner dynamism of this intuition, that love is not a passing pleasure or a more or less intense emotion, but the root tendency and very meaning of his being alive. He becomes both an "ontological" and an "erotic" man; he is man anew.

And not only does he know, by virtue of his primordial intellectual grasping of existence, that God exists and is the absolute Being, the self-subsisting *Esse*. He also knows that because of this very fact, God is absolute ontological generosity, the self-subsisting Love; and that such transcendent Love inherently causes, permeates and activates every creature, which in answer loves God more than itself. This basic love for God, this natural and universal eros, is the very virtue and innermost vitality in which all beings desire and love, act and strive.

II. A THEOCENTRIC HUMANISM

In the preceding pages I have emphasized our new awareness of the eternal approach to God. Summing up what I have often tried to point out, I should like now to outline what may be called, properly speaking, a new approach to God, not in the field of knowledge but in the field of culture and in the historical life of man.

Every great age of culture receives its deepest meaning and direction from a particular constellation of spiritual factors or dominating ideas; let us say, from a particular historical heaven. And the most significant factor to be considered in such moving appearances of the zodiac of history is the peculiar approach to God characterizing a given period of culture. What are, from this point of view, the main characteristics of the human approach to God, or of the human attitude toward God, in the new age of civilization that is emerging?

The Medieval Age was a humble and magnanimous age. I would

say that, at the end of this sacral era, man experienced not humility but humiliation. Whereas new forces awakened in history,
he felt overwhelmed and crushed by the old structures of a civilization which had conceived of itself as a God's stronghold built upon
earth. From the Renaissance on, he endeavored to become aware
of and establish his own dignity through the sole effort of his own
reason, by liberating himself both from the old structures of the
world, and from all sorts of disciplines and authorities which confronted him, in the name of God, as being the keystone of these
structures. He isolated himself progressively from God. God, the
heavenly God of Christianity, or the immanent and evolving God
of pantheism, was but the supreme guarantor of our own greatness
and power. We expected progress and happiness from the effort of
man centered upon himself and set apart from God. We realized
our own dignity; we became the masters of nature. But we were
alone. The age was an age of anthropocentric humanism. It ended
in human devastation.

If civilization is to be saved, the new age must be an age of theocentric humanism. Today human dignity is everywhere trampled
down. Still more, it crumbles from within, for in the mere perspective of science and technology we are at a loss to discover the
rational foundations of the dignity of the human person and to
believe in it. The task of the emergent civilization (which will
doubtless not appear tomorrow but which may possibly appear the
day after tomorrow) will consist in refinding and refounding the
sense of that dignity, in rehabilitating man in God and through
God, not apart from God. This means a complete spiritual revolution. Then all the conquests of the preceding epoch will be both
purified and saved, redeemed from the errors of this epoch and
transfigured—brought to a new flowering. The age will be an age
of dignification of the creature, in its living relation with the
Creator, as vivified by Him, and as having in Him the justification
of its very existence, its labor on earth, its essential claims and its
trend toward freedom. It will be again, at least for those capable
of understanding, an age of humility and magnanimity, but with
a new awareness of human potentialities and of the depth, magnitude and universality of human problems. The new approach to
God will be a new approach to the true God of the Judaeo-Christian tradition, the true God of the Gospel, Whose grace, perfecting
nature and not destroying it, transcends reason in order to
strengthen, not to blind or annihilate it, makes moral conscience

progress in the course of time, and leads human history, that is, the ceaseless and ceaselessly thwarted effort of mankind toward emancipation, in the direction of its supratemporal accomplishment. This new approach will proceed neither in the adoration of creatures, which was the foolishness of our time, nor in that bitter contempt which too many Christians mistake for the divine madness of the saints. It will manifest itself in a deeper respect for and understanding of the creature and in a greater attentiveness to discover in it every vestige of God.

Hence appear a number of consequences which I should like merely to enumerate. Doubtless metaphysical anguish, the great anguish of Augustine and Pascal, will always play its part in the human search for God. Yet it seems that in the present situation of mankind it is rather through the practical effort to rediscover man, through the actual experience of the basic conditions for personality, justice, freedom, respect and love for our fellow men, that ordinarily we shall be led to the rediscovery of God. On the other hand, it appears that the controversial front of religious thought has henceforth shifted. The main issue now is to promote rather than to humble reason. Religious thought will not so much have to defend itself against philosophical (critical) reason, as at the time of the Enlightenment, as it will have to defend philosophical (ontological) reason both against sheer irrationalism or a metaphysics of despair and such ultimate fruits of rationalism as pseudo-scientific positivism and dialectical materialism. It will have to defend the existence of supernatural reality less against naturalistic exaltation than against naturalistic destruction of nature. In the structure of human knowledge theology occupies and will always occupy the highest position. Yet with regard to the role played in fact by the various kinds of wisdom in the inner stimulations of culture, it is mainly through Christian philosophy that the new civilization will be spurred, at least to the extent that it will be Christianly inspired. The momentous question will be more than ever: What is man? I mean man not only essentially, but existentially. In the very perspective of religious thought there must be developed a philosophical ethics, as distinguished from moral theology and encompassing anthropology as well as sociology. The notion of natural law, cleansed of the spurious interpretations of a naïve rationalism that preyed upon it, will be re-examined and restored. Whereas for centuries the crucial issues for religious thought were the great theological controversies centered on the dogmas of faith, the crucial issues will now deal with political theology and political philosophy.

Yet since the preaching of the gospel, what has had, in the supreme regions of knowledge, and will always have, a characteristic and all-pervading significance for a given period of civilization, is the peculiar way in which the human mind is able to grasp the mystery of human freedom and divine grace. I think that the emergent civilization will not fail to have its say in the matter. At the same time the reverse mystery, which displays our capacity for refusal and nothingness, the problem of evil, will be scrutinized anew in its metaphysical and psychological recesses and implications.

Finally, shall we seek to determine the deepest characterization, from the spiritual point of view, of the new age we are considering? It would be necessary to make clear that the spiritual dynamism at work in human culture implies a twofold movement. First, there is the movement of descent, the movement by which the divine plenitude, the prime source of existence, descends into human reality to permeate and vivify it. For God infuses in every creature goodness and lovability together with being, and has the *first* initiative in every good activity. Then there is the movement of ascent, which is the answer of man, by which human reality takes the *second* initiative, activates itself toward the unfolding of its energies and toward God. Speaking absolutely, the first movement is obviously what matters most; to receive from God is of greater moment for man than to give to God, and he can only give what he has received.

At this point we would observe that the great error of modern times, from the Renaissance on, has been to believe that the second movement matters more than the first, or to expect from man the *first* initiative; let us say to forget that the word of God always precedes man's answer, and finally to consider the answer to be the first utterance.

And we would conclude that a new age of civilization will realize again that the descent of divine plenitude into man matters more than the ascent of man toward self-perfection. In this new age the movement by which the human being answers God's movement of effusion would not take place, as in the Middle Ages, in a childlike, ignorant-of-itself humanity. Its new simplicity would be a mature and experienced, self-awakened simplicity, enlightened by what might be called a free and evangelical introspection.

Such will be, I believe, the new approach to God peculiar to this age. Man will understand that he ascends toward his own fullness and toward God all the better because he himself espouses the movement of descent of the uncreated Love and in so doing gives all that he is and possesses. He will understand that he can build only in order to deal out such an effusion. Gospel generosity, by accustoming human life to the divine ways, appears at the same time as a manifestation of the "philanthropy of our God," as St. Paul puts it,* and corresponds to that rehabilitation and dignification of the creature in God of which I spoke above. Man will find anew his internal unity by preferring once and for all the evangelical loss of himself which is produced by love—that readiness to give everything, the mantle and the tunic and the skin—to the rationalist self-achievement which is the conquest of illusion and delusion, and to the irrationalist self-achievement which is a loss of oneself into despair and absurdity.

III.   FAITH VS. ATHEISM

The Dialectic of Anthropocentric Humanism

The dialectics of anthropocentric humanism developed within three centuries. Man's approach to God changed accordingly. For the notion of God—to the extent that it ceases to be encompassed and kept pure by revelation—is connected with the general state of culture, and its fate then conforms to that of culture.

At the first moment of humanistic dialectics, God, as we noted above, became the guarantor of man's domination over matter. He was a transcendent God, but imprisoned in his transcendence and forbidden to interfere in human affairs. He became a decorative God, the God of the classical rationalist world.

At the second moment, with Romanticist philosophy and the great Idealist metaphysicians, God became an idea. He was an immanent God engulfed in the dialectical progress of the self-asserting Idea and the evolving world. This God of pantheism and of the romanticist world was but the ideal borderline to which tended the development of mankind. He was also the absolute, total and unbending justification of good and evil—of evil fully as much as of good—of all the crimes, oppressions and iniquities of history as well as of its conquests and progress, particularly its progress in taking hold of material goods and power.

*Ep. to Titus, III, 4. (Greek text.)

At a third moment, Feuerbach was to discover that God—such a God—alienated man from himself; Marx, that He was but an ideological mirror of the alienation or dehumanization of man accomplished, he thought, by private property. And Nietzsche was to become exhilarated by the mission with which he felt himself endowed, namely, to proclaim the death of God. How could God still live in a world from which His image, that is, the free and spiritual personality of man, seemed definitely destined to disappear? God as dead, God in the grave, was the God of the final agony and self-destruction of an age of civilization which had proclaimed the self-sufficiency of man. Atheism is the final end of the inner dialectics of anthropocentric humanism.

Practical Atheism and Absolute Atheism

Thus, we are confronted with the problem of atheism, the significance of which I shall discuss in the following chapter. There are several kinds of atheism. With respect to the first act of freedom* I have distinguished between pseudo-atheism and true or absolute atheism. Let us say now that in point of fact the division is threefold. There are *pseudo-atheists* who believe that they do not believe in God and who in reality unconsciously believe in Him, because the God whose existence they deny is not God but something else. There are *practical atheists* who believe that they believe in God (and who perhaps believe in Him in their brains) but who in reality deny His existence by each one of their deeds. Out of the living God they have made an idol. There are *absolute atheists* who actually deny the existence of the very God in Whom the believers believe and who are bound to change entirely their own scale of values and to destroy in themselves everything that connotes His name.

What is the meaning of this absolute atheism? Practical atheism does not pose any special problem for the philosopher, except the problem of the possibility of a deluded conscience and of the disagreement or cleavage between the intellect and the will, theoretical belief and actual behavior; or, in theological terms, between faith (dead faith) and charity. Dead faith is faith without love. The practical atheist accepts the fact that God exists—and forgets it on all occasions. His case is a case of voluntary, stubborn forgetting.

Quite different is the case of the absolute atheist. He does not forget God, he steadily thinks of Him—in order to free himself

*See Chapter VI.

from Him. When he has acquired the intellectual persuasion that God does not exist, his task and endeavor is not finished; this very negation delivers him over to an inner dialectic which obliges him ceaselessly to destroy any resurgence in himself of what he has buried. For in denying God he has explicitly denied Transcendence. But in actual fact the good which every being desires, even without knowing it, is in the last analysis self-subsisting Good; and thus, in actual fact, the dynamism of human life, because it tends toward good and happiness, even if their true countenance is not recognized, tends implicitly, willy-nilly, toward Transcendence. Doubtless the absolute atheist may ascribe to superstition, or to human stupidity, or to human "alienation," every vestige or trace of Transcendence he contemplates in the common behavior and beliefs, and the individual or social life, of men. Yet within himself is the real drama. In proportion as the dialectic of atheism develops in his mind—each time he is confronted with the natural notion of and natural tendency to an ultimate End, or with the natural notion of and natural attention to absolute values or unconditioned standards, or with any metaphysical anxiety—he will discover in himself vestiges of Transcendence which have not yet been abolished. He must get rid of them. God is a perpetual threat to him. His case is not a case of practical forgetting, but a case of deeper and deeper commitment to refusal and fight.

Thus absolute atheism is in no way a mere absence of belief in God. It is rather a refusal of God, a fight against God, a challenge to God. And when it achieves victory it changes man in his own inner behavior, it gives man a kind of stolid solidity, as if the spirit of man had been stuffed with dead substance, and his organic tissues turned into stone. As I shall try to point out in the next chapter, atheism begins with a kind of new start in moral activity, a determination to confront good and evil in an absolutely free experience, by casting aside any ultimate end—a determination which is mistaken for enfranchisement and moral maturity and boils down in reality to the complete giving of self to some earthly "Great Being": either Mankind as for Auguste Comte, or, as for others, a Work to be done or a Party to serve. At the same time the relation to the absolute Good which the moral good essentially implies is abolished, and as a result the very nature of the moral good is changed and is replaced by an idol.* As I noted a while ago, the appearance of absolute atheism in human thought—with that vio-

*See above pp. 84–85.

lence which manifested itself at first in the philosophers of the
"Hegelian Left"—was the conclusion of a progressive degradation
of the idea of God. It heralded the beginning of a new age in
which the process of death and the process of resurrection will
develop together, confronting each other and struggling against
each other.

With regard to culture, atheism is a mirror of the state to which
the human being has been reduced. For since man is the image of
God, it is but natural that he thinks of God according to the state
in which that image presents itself at a given moment of culture.
Absolute atheism means that the personality of man is definitely
endangered; and that all the masks, the words, the shams, the
facades, the palliatives, the plasters and cosmetics with which human conscience tries to deceive itself and to give us the appearance
of men are henceforth useless and will be cast away. Picasso's art,
in its present character, is the true art of atheism; I mean of that
thorough defacement of contemporary man, which is mirrored in
atheism. We are no more persons than the distorted, imbecile faces
of those ferocious females are true human faces.

Absolute atheism is also a translation into crude and inescapable
terms, a ruthless counterpart, an avenging mirror, of the practical
atheism of too many believers who betray their belief—Christians
who keep in their minds the settings of religion, for the sake of
appearances or outward show, or because of the class or family
advantages that religion seems to them to protect, but who deny
the gospel and despise the poor, pass through the tragedy of their
time only with resentment against anything that endangers their
interests and fear for their own prestige or possessions, contemplate
without flinching every kind of injustice if it does not threaten
their own way of life. Only concerned with power and success, they
are either anxious to have means of external coercion enforce what
they term the "moral order," or else they turn with the wind and
are ready to comply with any requirement of so-called historical
necessity. They sport a clear conscience, and live and act as if God
did not exist. Such men and women invoke the name of God and
do not believe in Him in their hearts. They live on empty formulas
and stereotyped phrases, on mental clichés. They cherish every
kind of sham that will flatter and deceive them. They await the
deceivers. They are famished for deception, because first they themselves are trying to deceive God.

In their own existence absolute atheists have substituted the cosmic dynamism of nature for the supratemporal life of the soul. Spiritually they are the walking dead, wagging powerful hands. At least they appear as they are. In some of them, moreover, the process of death is not yet complete; there still remains a hidden germ of life, a living thirst. And this subsisting germ, thwarted, denudated, stripped of every rational support, calls for an inner transformation all the more desperately as it resists the destruction and havoc which atheism has brought everywhere else into the spiritual substance of man. Such errant persons, if they receive the grace of faith, may become Christians for whom nothing is of account except God and the gospel. For them atheism will have been a sort of hellish purification.

Practical atheists also have buried their souls. But they have the appearance and color of life although they are dust within. The gospel terms them whited sepulchers. It would be too optimistic to pretend that their time has passed. Yet to say that they will be of no great use in the coming struggles and hazards of civilization seems to be an understatement.

The Requirements of Living Faith

Atheists and believers are crossing together the threshold of the future. They will travel a long way, each asserting his own position against the other, each endeavoring to inculcate the human mind and civilization with his particular philosophy. Under penalty of death civilization will have to overcome atheism and free itself of its inspiration. This cannot be done by external means of pressure, nor will the finest propaganda serve to achieve it. The workings of reason—deep and thorough intellectual enlightenment—are necessary. But first of all the testimony of love is needed. If it is true that absolute atheism is primarily the fruit and condemnation of practical atheism, and its reflected image in the mirror of divine wrath, then it must be said that the cardinal prerequisite for getting rid of absolute atheism is first to get rid of practical atheism. A decorative Christianity is henceforth not enough. A living Christianity is necessary to the world. Faith must be actual, practical, existential faith. To believe in God must mean to live in such a manner that life could not possibly be lived if God did not exist. For the practical believer, gospel justice, gospel attentiveness to everything human must inspire not only the deeds of the saints, but the structure and institutions of common life, and must penetrate to the depths of terrestrial existence.

This is not conceivable, even in the imperfect ways of humanity and amid the hard conflicts of the coming age, if in those who believe in God the true sources are not alive, and if the life they must give to the world does not flow down into them from the heights of God-given wisdom. A great deal of wisdom, a great deal of contemplation will be required in order to make the immense technological developments of our day truly human and liberating. At this point one should recall Henri Bergson's observations on the mutual need which "mystics" and "mechanics" have of each other, and on the *supplément d'âme,* the "increase in soul" that must vivify the body of our civilization, a body now become too large. Contemplative life, perhaps in new forms, and made available not only to the chosen few but to the common man if he actually believes in God, will be the prerequisite of that very activity which tries to make the leaven of the gospel penetrate every portion of the world.

As I pointed out many years ago,* the deepest requirement of a new age of civilization, to the extent to which Christianity inspires it, will be the sanctification of secular life. For pagan antiquity, *holy* was synonymous with *sacred;* that is, with what had been set apart to be physically, visibly, socially assigned to the service of God. But the gospel has made moral life and sanctity retire into the inner world of the hearts of men, into the secrecy of the invisible relations between the divine Personality and the human personality. Both, the men involved in the secular or temporal order and those involved in the sacred order, must tend to the perfection of human life; that is, to the perfection of love, and to inner sanctity.

In these perspectives we may understand that a new "style" of sanctity (I do not speak of a new "type" of sanctity, for sanctity has its eternal type in the person of Christ), a new step in the sanctification of secular life, is needed for the rejuvenation of the world. Not only will the spirit of Christ overflow into secular life, and seek for witnesses among those who labor in yards and factories, in social work, politics or poetry, as well as among monks dedicated to the search for perfection; but a kind of divine simplification will help people to realize that the perfection of human life does not consist in a stoic athleticism of virtue or in a humanly calculated application of holy recipes, but rather in a ceaselessly increasing love, despite our mistakes and weaknesses, between the

*Cf. *Humanisme Intégral,* Paris, 1936 (*True Humanism,* 1938).

H

Uncreated Self and the created Self. There will be a growing consciousness that everything depends on that descent of the divine plenitude into the human being of which I spoke above, and which performs in man death and resurrection. There will be a growing consciousness that man's sanctification has its touchstone in the love of his fellow man, which requires him to be always ready to give what he has—and himself—and finally to die in some manner for those he loves.

CHAPTER EIGHT

THE MEANING OF

CONTEMPORARY ATHEISM

THE subject discussed in this chapter involves many deep and intricate problems. I do not pretend to dogmatize about them; the views that I shall put forward are no more than tentative views, which originate in a desire to look for the hidden spiritual significance which lies within the present agony of the world.

I. VARIOUS KINDS OF ATHEISM

Let us try, first, to establish in a more systematic way the distinction, indicated in the two previous chapters, between the diverse forms of atheism. This distinction can be made from either of two points of view: from the point of view of the attitude of the human being who professes himself to be an atheist; or from the point of view of the logical content of various atheistic philosophies.

From the first point of view, or with regard to the manner in which atheism is professed, I have already remarked that there are, in the first place, *practical atheists,* who believe that they believe in God but who in actual fact deny His existence by their deeds and the testimony of their behavior. Then there are *pseudo-atheists,* who believe that they do not believe in God but who in actual fact unconsciously believe in Him, because the God whose existence they deny is not God but something else. Finally there are *absolute atheists,* who really do deny the existence of the very God in Whom the believers believe—God the Creator, Savior and Father, Whose name is infinitely over and above any name we can utter. Those absolute atheists stand committed to change their entire system of values and to destroy in themselves everything that could possibly suggest the name they have rejected; they have chosen to stake their all against divine Transcendence and any vestige of Transcendence whatsoever.

From the second point of view, that is, with regard to the logical content of various atheistic philosophies, I would divide atheism into negative and positive atheism.

By *negative atheism* I mean a merely negative or destructive process of casting aside the idea of God, which is replaced only by a void. Such a negative atheism can be shallow and empirical, like the atheism of the *libertins* in the XVIIth century—then it digs a hollow in the center of the universe of thought which has taken shape through the centuries around the idea of God, but it does not bother about changing that universe; it is merely concerned with making us live a comfortable life, enjoying the freedom of doing exactly as we please. On the other hand, negative atheism can be lived at a profound and metaphysical level: in which case the hollow it creates at the heart of things extends to and lays waste our whole universe of thought; the freedom it claims for the human Self is absolute independence, a kind of divine independence that this Self, like Dostoievsky's Kirilov, has no better way of affirming than by suicide and voluntary annihilation.

By *positive atheism* I mean an active struggle against everything that reminds us of God—that is to say, antitheism rather than atheism—and at the same time a desperate, I would say heroic, effort to recast and reconstruct the whole human universe of thought and the whole human scale of values in accordance with that state of war against God. Such positive atheism was the tragic, solitary atheism of a Nietszche; such is today the literary, fashionable atheism of existentialism; such is the revolutionary atheism of dialectical materialism. The latter is of special interest to us, because it has succeeded in getting a considerable number of men to accept whole-heartedly this new kind of faith, and to give themselves to it with unquestionable sincerity.

Now when I speak of contemporary atheism, I have in mind atheism seen under the last aspect I have just mentioned; I consider it the most significant form of atheism, one which spells a new and unheard of historic event because it is an atheism at once *absolute and positive*. Human history has been confronted, for almost a century now, with the stormy bursting forth of an atheism which is both *absolute* (making man actually deny God Himself) and *positive* (anti-theism, demanding to be lived in full by man and to change the face of the earth). I have outlined in the preceding chapter* the ideological process which terminated in this atheism which is both absolute and positive.

II. THE TWO-FOLD INCONSISTENCY OF CONTEMPORARY ATHEISM

An Act of Faith in Reverse Gear

After these preliminary signposts I should like to point out that today's absolute-positive atheism involves a dual inconsistency.

How does absolute-positive atheism come to birth in the mind of a man? At this point we are faced with a remarkable fact. A man does not become an absolute atheist as a result of some inquiry into the problem of God carried on by speculative reason. No doubt he takes into account the negative conclusions afforded in this connection by the most radical forms of rationalist or positivist philosophy; he does not neglect, either, the old platitude which will have it that the scientific explanation of the universe purely and simply got clear of the existence of God. But all that is for him a second-hand means of defense, not the prime propelling and determining incentive. Neither those philosophical conclusions nor that nonsensical commonplace does he submit to any critical examination. He takes them for granted. He believes in them. And why? By virtue of an inner act of freedom, in the production of which he commits his whole personality. The starting point of absolute atheism is, in my opinion, a basic act of moral choice, a crucial free determination. If at the moment when he takes stock of himself and decides upon the whole direction of his life, a man confuses the transition from youth to manhood with the refusal not only of childhood's subordinations but of any subordination whatsoever; if he thus considers the rejection of any transcendent law as an act of moral maturity and emancipation; and if he decides to confront good and evil in a totally and absolutely free experience, in which any ultimate end and any rule coming from above are cast aside forever—such a free moral determination, dealing with the primary values of existence, will mean that this man has entirely excluded God from his own universe of life and thought. Here is, in my opinion, the point at which absolute atheism begins in the depths of a man's spiritual activity.

But what is this I have just been describing if not a kind of act of faith, an act of faith in reverse gear, whose content is not an

*See pp. 96–97.

adherence to the transcendent God but, on the contrary, a rejection
of Him?

Thus it is that absolute atheism is positive atheism. As I stated
above,* and this must be stressed once again: "It is in no way a
mere absence of belief in God. It is rather a refusal of God, a fight
against God, a challenge to God." The absolute atheist is delivered
over "to an inner dialectic which obliges him ceaselessly to destroy
any resurgence in himself of what he has buried. . . In proportion as the dialectic of atheism develops in his mind—each time
he is confronted with the natural notion of and tendency to an
ultimate End, or with the natural notion of and natural interest in
absolute values or unconditioned standards, or with some metaphysical anxiety—he will discover in himself vestiges of Transcendence which have not yet been abolished. He must get rid of
them. God is a perpetual threat to him. His case is not a case of
practical forgetting, but a case of deeper and deeper commitment
to refusal and fight." He is bound to struggle against God without
pause or respite, and to change, to recast everything in himself
and in the world on the base of that anti-theism.

Now what does all this mean? Absolute atheism starts in an act
of faith in reverse gear and is a full-blown religious commitment.
Here we have the first internal inconsistency of contemporary
atheism: it proclaims that all religion must necessarily vanish away,
and it is itself a religious phenomenon.

An Abortive Protest and Rupture

The second inconsistency is very like the first one. Absolute
atheism starts as a claim of man to become the sole master of his
own destiny, totally freed from any "alienation" and heteronomy,
made totally and decisively independent of any ultimate end as
well as of any eternal law imposed upon him by any transcendent
God. According to atheistic theorists, does not the idea of God
originate in an alienation of human nature separated from its true
subject, and transmuted into an ideal and sublimated image whose
very transcendence and sovereign attributes ensure man's submission to an enslaved state of existence? Is it not by getting rid of
that sublimated image and of any transcendence, that human nature
will achieve the fullness of its own stature and freedom and bring
about the final "reconciliation between essence and existence?"

But what is the actual end-all of the philosophy of absolute

*Chapter VII, p. 98.

Immanence which is all one with absolute atheism? Everything which was formerly considered superior to time and participating in some transcendent quality—either ideal value or spiritual reality —is now absorbed in the movement of temporal existence and the all-engulfing ocean of Becoming and of History. Truth and justice, good and evil, faithfulness, all the standards of conscience, henceforth perfectly relativized, become radically contingent: they are but changing shapes of the process of History, just as for Descartes they were but contingent creations of divine Freedom. The truth, at any given moment, is that which conforms with the requirements of History's begettings. As a result truth changes as time goes on. An act of mine which was meritorious today will be criminal tomorrow. And that is the way my conscience must pass judgment on it. The human intellect and moral conscience have to become heroically tractable.

And what of the Self, the person, the problem of human destiny? A total rejection of Transcendence logically entails a total adherence to Immanence. There is nothing eternal in man; he will die in the totality of his being; there is nothing to be saved in him. But he can give himself, and give himself entirely, to the Whole of which he is a part, to the boundless flux which alone is real and which bears the fate of mankind. By virtue of his decisive moral experience itself, and of that primary moral choice—against any ultimate End—which I have tried to describe, and which commits the human personality far more profoundly than individualistic egoism or epicureanism can do, the absolute or positive atheist hands himself over, body and soul, to the ever-changing and all-engulfing Whole—be it the social or the cosmic totality. It is not only that he is satisfied to die in it, as a blade of grass in the loam, and to make it more fertile by dissolving in it. He is also willing to make of his own total being, with all its values and standards and beliefs, an offering given, as I said above, to that great Minotaur that is History. Duty and virtue mean nothing else to him than a total submission and immolation of himself to the sacred voracity of Becoming.

Here we are confronted with a new variety of mystical "pure love"—giving up every hope for personal redemption—a real unselfishness, self-denial and self-sacrifice, a total and absolute disinterestedness—but a monstrous one, paid for at the price of the very Self, and the existence and dignity of the human Person: at the price of that which, in each one of us, is an end in itself and the image of God. Christ had said: "He who loses his own soul for Me, shall find it,"* because losing one's own soul for God is delivering it over to absolute Truth and Goodness and Love, to the eternal Law itself which transcends all the contingency and mutability of Becoming. The positive atheist delivers over his own soul—and not in order to save it—to a worldly demiurge crazy for human minds to bend and bow and yield at the event's sweet will.

I am not belittling the spiritual significance of the moral attitude of the absolute atheist. On the contrary, I am emphasizing the kind of mystical disinterestedness, and the elements of greatness and generosity which are implied in it. But I say that this moral attitude also involves a basic inconsistency, and that the whole process is in the end a failure. That rupture with God began as a claim to total independence and emancipation, as a proud revolutionary break with everything that submits man to alienation and heteronomy. It ends up in obeisance and prostrate submission to the all-powerful movement of History, in a kind of sacred surrender of the human soul to the blind god of History.

III.   THE ATHEIST AND THE SAINT

The Initial Act of Rupture Brought About by the Saint

The failure I have just mentioned reveals to us a fact which has, to my mind, a deep significance: I mean the fact that absolute atheism has a revolutionary power which materially speaking is exceedingly strong, but spiritually speaking is very weak indeed, minute, and deceptive; I mean the fact that its radicalism is an inevitably self-deluded radicalism, for a genuinely revolutionary spirit does not kneel before History, it presumes to make history; I mean the fact that absolute atheism falls short of that uncompromising protest, of that absolute non-compliance the semblance— and the expectation—of which make it seductive for many people.

Thus, we arrive at the point I should like especially to discuss. Which of these two, the Atheist or the Saint, is the more uncompromising and thorough-going, the harder, the more intractable; which has his axe more deeply embedded in the root of the tree? Which brings about the more complete and far-reaching, the cleaner and more radical break?

Let us try to imagine what takes place in the soul of a saint at the crucial moment when he makes his first irrevocable decision.

*Matth. 10, 39.

Let us consider St. Francis of Assisi when he threw away his rai-
ment and appeared naked before his bishop, out of love for poverty;
or St. Benedict Labre when he decided to become a verminous
beggar wandering along the roads. At the root of such an act there
was something so deep in the soul that it hardly can be expressed,
I would say a simple refusal—not a movement of revolt which is
temporary, or of despair, which is passive—rather a simple refusal,
a total, stable, supremely active refusal to accept things as they are:
here it is not a question of knowing whether things and nature and
the face of this world are good in their essence—to be sure they
are good; being is good insofar as it is being; grace perfects nature
and does not destroy it—but these truths have nothing to do with
the inner act of rupture, of break, that we are now contemplating.
This act is concerned with a fact, an existential fact: Things as
they are are not tolerable, positively, definitely not tolerable. In
actual existence the world is infected with lies and injustice and
wickedness and distress and misery; the creation has been so marred
by sin that in the nethermost depths of his soul the saint refuses
to accept it as it is. Evil—I mean the power of sin, and the universal suffering it entails, the rot of nothingness that gnaws everywhere—evil is such, that the only thing at hand which can remedy
it, and which inebriates the saint with freedom and exultation and
love, is to give up everything, the sweetness of the world, and what
is good, and what is better, and what is pleasurable and permissible,
in order to be free to be with God; it is to be totally stripped and
to give himself totally in order to lay hold of the power of the
Cross; it is to die for those he loves. That is a flash of intuition and
of will over and above the whole order of human morality. Once
a human soul has been touched by such a burning wing, it becomes
a stranger everywhere. It may fall in love with things, it will never
rest in them. To redeem creation the saint wages war on the entire
fabric of creation, with the bare weapons of truth and love. This
war begins in the most hidden recesses of his own soul and the most
secret stirrings of his desire: it will come to an end with the advent
of a new earth and new heaven, when all that is powerful in this
world will have been humiliated and all that is despised will have
been exalted. The saint is alone in treading the winepress, and of
the peoples there is no man with him.*

And I would say that in that war of which I have just spoken
his God has given him the example. For, in calling the intellectual

*Isaiah, 63, 3.

creatures to share in His own uncreated life, God uproots them from the very life of which they are possessed as rooted in nature. And Jews know that God is a hidden God, Who conceals His name and manifests Himself to mankind in prodigies and in the stormy visions of the prophets, in order to renew the face of the earth, and Who has separated for Himself His people from all the nations of the world. And Christians know that God is both so dissatisfied with that lost world which He had made good and which evil has ruined —and at the same time so carried away by love—that He has given His Son and delivered Him over to men, in order to suffer and to die, and in this way redeem the world.

The Great God of Idolaters

To this true God the saint is entirely given. But there are false gods; even, as I shall shortly say, there is a spurious and distorted image of God that can be called the King or Jove of all false gods, the great god of the idolaters. With regard to *this* god, the saint is a thorough atheist, the most atheistic of men—just because he adores *only* God.

Let us dwell a moment on this point. And let us consider the merely rational, merely philosophical concept of God. This concept is twofold: there is the true God of the philosophers, and there is the false god of the philosophers. The true God of the philosophers is but the true God Himself, the God of the saints, the God of Abraham, Isaac and Jacob—imperfectly and inchoatively known, known in those attributes only which can be reached by our natural forces: Such a merely rational notion of God is in actual fact open to the supernatural.

But now suppose for yourselves a merely rational notion of God which would know the existence of the Supreme Being, but would disregard at the same time what St. Paul called His glory, deny the abyss of freedom which is meant by His transcendence, and chain Him to the very world He has made. Suppose for yourselves a merely rational—and warped—notion of God which is closed against the supernatural, and makes impossible the mysteries that are hidden in God's love and freedom and incommunicable life. Here we would have the false god of the philosophers, the Jove of all false gods. Imagine a god bound to the order of nature who is no more than a supreme warrant and justification of that order, a god who is responsible for this world without the power of re- deeming it, a god whose inflexible will, that no prayer can reach, is pleased with and hallows all the evil as well as all the good of the universe, all the trickery, wickedness and cruelty together with all the generosity which are at play in nature, a god who blesses iniquity and slavery and misery, and who sacrifices man to the cosmos, and makes the tears of the children and the agony of the innocents a stark ingredient of, and a tribute offered without any compensation to the sacred necessities of eternal cycles or of evolution. Such a god would be the unique supreme Being but made into an idol, the *naturalistic* god of nature, the Jupiter of the world, the great god of the idolaters and of the powerful on their thrones and of the rich in their earthly glory, the god of success which knows no law, and of mere fact set up as law.

I am afraid that such was the God of our modern rationalistic philosophy, the God perhaps of Leibniz and Spinoza, surely the God of Hegel.

Such was also, in quite another mood, not rationalistic, but magical, the God of Pagan antiquity, or rather one of the countenances of that double-faced God. For the pagan God was ambiguous; on the one hand he was the true God of nature and reason, the unknown God of Whom St. Paul spoke to the Athenians; and on the other hand he was the false god of naturalism, the self-contradictory god I have just described, and who does get on very well with the Prince of this world.

It could be added that among Christian sects, some wild Gnostics, especially the followers of Marcion, who regarded the God of the Old Covenant as an evil world-maker in conflict with the Redeemer, mistook for the Creator the same false god I have been discussing, the same absurd Emperor of the world.

And this brings me to the point I want to drive home. The saint, when he brings about the great act of rupture which I stressed earlier, rejects by the same stroke, breaks and annihilates, with an irresistible violence, this spurious Emperor of the world, this false god of naturalism, this great god of the idolaters, the powerful and the rich, who is an absurd counterfeit of God, but who is also the imaginary focus whence the adoration of the cosmos radiates, and to whom we pay tribute each time we bow down before the world. With regard to this god the saint is a perfect atheist. Well, were not the Jews and the first Christians often called atheists by the pagans at the time of the Roman Empire? There was a hidden meaning in this slander.*

*St. Justin said: "We are called atheists. And yes we confess it, we are atheists of those so-called gods." 1st *Apology*, VI, n. 1.

The Case of the Absolute Atheist

But let us turn at present to our modern atheists, our true and actual atheists—what can we say about them? I would suggest that, in the sense I have just emphasized, the absolute atheist is *not atheist enough*. He, too, is indignant against the Jupiter of this world, against the god of the idolaters, the powerful and the rich; he too decides to get rid of him. But instead of hurling against that false god the strength of the true God, and of giving himself to the work of the true God, as the saint does, the atheist, because he rejects the true God, can only struggle against the Jupiter of this world by calling on the strength of the immanent god of History, and by dedicating himself to the work of that immanent god.

It is indeed because he believes in the revolutionary disruptive power of the impetus of History, and because he expects from it the final emancipation of man, that the atheist delivers over his own soul to the blind god of History. Yet he is caught in a trap. Wait a while, and the blind god of History will appear just as he is— yes, the very same Jupiter of this world, the great god of the idolaters and the powerful on their thrones and the rich in their earthly glory, and of success which knows no law, and of mere fact set up as law. He will reveal himself as this same false god in a new disguise and crowned by new idolaters, and meting out a new brand of power and success. And it is too late for the atheist. As we saw at the beginning, he is possessed by this god. He is on his knees before History. With respect to a god who is not God, he is the most tractable and obedient of the devotees.

And so his break with this world of injustice and oppression was but a shallow and temporary break. More than ever he is subservient to the world. In comparison with the saint, who consummates in his own flesh his initial rupture with the world, and every day dies unto himself, and is blessed with the beatitudes of the poor and the persecuted and all the other friends of God, and who enjoys the perfect freedom of those who are led by the Spirit, the atheist is, it seems to me, a very poor replica of the liberated mind and the heroic insurgent. Nevertheless, as I have tried to point out, it is by an ill-directed longing for inner freedom and for non-acceptance of things as they are that he has been led astray. A somewhat paradoxical, yet, in my opinion, true statement about absolute atheism would be to say that it deprives God and mankind of some potential saints, in bringing to bankruptcy their attempt at heroic freedom, and turning their effort to break with the world into a total and servile subservience to the world. With all his sincerity and devotion, the authentic, absolute atheist is after all only an abortive saint, and, at the same time, a mistaken revolutionist.

IV.   THE SAINT AND TEMPORAL HISTORY

A Lost Opportunity

There is now another paradox, this time in an opposite direction. If we look at the saint, it seems that the inner act through which he achieves his total break with the world and total liberation from the world, making him free from everything but God, will inevitably overflow from the realm of spiritual life onto the realm of temporal life. Thus, if he is not dedicated solely to a contemplative state of existence, he will be led to act as a ferment of renewal in the structures of the world, as a stimulating and transforming energy in social matters and in the field of the activities of civilization.

And this is true, of course. As a matter of fact, it is what has been taking place for centuries. The Fathers of the Church were great revolutionaries. Thomas Aquinas in the order of culture, St. Vincent de Paul in the social field, were eminent examples of genuine radicals, whose initiative brought about decisive changes in the history of civilization. For centuries temporal progress in the world has been furthered by the saints.

Yet, here is the paradox that I just mentioned—the day when, in the course of modern history, a particularly inhuman structure of society, caused by the Industrial Revolution, made the problem of social justice manifestly crucial; when, at the same time, the human mind became aware of the *social* as a specific object of knowledge and activity, and when the first attempts to create workers' organizations provided the beginnings of a historical force capable of acting upon social structures—then was it not the moment for the saints to take the lead in the protest of the poor and in the movement of labor toward its historical coming of age? In actual fact, except for a few men of faith, like Ozanam in France and Toniolo in Italy (they are not yet canonized, but some day they might be), the task, as we know, was not conducted by saints. It even happened that atheists, instead of saints, took the lead in social matters, much to the misfortune of all.

Why such a tragic vacancy? It seems difficult not to see in it a

kind of punishment of the Christian world, which for a long period
has more or less failed Christianity in its practical behavior, and
despised the lessons of the saints, and abandoned to their fate, here
below, that great flock which also belongs to Christ, that immense
herd of men whom destitution and unlivable conditions of existence
kept chained to hell on earth. Let us not be mistaken. During the
time of which I am speaking, the saints were not lacking on the
earth; there was a considerable flowering of saints in the last century. But they did not pass beyond the field of spiritual, apostolic
or charitable activities: they did not cross the threshold of temporal, social, secular activity. And thus the gap was not filled, because in the historical age which is ours, the indirect repercussion
of the inner renewal of conscience upon the external structures of
society is definitely not enough, although it answers a basic need
and has made progressively more possible such social changes as
the abolition of slavery. A specifically social activity, an activity
which directly aims at improving and recasting the structures of
temporal life, is also needed.

Why has this kind of activity been neglected by a great many
Christians in the past? Is it on account of their supposed contempt
for the world, as people say? Nonsense! The saints break with the
world, but they have no contempt for creation; that they leave to
apprentices. As for the general run of Christians, one need but look
at them—at ourselves—(as François Mauriac reminded us rather
bluntly in the second *Semaine des Intellectuels Catholiques*)* to be
assured that we do not despise the world in the least and that we
are "of the earth," as it is said in the new devotional jargon. No;
the reason for which activities directly aiming at the structural
changes required by social justice have been lacking for so many
centuries, is quite simple: the means of exercising such activities
were non-existent. In the seventeenth century Saint Vincent de Paul
could found hospitals but he could not found trade unions. It was
only after the Industrial Revolution and the way in which it developed that the possibility of directly social activity could enter
people's imaginations, and that such a directly social, and not only
spiritual or charitable, activity has become a crying need.

Perhaps a concrete example will help to make clear the difference
between the two kinds of activity I have mentioned. A poor priest
named Cottolengo, who was a saint (though his name is not to
be found in the *Encyclopaedia Britannica*) founded in Turin, in

*See *Foi en Jésus-Christ et Monde d'aujourd'hui*. Editions de Flore. Paris, 1949.

the first half of the past century, a hospital that rapidly grew into a sort of huge city of all kinds of infirmity and human misery; hundreds of the poor were fed and cared for every day. But Cottolengo had established the rule that none of the money contributed for the support of his Institute should ever be saved and invested. Money each day received from the Providence of God should be spent each day, for "sufficient unto the day is the evil thereof."* There is even a story that one evening, as he saw that his assistants had set aside a certain amount of money for the morrow, Cottolengo threw that money out of the window—which in our modern world is the height of insanity, and perhaps of sacrilege. This course of action was in itself perfectly revolutionary, and all the more revolutionary in that it succeeded (Cottolengo's work has thrived in an astounding manner; it is now one of the most important institutions in Turin). Yet such a course of action, for all its spiritual significance, remained of no social consequence. It transcended the social problem. The social problem must be managed and solved in its own order. For half a century men of good will have realized better and better that the temporal mission of those who believe in God is to take over the job. Still, we must not forget that, even in the simple perspective of the temporal community, Christian social action is not enough; political action is even less so, however necessary both of them may be. What is required of those who believe in God is a witness of God; and what the world demands and expects of the Christian is first and foremost to see the love of truth and brotherly love made genuinely present in and through man's personal life—to see a gleam of the Gospel shining in the one place where the crucial test and crucial proof are to be found, namely the obscure context of relations from person to person.

The Christian World is Neither Christianity Nor the Church

I have just spoken of the historical deficiencies of the Christian world. Parenthetically, in order to avoid any misunderstanding, I should like to point out that by these words, "the Christian world," I am designating a sociological category, which is involved in the order and history of temporal civilizations, and is a thing of this world. The Christian world is neither Christianity nor the Church. The failures of the Christian world have no power to tarnish the Church or Christianity.

There has been, moreover, a good deal of confusion on this score.

*Matth. 6, 34.

Neither Christianity nor the Church have a mission to make men happy, their business is to tell them the truth—not to bring about justice and freedom in the political society, but to give mankind salvation and eternal life. No doubt this lays upon them the additional task of quickening the energies of justice and love in the depths of temporal existence and thus making that existence more worthy of man. Yet the successful accomplishment of such a task depends on the way in which the divine message is received. It is at this point that we are confronted with the responsibilities of the Christian world, that is, of the social groups of Christian denomination at work in secular history.

It is nonsense to reproach the Christians, as we often see it done today, with not having baptized "the Revolution," and with not having devoted their whole energies to "the Revolution." The messianic myth of "the Revolution" is a secularized perversion of the idea of the advent of God's Kingdom; it is apt to warp the course of human history, and to turn into failures the particular, genuine and genuinely progressive revolutions—the revolutions without a capital R—that are bound to follow one another as long as human history endures. But it is not nonsense to reproach Christians in the world with having failed to bring about at certain given times such needed particular revolutions. It is not nonsense to reproach them, more generally, with being sinners—they know very well that they are—who more or less always betray Christianity. Most important of all, it is certainly not nonsense to reproach the many people in modern times who are paying lip-service to the God in Whom they think they believe, with being in fact practical atheists.

Men Today Need Signs

According to one of our previous remarks,* if a new age of civilization is to come rather than a new age of barbarism, the deepest requirement of such an age will be the sanctification of secular life, a fecundation of social, temporal existence by spiritual experience, contemplative energies and brotherly love.

I dare say that we have not yet reached that stage. For the moment we are at the lowest point; human history today is in love with fear and absurdity, human reason with despair. The powers of illusion are spreading all over the world, throwing all compasses off direction. The faculty of language has been so dishonored, the

*Chapter VII, pp. 94–96, 101–102.

meaning of words so thoroughly falsified; so many truths, met with
at every corner in press or radio reports, are at each moment so
perfectly mixed with so many errors similarly advertized, and
trumpeted to the skies, that men are simply losing the sense of truth.
They have been lied to so often that they have become addicted,
and need their daily dose of lies as a daily tonic. They look as if
they believed in all this; but they are beginning to lead a kind of
clandestine mental life in which they will believe nothing they are
told, but will rely only upon savage experience and elementary instincts. They are surrounded on all sides by spurious marvels and
false miracles, which dazzle and blind their minds.

Things being as they are, it seems clear that the wisest reasonings
and the most eloquent demonstrations and the best managed organizations are definitely not enough for the men of this time. Men
today need *signs*. They need deeds. Above all they need tangible
signs to reveal to them the reality of things divine. Yet there is
everywhere a considerable shortage of thaumaturges, though they
probably are the kind of a commodity we need the most.

At this point I should like to bring back to our minds a saying
of Pascal. "We always behave," Pascal has said, "as if we were
called upon to make the truth triumph, whereas we are called upon
only to struggle for it."

It does not rest with us to give men miracles. It is up to us to
practice what we believe.

Here it seems well to stress one of the deepest meanings of
absolute atheism. In so doing we shall but be brought back to the
conclusion of the preceding chapter. As I put it, absolute atheism
is "a translation into crude and inescapable terms, a ruthless counterpart, an avenging mirror, of the practical atheism of too many
believers who do not actually believe." It is both the fruit and the
condemnation of practical atheism, its image reflected in the mirror
of divine wrath. If this diagnosis is true, then we must go on to say
that it is impossible to get rid of absolute atheism without first getting rid of practical atheism. Furthermore this has become clear to
everyone that from now onwards a decorative Christianity is not
enough, even for our existence in this world. The faith must be an
actual faith, practical and living. To believe in God must mean to
live in such a manner that life could not possibly be lived if God
did not exist. Then the earthly hope in the Gospel can become the
quickening force of temporal history.

I

PART II

FAITH AND THE
HUMAN COMMUNITY

CHAPTER NINE

TO EXIST WITH THE PEOPLE

WHENEVER we have to deal with the ingredients of human history, we are prone to consider matters from the point of view of *action* or of the *ideas* which shape action. Yet it is necessary to consider them also—and primarily—from the point of view of *existence.* I mean that there is another, and more fundamental, order than that of social and political action: it is the order of communion in life, desire and suffering. In other words there must be recognized, as distinct from the category *to act for* or *to act with,* the category *to exist with* and *to suffer with* which concerns a more profound order of reality.

To act for belongs to the realm of mere benevolence. *To exist with* and *to suffer with,* to the realm of love in unity. Love is given to an existing, concrete being. Despite what Pascal says, one loves persons, not "qualities." The one I love, I love him, right or wrong; and I wish to exist with him and suffer with him.

To exist with is an ethical category. It does not mean to live with someone in a physical sense, or in the same way as he lives; and it does not mean loving someone in the mere sense of wishing him well; it means loving someone in the sense of becoming one with him, of bearing his burdens, of living a common moral life with him, of feeling with him and suffering with him.

If one loves that human and living thing which is called "the people," and which, like all human and living things is, I know, very difficult to define, but all the more real, then one's first and basic wish will be to exist with the people, to suffer with the people, and to stay in communion with the people.

Before doing them good, or working for their good, before following or rejecting the political line of this or that group which claims to be supporting their interests, before weighing conscientiously the good and evil to be expected from the doctrines and historical trends which ask for their support and choosing amongst them, or in certain exceptional cases, rejecting them all—before doing any of these things one will have chosen to exist with the people, to suffer with the people, to assume the people's hardships and destiny.

I.   CLASS, RACE, PEOPLE

Insofar as the notions of class and race affect the consciousness and political debates of our day, *class* is a social-economic concept, and *race* (whatever its scientific value, which I consider very slight) is a social-biological concept. In both these concepts, but more especially in the second, the "social" is qualified by one of the inferior elements which go to make up the concepts in question. The notion of *people* is a social-ethical idea, with the word "ethical" only emphasizing and repeating the very word "social."

The word *people* can designate the whole multitude; it can also designate the lower levels of society. Neither definition exactly corresponds to the sense that the people have of themselves. If this sense or instinct were used as a guide, it would doubtless be found to refer to a certain loosely-bounded community, smaller than the whole multitude, and at the same time possessed of characteristics more deep-rooted and more typically human than those of "the lower levels of society." To be sure, in a negative sense the people appear to be the mass of the non-privileged ones; in a positive sense they are, I believe, that moral community which is centered on manual labor (allowing for the imprecision that such a description entails)—a moral community made up of the bulk of those who labor with their hands, farmers and workers, and also of the various elements which in point of fact are socially and morally bound up with them. By using the term moral community, I imply that the central characteristic I just mentioned—the function of manual labor—is not enough to define the people. We must take into account a certain historical patrimony connected with labor, and made up of sorrows, efforts and hopes—the dimension of past *time* and memory comes in.—We must similarly take into account a certain common call as well as a certain inner moral behavior—the dimension of *consciousness* comes in also—a certain way of understanding and living out suffering, poverty, hardship and especially work itself, a certain conception of how a man must help or correct another, look at joy and death, belong to the anonymous mass and have his name within it, a certain way of being "always the same ones who get killed."

II. THE CONNOTATIONS OF THE WORD "PEOPLE"

I believe that the concept of the people as understood today (at least where it is understood in the ethical-social and not racial sense) is derived from Christian and, so to speak, "parochial" sources. The idea of "the little people of Our Lord," or of the people of the poor to whom the promise of the Beatitudes has been made and who enjoy an "eminent dignity" in the *communion of saints,* was gradually transferred from the spiritual order, in which it belongs, to the temporal order, and there, awakening the sense of the above-mentioned moral community, it contributed to the formation of the concept, this time an ethical-social one, of the working people—which is neither antiquity's rather civic and national idea of the *populus* nor yet its idea of the *plebs.*

The result was what Auguste Comte would have called "a happy ambiguity" between the idea of the poor, the wretched, the disinherited, and the idea of the husky worker. This ambiguity can give rise to a spurious sentimentalism and romanticism, insofar as the first idea is considered a natural category in society, defined by the compassionate thrill or else by the resentment it awakens. It remains a well-founded ambiguity in the sense that as a matter of fact the husky worker usually has no inheritance and is condemned to a condition of poverty (in which today's middle classes are sharing as well as the proletariat). Be it added that the greatest mass of men represents a mass of non-privileged conditions of existence (which means, in the present state of the universe, not only poverty, but also, for a terribly large number of people, under-nourishment, servitude and oppression).

Afterwards many other factors were to intervene. At the time when modern capitalism reached its peak, Karl Marx, because he paid preponderant attention to the economic structure of society, froze the notion of class (proletariat) and that of the people, and tried to make the former absorb the latter. Today we see that this was an artificial operation, contrary to the nature of things. Neither the concept of *class*—nor (and still less) the concept of *race*—only the broader concept of *the people,* is possessed of a primordial social value on a genuinely human level.

As I noted in another book, an important historical gain was made during the nineteenth century: "the growing consciousness of the dignity of work and of the worker, of the dignity of the human person in the worker as such." Such a gain was primarily spiritual in na-

ture. As a matter of fact what actually developed was the consciousness of the collective personality of the people still more than class
consciousness. The dimension of consciousness is in this case as always linked with that of past time and memory. It is through the
slow work of the labor movement in all its historical complexity
that there came into being, first for the proletariat and then, gradually, for the other elements which make up the people, an awareness
of a developing personality, the necessary condition for the future
birth of a personalistic democracy.

III.   A FUNDAMENTAL CHOICE

It may happen that at certain critical times one wonders *where*
the people really are; just as at the time of the great schism the
Catholic could wonder: where really is the Church? The practical
difficulty of discerning a reality does not obliterate the latter. Who-
ever loves the people knows that the good of the political society,
or of the nation, or of what is eternal in man, may demand that
he refuse to countenance certain ideas or historical trends acting
in the people, but he also knows that for all that he is not required
to break his temporal communion with the people, or to cease to
exist with the people: on the contrary, existence with the people is
involved in the very good of the earthly community, and in the
very good of the Kingdom of God militant here below. Separated
from existence with the people, the common good of the political
community would become artificial and fragile, and the mission of
the Church (her very life) would not be fulfilled.

If the ideas and historical trends (sometimes the worst ideas and
trends) which at a certain time are acting upon the people are
contrary to truth and to the good of man, I shall fight against them
and do my utmost to change them; but I shall not, for all that,
cease to exist with the people if I have once chosen so to exist.

And why should I have chosen to exist with the people? Because
(speaking in religious and Christian terms) it is to the people, to
the people first, that the Gospel must be preached; it is the people
whom Christ loved. And is it possible to evangelize those with whom
one does not exist and does not suffer? What the sacred vocabulary
termed "the multitudes," on whom Christ had compassion, is called
"the masses" in the secular and temporal vocabulary.

Moreover, speaking in ethical-social terms, however great the
error and evil within the people may be, the people remain the
great granary of vital spontaneity and non-pharisaic living force.

The actual quantitative fact of their constituting the mass is important here, for it is within the mass that life takes root.

And finally, at the present moment in the world's history, the people, in their rise to historical adulthood, are the human reserve of a new civilization. Either civilization rests on the slavery of the masses, or it must be in continuity with their development.

IV. TO EXIST WITH AND SUFFER WITH THE PEOPLE

The Church is the Kingdom of God "in a state of pilgrimage and crucifixion." Concerned, not with managing temporal matters, but with guiding men toward supernatural truth and eternal life, the Church as such, in her very life and spiritual mission, exists and suffers with the people; nor can she do otherwise. If we better understood the mystery of the Church we would understand that, amidst the vicissitudes of temporal societies and civilizations, what the Church seeks and requires over and above all is *not to be separated* from the people. Anything would be better than such unnatural separation! For her will and mission is to give to the people the vivifying Blood of Jesus Christ.

This is where the devil plays his hand. Using his wiles to confuse the minds not only of the enemies of the Church, but also of some of her friends (especially those who, without *being* Christian, claim that they "defend Christianity"—for the sake of things other than Christ's glad tidings), the Deceiver causes them to mistake this true, holy, evangelical will of the Church, for the illusion of the very opposite, the pernicious illusion of those governments or those social strata which tried at times to dominate the people by means of the Church. But, whether in life or in dreams, illusions do not endure. And the gates of Hell, whether left or right, shall not prevail against the Church.

The proper order of the Church is the spiritual order. Now, in the temporal order, the Christians, *as members of the earthly community,* have to exist with the people and suffer with the people, this time with respect to the temporal aims of the history of mankind, and in order to work with the people toward their achievement.

Clearly every Christian individually taken is under no moral obligation to "exist with the people" in the temporal sense which I am stressing at present. To posit such an obligation would be to jumble the issues and confuse the religious with the social, the spiritual with the temporal. What I am saying is that if, in a collective manner, and in most instances the social and temporal groups of Christian denomination do not exist in this way with the people, then a deep-rooted disorder is introduced into the world, and will be paid for at great cost.

Pope Pius XI's statement on "the great scandal of the nineteenth century" has often been quoted, and rightly so. The working class turned away from the Church because the Christian world had turned away from the working class. For the people to exist with Christ it is necessary that Christians exist with the people.

A hopeful sign is that more and more Christians are understanding these things. May I be allowed to allude in this connection to the "working fraternities" of men or women engaged in religious orders, which are now developing in France?* They really exist with the people, they share in their labor and pain and poverty, they are starting an extraordinary renewal.

The strength of the Marxist revolutionists stems much less from their ideology than from the fact that, while endeavoring everywhere to disintegrate the labor movement, they exist with the people —to the confusion of the people. They claim that in order to exist with the people it is necessary to join their party or cooperate with it. That's a lie. The shibboleth "unity of action of the working class," which they put forward when it is to work for their benefit, is but a political perversion of the genuine concept of existential communion with the people. Obviously one can exist with the people while loathing Communism. But anyone who wants to substitute in actual existence a just vision of things for Marxist and materialist ideologies must first exist with the people. In order efficaciously to apply the social doctrine of Papal encyclicals, there is a previously required condition: namely, to exist with the people.

The weakness of many makeshift political movements is caused by the fact that they have not fulfilled this condition. I do not mean as regards the recruiting of more or less numerous members among the people; I am speaking of something much deeper, which takes place within the soul as I have tried to explain earlier. The tragedy of Mussolini was that hoping to *act for* the people (for this man, for a while, loved the people, that Italian people endowed with such great qualities), he ceased to *exist with* the people. Shortly he was to exist only with the State.

---

*I am thinking especially of the "Little Brothers" and "Little Sisters" (*Petits Frères et Petites Soeurs de Jésus*) who follow the teachings and inspiration of Father de Foucauld.—See the remarkable book by their founder and Prior, Father R. Voillaume, *Au Coeur des Masses*, Paris, 1950, ed. du Cerf.

V. POLITICAL ACTION AND EVANGELIC ACTION

It is evident that the normal result of existing with the people is political and social action with and for the people, and an effort to foster the progress of social justice. This is not simply a task of technical adjustment or material improvement. It requires an idea of the dignity of the human person, and of the spiritual value of justice, freedom, and neighborly love. The task is to help prepare for a new order while being intent on the spirit of the Gospel.

Now we are not unaware that such a task may possibly be made unfeasible in certain tragic circumstances—I think of peoples submitted to· the ruthless power of some totalitarian dictatorship, an ordeal that the nations behind the iron curtain are suffering at present. What, then, is the situation of a Christian conscious of his responsibility toward the people? Let us take the example of the most perfect case of political regression, namely, the case of the life inside a concentration camp. Those who suffered agony in the *univers concentrationnaire* know that Büchenwald or Ravensbrück were not only shambles, but a kind of society, "a nightmare of a society, in which the conquest of power was a life-and-death issue, as the merciless struggle between the *greens* and the *reds*—that is, between the common law prisoners and the political prisoners—has shown."*

Let us not speak of people who chose to accept any kind of rotten means—spying, cruelty, betrayal, co-operation with oppressors and torturers, direct or indirect murder of fellow prisoners—to seize the upper hand in such a degraded society. There were other people, generally Christians, who also undertook a sort of political struggle to dodge the ferocious discipline of their jailers, but who in so doing endeavored to submit to the exigencies of moral law the decisions they were obliged to make in the midst of barbarous circumstances.

Yet other Christians took the position that any political action was condemned, there, to come to terms with evil; in other words, they thought that they were confronted with a "catastrophe of the political order." At least it was a fact for them, given either their particular temperament or their awareness of a higher calling.

For those who in a given historical situation, would find themselves faced with such a catastrophe of the political order, the ways of political action would cease to exist—against their will, and, so to speak, through violence. Yet there would remain the order of

*Cf. *Man and the State*, p. 72.

evangelic action. Then there would awaken within those men, as required by events themselves, those so to speak sacerdotal potentialities the grace of Christ sows in each of us. It is to action of an evangelic and "sacerdotal" order that they would devote themselves, to the pure service of their neighbors, to the works of Antigone—which bear witness, despite any oppression, to brotherly love and devotion, and introduce us into the deepest communion, and demand, fully as much as political works, that one risk one's life or even lay it down. This would still be existing and suffering with the people but acting with the people only on an evangelic and almost sacerdotal plane.

Such evangelic action has always been needed. Given the pace at which the world is going, it will probably become more and more necessary. But as long as a spark of civilization is alive, men will not be obliged to fall back on these means alone. Political action is demanded by man's very nature. Freedom must be saved. And to save freedom the world today desperately longs to have political action itself, in its own field, penetrated and quickened by evangelic inspiration—through the instrumentality of Christians who exist with the people.

CHAPTER TEN

THE CHRISTIAN TEACHING

OF THE STORY

OF THE CRUCIFIXION

This chapter is made up of a letter directed by the author to Mr. Hayim Greenberg, editor of Jewish Frontier, *and published in the August, 1944, issue of this periodical, under the title* A Catholic View of the Crucifixion. *It refers to the* Letter to a Christian Minister, *which Mr. Hayim Greenberg had published in the August, 1939 issue.*

I THANK you cordially for having sent me your moving and inspiring "Letter to a Christian Minister." Not only did I read it with the keenest interest, but I greatly admire the way in which you have expressed the Christian understanding of the mystery of Christ's crucifixion by God's people. I cannot help thinking that in the very fact that a Jewish scholar, acquainted with the purest and deepest insights of his tradition, has come "from the outside" to such a grasp of the Christian point of view, there is an invaluable sign of the kinship between the Christian spirit and the Jewish spirit. In any case, for a Christian aware of the significance of his own creed, Christ's condemnation and death are a divine mystery, the most awesome irruption of God's secret purposes into human history, a mystery which can be looked at only in the light of supernatural faith, and you are perfectly right in stating that "as long as your pupils will think of this problem in terms of a lynching party or of a judicial frameup, they will remain on a low, nonmetaphysical plane that has nothing to do with Christianity."

Precisely because I am so profoundly in agreement with you on the fundamentals of the question, I think you will allow me to add a few remarks. And first, a criticism: the expression of "tragic guilt" is only an approximate and deficient one, for it deals with the basic concept of fate. Now from the Christian outlook (as well as from the outlook of the Old Testament) guilt is not made inevitable by fate. It is involved in the unbreakable plan of eternal wisdom, yet human freedom stays real under the will of God, and does freely the good which God has eternally decided to predetermine, the evil which He has eternally decided to permit.* (In the same way, Christ did not choose Judas as the betrayer. He knew those He has chosen—the Greek text uses the plural, John 13, 18. "I speak not of you all. I know [those] whom I have chosen." Judas was not among them, he was known as the non-chosen.) † Nowhere more than in the condemnation of Christ did the exercise of human freedom appear supremely dominated by the transcendent power and foreseeing mercy of God, in a way infinitely more pathetic than Greek tragic destiny. It made Paul bend his knees in adoration. Yet freedom and responsibility remained, and therefore, guilt.

This guilt was that of a few persons, the princes of the priests, and, to a certain extent, the mob of those days, blind and cruel as the killers of the prophets had been. The Christian, knowing that Christ is the Second Person of the divine Trinity, has good reason to call this guilt a crime of deicide. It was so in fact. But it was not so with regard to the conscience of the judges. If they had known He was the Son of God, they would not have condemned Him; for their fault was essentially lack of faith and blindness of heart, and so they did not recognize the One whom the prophets had announced. At this point, Christian teachers should emphasize the saying of St. Peter: "I know that ye did it in ignorance, as did also your rulers"‡ as well as the words of Jesus on His cross: "They know not what they do."

Moreover, it is obvious, when we read the Acts and St. Paul's Epistles, that the apostles' reproach to the Jews was not so much the crucifixion as their failure to believe in that very Christ Whom their priests had crucified, and Who had risen from the dead. Their reproaches to the Jews were no more anti-semitic—and no less vehement—than those of Moses.

---

*Cf. *Existence and the Existent*, chapter IV.

†He was known as the non-chosen *for eternal life*. With respect to the apostolate, Judas was chosen with the twelve; and Jesus knew from the very first that Judas would betray Him (St. John, 6, 65).—"Have I not chosen you twelve, and one of you is a devil?" (*Ibid.*, 71).—But Jesus chose him because He loved him, not because He knew that Judas would betray Him.

‡Acts, 3, 17.

Now here takes place, from the Christian point of view, another mystery, the mystery of the solidarity of Israel as a people with its spiritual leaders, for whose fault the people were to pay for centuries. For the people of Israel is a *corpus mysticum,* a Church-nation. The Christian believes that by reason of this paramount of all clerical crimes—the blindness of their spiritual leaders—Israel failed in its mission, and the Jews were deprived of the actual exercise of their privileges, and were abandoned to the world, and will remain thus dispossessed as long as they do not believe in their crucified Messiah. The ordeals suffered by a nation as a result of the faults of its political leaders are but a weak and watered-down image of such solidarity. Here, in the eyes of a Christian, it is with the spiritual mis-step of a consecrated people, and with the consequences inevitably involved, that we are confronted. And because God is the supreme ruler of human history, such consequences—the temporary dispossession of Israel—may be viewed in the line of those "chastisements" which God never spared His beloved people. Yet this concept is only valid from the highest metaphysical and transcendent standpoint, and divine punishment is only the normal, mysterious fructification of human deeds, and the patience of God waiting for man's return. Not only must we point out, as you rightly do, that every Jew of today is as innocent of the murder of Christ as every Catholic of today is of the murder of Jeanne d'Arc or the imprisonment of Galileo. But over and above all it must be stated that those who want to "punish" the Jews—who are in the hands of *their* and *our* God—for the murder of Golgotha, make themselves guilty of blasphemy and sacrilege; they stupidly encroach for the sake of their own human wickedness upon the hidden purposes of God, they flaunt the love with which He waits for His people, they offend with their bloody hands eternal Wisdom itself.

At this point we must observe that certain rhetorical commonplaces—such as the expression, "the deicide race"—which have been used for centuries in the vocabulary of Christian Gentiles, perhaps through some anti-Semitic motive, perhaps by mere coarseness of thought, are pregnant in any case with anti-Semitic potentialities, which may burst out into the worst feelings in the poisonous atmosphere of our day. Christian teachers have a duty to rule out such expressions which are definitely nonsense, as well as to purify carefully their language of similar improprieties due to human

thoughtlessness and to the indifference of Gentiles heedless of what
did not directly concern themselves.

Who killed Christ? The Jews? The Romans? I have killed Him,
I am killing Him every day through my sins. There is no other
Christian answer, since He died voluntarily for my sins, and to
exhaust the justice of God upon Himself. Jews, Romans, executioners, all were but instruments, free and pitiable instruments, of
His will to redemption and sacrifice. That is what Christian teachers
ought to inculcate in their pupils.

Shall we look for the deepest impulse toward that monstrosity—
Christians who are anti-Semites? They are seeking an alibi for their
innermost sense of guilt, for the death of Christ of which they want
to clear themselves: but if Christ did not die for their sins, then
they flee from the mercy of Christ! In reality they want *not to be
redeemed*. Here is the most secret and vicious root by virtue of
which anti-Semitism dechristianizes Christians, and leads them to
paganism.

The golden rule of Christian teaching in this matter is perfectly
simple: one need only cling to St. Paul. St. Paul has been especially commissioned to convey to us the enlightenment of divine
inspiration, the views of our God on that subject; it is a shame that
so many Christians do not know the statements of the Apostle to
the Gentiles. Never did I realize so acutely the essentially anti-
Christian madness of anti-Semitism as when preparing a book on
St. Paul and gathering together his texts on the mystery of Israel.
St. Paul teaches that "the gifts and the call of God are without
repentance," so that the people of Israel continue "ever beloved
for the fathers' sake."* He would wish to be anathema himself
from Christ on behalf of his brethren, "my kinsmen according to
the flesh, who are Israelites, whose is the adoption and the glory
and the covenants and the legislation and the liturgy and the
promises, whose are the fathers, and of whom is Christ according
to the flesh."†

"I say, then, have they stumbled to their fall? Heaven forbid!
But by their lapse salvation is come to the Gentiles, that the latter
may 'rouse them to jealousy.' And if their mis-step is the riches of
the world, and their diminution the riches of the Gentiles, how
much more their fulness?"‡ (*non conversio, sed plenitudo*, not con-

*Rom. 11, 28, 19.
†Rom. 9, 3–5.
‡Rom. 11, 11–12.

version, but fulness; Cornelius a Lapide, the famous commentator, stresses this point).

"If their dispossession hath been the reconciliation of the world, what will the reintegration of them be but life from the dead? If the first fruit of the bough is holy, so are the branches."* "If thou hast been cast off from that which is by nature a wild olive tree, and hast been grafted contrary to nature, into the good olive tree, how much more shall these, the natural branches, be grafted back into their own olive tree! For I would not have you ignorant, brethren, of this mystery (lest ye be wise in your own conceits), that hardening in part has happened in Israel, until the fulness of the Gentiles be entered in; and thus all Israel shall be saved, according as it is written. . . Just as yourselves at one time disobeyed God, but now have found mercy through their disobedience, so they too have now disobeyed through the mercy shown to you, in order that they too, as it is, may find mercy. For God hath imprisoned all alike in disobedience, in order that He may have mercy on all. O the depths of the riches of the wisdom and of the knowledge of God! How inscrutable are His judgments, and how untraceable His ways!"†

That is the genuine Christian view, the only genuine Christian view, of the mystery of Christ's rejection of the chosen people. It is in this light, and with feelings of brotherly love for the branches of the olive tree of which Christian Gentiles have been made part, that the drama of the crucifixion should be told by Christian teachers. St. Paul goes on to say: "For Christ is our peace, He that hath made both one, and hath broken down the dividing barrier of enmity. He hath brought to naught in His flesh the law of commandments framed in decrees, that in Himself He might create of the two [the Jew and the Gentile] one new man, and make peace and reconcile both in one body to God through the cross, slaying by means thereof their enmity."‡

*Rom. 11, 15–16.
†Rom. 11, 24–33.
‡Ephes. 2, 14–16.

K

CHAPTER ELEVEN

THE END

OF MACHIAVELLIANISM

I. MACHIAVELLI'S MACHIAVELLIANISM

M Y purpose is to discuss Machiavellianism. Regarding Machiavelli himself, some preliminary observations seem necessary. Innumerable studies, some of them very good, have been dedicated to Machiavelli. Jean Bodin, in the sixteenth century, criticized *The Prince* in a profound and wise manner. Later on Frederick the Great of Prussia was to write a refutation of Machiavelli in order to exercise his own hypocrisy in a hyper-Machiavellian fashion, and to shelter cynicism in virtue. During the nineteenth century, the leaders of the conservative "bourgeoisie," for instance the French political writer Charles Benoist, were thoroughly, naïvely and stupidly fascinated by the clever Florentine.

As regards modern scholarship, I should like to note that the best historical commentary on Machiavelli has been written by an American scholar, Professor Allan H. Gilbert.* As regards more popular presentations, a remarkable edition of the *Prince* and the *Discourses* has been issued by the Modern Library.

Mr. Max Lerner, in the stimulating, yet somewhat ambiguous Introduction he wrote for this edition of the *Prince* and the *Discourses,* rightly observes that Machiavelli was expressing the actual ethos of his time, and that as "power Politics existed before Machiavelli was ever heard of, it will exist long after his name is only a faint memory." This is perfectly obvious. But what matters in this connection is just that Machiavelli *lifted into consciousness* this

---

Machiavelli's Prince and its Forerunners, The Prince *as a Typical Book* De Regimine Principum, by Allan H. Gilbert, Duke University Press, 1938. I think that Professor Gilbert is right in locating the *Prince* in the series of the classical treatises *De Regimine Priciptum.* Yet the *Prince* marks the end of this series, not only because of the political changes in society, but because its inspiration utterly reverses and corrupts the medieval notion of government. It is a typical book *De Regimine Principum,* but which typically puts the series of these books to death.

ethos of his time and this common practice of the power politicians of all times. Here we are confronted with the fundamental importance of the phenomenon of *prise de conscience,* and with the risks of perversion which this phenomenon involves.

Before Machiavelli, princes and conquerors did not hesitate to apply on many occasions bad faith, perfidy, falsehood, cruelty, assassination, every kind of crime of which the flesh and blood man is capable, to the attainment of power and success and to the satisfaction of their greed and ambition. But in so doing they felt guilty, they had a bad conscience—to the extent that they had a conscience. Therefore, a specific kind of unconscious and unhappy hypocrisy —that is, the shame of appearing to oneself such as one is—a certain amount of self-restraint, and that deep and deeply human uneasiness which we experience in doing what we do not want to do and what is forbidden by a law that we know to be true, prevented the crimes in question from becoming a rule, and provided governed peoples with a limping accommodation between good and evil which, in broad outline, made their oppressed lives, after all, livable.

After Machiavelli, not only the princes and conquerors of the *cinquecento,* but the great leaders and makers of modern states and modern history, in employing injustice for establishing order, and every kind of useful evil for satisfying their will to power, will have a clear conscience and feel that they accomplish their duty as political heads. Suppose they are not merely skeptical in moral matters, and have some religious and ethical convictions in connection with man's personal behavior, then they will be obliged, in connection with the field of politics, to put aside these convictions, or to place them in a parenthesis; they will stoically immolate their personal morality on the altar of the political good. What was a simple matter of fact, with all the weaknesses and inconsistencies pertaining, even in the evil, to accidental and contingent things, has become, after Machiavelli, a matter of right, with all the firmness and steadiness proper to necessary things. A plain disregard of good and evil has been considered the rule, not of human morality— Machiavelli never pretended to be a moral philosopher—but of human politics.

For not only do we owe to Machiavelli our having become aware and conscious of the immorality displayed, in fact, by the mass of political men, but by the same stroke he taught us that this very immorality is the very law of politics. Here is that Machiavellian perversion of politics which was linked, in fact, with the Machia-

vellian *prise de conscience* of average political behavior in mankind.
The historic responsibility of Machiavelli consists in having *accepted,*
recognized, indorsed as normal the fact of political immorality, and
in having stated that good politics, politics conformable to its true
nature and to its genuine aims, is by essence non-moral politics.

Machiavelli belongs to that series of minds, and some of them
more profound than his, which all through modern times have
endeavored to unmask the human being. To have been the first in
this lineage is the greatness of this narrow thinker eager to serve the
Medici as well as the popular party in Florence, and disappointed
on both counts. Yet in unmasking the human being he maimed its
very flesh, and wounded its eyes. To have thoroughly rejected ethics,
metaphysics and theology from the realm of political knowledge
and political prudence is his very own achievement, and it is also
the most violent mutilation suffered by the human practical intellect
and the organism of practical wisdom.

II. BECAUSE MEN ARE BAD

Radical pessimism regarding human nature is the basis of Machiavelli's thought. After having stated that "a prudent ruler ought not
to keep faith when by so doing it would be against his interest, and
when the reasons which made him bind himself no longer exist,"
he writes: "If men were all good, this precept would not be a good
one; but *as they are bad,* and would not observe their faith with
you, so you are not bound to keep faith with them." Machiavelli
knows that they are bad. He does not know that this badness is not
radical, that this leprosy cannot destroy man's original grandeur,
that human nature remains good in its very essence and its root-
tendencies, and that such a basic goodness joined to a swarming
multiplication of particular evils is the very mystery and the very
motive power of struggle and progression in mankind. Just as his
horizon is merely terrestrial, just as his crude empiricism cancels for
him the indirect ordainment of political life toward the life of souls
and immortality, so his concept of man is merely animal, and his
crude empiricism cancels for him the image of God in man—a can-
cellation which is the metaphysical root of every power politics and
every political totalitarianism. As to their common and more frequent
behavior, Machiavelli thinks, men are beasts, guided by covetousness
and fear. But the prince is a man, that is, an animal of prey endowed with intelligence and calculation. In order to govern men,
that is, to enjoy power, the prince must be taught by Chiron the

centaur, and learn to become both a fox and a lion. Fear, animal
fear, and animal prudence translated into human art and awareness, are accordingly the supreme rulers of the political realm.

Yet the pessimism of Machiavelli is extremely removed from any
heroical pessimism. To the evil that he sees everywhere, or believes
he sees everywhere, he gives his consent. He consents, he aspires to
become a clearsighted composite of fox and lion. "For how we live,"
he says, "is so far removed from how we ought to live, that he who
abandons what is done for what ought to be done, will rather learn
to bring about his own ruin than his preservation." Therefore we
have to abandon what *ought to be done* for *what is done,* and it is
necessary for the prince, he also says, "to learn how not to be good,
and to use this knowledge and not use it, according to the necessity
of the case." And this is perfectly logical if the end of ends is only
present success. Yet such an abandonment, such a resignation would
be logical also, not only for political life, but for the entire field of
human life. Descartes, in the provisory rules of morality which he
gave himself in the *Discours de la Méthode,* made up his mind to.
imitate the actual customs and doings of his fellow-men, instead of
practicing what they say we ought to do. He did not perceive that
this was a good precept of immorality; for, as a matter of fact, men
live more often by senses than by reason. It is easy to observe with
Mr. Max Lerner that many Church princes, like the secular princes,
and above all that Alexander VI whom Machiavelli gives often as
an example, were among the principal followers of Machiavelli's precepts. But never has any catechism taught that we must imitate the
Church princes in our conduct, it is Christ that religion teaches us
to imitate. The first step to be taken by everyone who wishes to act
morally is to decide not to act according to the general customs and
doings of his fellow-men. This is a precept of the Gospel: "Do not
ye after their works; for they say, and do not. . ."*

III.   A CIVILIZED CYNICISM AND A PESSIMISM COMFORTED
BY AN OVERSIMPLIFIED IDEA OF MORALITY

The practical result of Machiavelli's teachings has been, for the
modern conscience, a profound split, an incurable division between
politics and morality, and consequently an illusory but deadly antinomy between what people call *idealism* (wrongly confused with
ethics) and what people call *realism* (wrongly confused with politics). Hence, as Mr. Max Lerner puts it, "the polar conflict between

*Matth. 23, 3.

the ethical and the ruthlessly realistic." I shall come back to this point. For the present I wish to note two kinds of complications which arise in this connection in the case of Machiavelli himself.

The first complication comes from the fact that Machiavelli, like many great pessimists, had a somewhat rough and elementary idea of moral science, plainly disregarding its realist, experiential, and existential character, and lifting up to heaven, or rather up to the clouds, an altogether naïve morality which obviously cannot be practiced by the sad yet really living and labouring inhabitants of this earth. The man of ethics appears to him as a feeble-minded and disarmed victim, occasionally noxious, of the beautiful rules of some Platonic and separate world of perfection. On the other hand, and because such a morality is essentially a self-satisfying show of pure and lofty shapes—that is, a dreamed-up compensation for our muddy state—Machiavelli constantly slips from the idea of well-do-ing to the idea of what men admire as well-doing, from moral virtue to appearing and apparent moral virtue; his virtue is a virtue of opinion, self-satisfaction and glory. Accordingly, what he calls vice and evil, and considers to be contrary to virtue and morality, may sometimes be only the authentically moral behavior of a just man engaged in the complexities of human life and of true ethics: for instance, justice itself may call for relentless energy—which is neither vengeance nor cruelty—against wicked and false-hearted enemies. Or the toleration of some existing evil—if there is no furthering of or co-operating with the same—may be required for avoiding a greater evil or for slowing down and progressively reducing this very evil. Or even dissimulation is not always bad faith or knavery. It would not be moral, but foolish, to open up one's heart and inner thoughts to any dull or mischievous fellow. Stupidity is never moral, it is a vice. No doubt it is difficult to mark exactly the limits between cunning and lying, and even some great Saints of the Old Testa-ment—I am thinking of Abraham—did not take great care of this distinction—this was a consequence of what may be called the twi-light status of moral conscience in the dawn-ages of mankind.* Yet a certain amount of cunning, if it is intended to deceive evil-disposed persons, must not be considered fox's wiles, but intellect's legitimate weapon. Oriental peoples know that very well, and even evangelic candor has to use the prudence of the serpent, as well as the simplicity of the dove (the dove tames the serpent, but the lion

*Cf. Raissa Maritain, *Histoire d'Abraham ou les Premiers Ages de la Conscience Morale*, Desclée De Brouwer, Paris, 1947.

does not tame the fox). The question is to use such cunning without
the smallest bit of falsehood or imposture; this is exactly the affair
of intelligence; and the use of lying—namely the large-scale indus-
trialisation of lying, of which the great dictatorships of our age have
offered us the spectacle—appears from this point of view, not only
as moral baseness, but also as vulgarity of mind and thorough degradation of intelligence.

The second complication arises from the fact that Machiavelli
was a cynic operating on the given moral basis of civilized tradition,
and his cruel work of exposure took for granted the coherence and
density of this deep-rooted tradition. Clear-sighted and intelligent
as he was, he was perfectly aware of that fact; that is why he would
pale at the sight of modern Machiavellianism. This commentator of
Titus Livius was instructed by Latin tradition, he was a partaker
as well as a squanderer of humanist learning, an inheritor as well
as an opponent of the manifold treasure of knowledge prepared by
Christian centuries, and degenerating in his day. Machiavelli never
negates the values of morality, he knows them and recognizes them
as they have been established by ancient wisdom, he occasionally
praises virtuous leaders (that is, those whose virtues were made
successful by circumstances). He knows that cruelty and faithless-
ness are shameful, he never calls evil good or good evil. He simply
denies to moral values—and this is largely sufficient to corrupt
politics—any application in the political field. He teaches his prince
to be cruel and faithless, according to the case, that is, to be evil
according to the case, and when he writes that the prince must learn
how not to be good, he is perfectly aware that not to be good is to
be bad. Hence his difference from many of his disciples, and the
special savour, the special power of intellectual stimulation of his
cynicism. But hence also his special sophistry, and the mantle of
civilized intelligence with which he unintentionally covered and
veiled for a time the deepest meaning, the wild meaning, of his
message.

IV. A MERELY ARTISTIC CONCEPT OF POLITICS

Finally, the "grammar of power" and the recipes of success written by Machiavelli are the work of a pure artist, and of a pure
artist of that Italian Renaissance where the great heritage of the
antique and Christian mind, falling in jeopardy, blossomed into the
most beautiful, delightful and poisonous flowers. What makes the
study of Machiavelli extremely instructive for a philosopher, is the

fact that nowhere is it possible to find a more purely artistic conception of politics.* And here is his chief philosophical fault, if it is true that politics belongs to the field of the "praktikon" (to do), not of the "poietikon" (to make), and is by essence a branch—the principal branch, according to Aristotle—of ethics. Politics is distinct from individual ethics as one branch from another branch on the same tree. It is a special and specific part of ethics, and it carries within itself an enormous amount of art and technique, for the role played by the physical elements to be known and utilized, the forces and resistances to be calculated, the role played by the *making,* or by the work to perform successfully, the role played by the moulding intelligence and imagination is much greater in political than in individual or even familial ethics. But all this amount of art and technique is organically, vitally and intrinsically subordinated to the ethical energies which constitute politics, that is to say, art is there in no manner autonomous, art is there embodied in, and encompassed with, and lifted up by ethics, as the physico-chemical activities in our body are integrated in our living substance and superelevated by our vital energies. When these merely physico-chemical activities are liberated and become autonomous, there is no longer a living organism, but a corpse. Thus, merely artistic politics, liberated from ethics, that is, from the practical knowledge of man, from the science of human acts, from truly human finalities and truly human doings, is a corpse of political wisdom and political prudence.

Indeed, Machiavelli's very own genius has been to disentangle as perfectly as possible all the content of art carried along by politics from the ethical substance thereof. His position, therefore, is that of a separate artistic spirit contemplating from without the vast matter of human affairs, with all the ethical cargo, all the intercrossings of good and evil they involve. His purpose is to teach his disciple how to conquer and maintain power in handling this matter as a sculptor handles clay or marble. Ethics is here present, but in the matter to be shaped and dominated. We understand from this point of view how the *Prince* as well as the *Discourses* are rich in true observations and sometimes in true precepts, but perceived and stated in a false light and in a reversed or perverted perspective. For Machiavelli makes use of good as well as of evil, and is ready to succeed with virtue as well as with vice. That specific concept of

*". . . In these things lie the true originality of Machiavelli; all may be summed up in his conviction that government is an independent art in an imperfect world." Alian H. Gilbert, *op. cit.,* p. 285.

virtù, that is, of brilliant, well-balanced and skilled strength, which was at the core of the morality of his time, as an aesthetic and artistic transposition of the Aristotelian concept of virtue, is always present in his work.* He knows that no political achievement is lasting if the prince has not the friendship of the people, but it is not the good of the people, it is only the power of the prince which matters to him in this truth perversely taught. The *Discourses*† eloquently emphasize the fundamental importance of religion in the state, but the truth or falsity of any religion whatsoever is here perfectly immaterial, even religion is offered as the best means of cheating the people, and what Machiavelli teaches is "the use of a national religion for state purposes," by virtue of "its power as a myth in unifying the masses and cementing their morale."‡ This is a perversion of religion which is surely worse and more atheistic than crude atheism—and the devastating effects of which the world has been able to see and enjoy in the totalitarian plagues of our day.

Here we are confronted with the paradox and the internal principle of instability of Machiavelli's Machiavellianism. It essentially supposes the complete eradication of moral values in the brain of the political artist as such, yet at the same time it also supposes the actual existence and actual vitality of moral values and moral beliefs in all others, in all the human matter that the prince is to handle and dominate. But it is impossible that the use of a supramoral, that is, a thoroughly immoral art of politics should not preduce a progressive lowering and degeneration of moral values and moral beliefs in the common human life, a progressive disintegration of the inherited stock of stable structures and customs linked with these beliefs, and finally a progressive corruption of the ethical and social matter itself with which this supramoral politics deals. Thus, such an art wears away and destroys its very matter, and, by the same token, will degenerate itself. Hence Machiavelli could only have rare authentic disciples; during the classical centuries of Henry VIII and Elizabeth, Mazarin and Richelieu, Frederick, Catherine

---

*According to a very just remark by Friedrich Meincke, the two concepts of *fortune* and *necessity* complete the trilogy of the leading ideas of Machiavelli: *Virtù, fortuna, necessità*. Cf. Friedrich Meinecke, *Die Idee der Staaträson*, München and Berlin, 1924, chapter I.

†Some authors magnify the divergences between the *Prince* and the *Discourses*. In my opinion these divergences, which are real, relate above all to the literary genus of the two works, and remain quite secondary. The *Discourses on the first ten Books of Titus Livius* owed it to their own rhetorical and academic mood as well as to Roman antiquity to emphasize the republican spirit and some classical aspects of political virtue. In reality neither this virtue (in the sense of the Ancients) nor this spirit ever mattered to Machiavelli, and his own personal inspiration, his quite amoral art of using *virtù* to master fortune by means of occasion and necessity are as recognizable in the *Discourses* as in the *Prince*.

‡Max Lerner, Introduction, p. xxxvii.

of Russia and Talleyrand, the latter was perhaps the only perfect
pupil of Machiavelli; finally Machiavelli's teachings, which imply
an essentially rational and well-measured, that is, an artistic use of
evil, were to give place to that use of every kind of seemingly useful
evil by great irrational and demonic forces and by an intelligence
no longer artistic but vulgar and brutal and wild, and to that im-
mersion of the rulers as well as of the ruled in a rotted ethics, calling
good evil and evil good, which constitute the common Machiavellianism of today.

V.   MACHIAVELLIANISM AND THE PHILOSOPHY OF THE
COMMON GOOD

But so much for Machiavelli. It is this common Machiavellianism
that I wish now to consider. In so doing, I should like briefly to
touch the three following points: first, the notion of common good
and the factual successes of Machiavellianism; second, the crucial
conflict which here constitutes the main problem, and the resolution thereof; third, the roots and the more subtle implications of
this resolution, which concern the specific structure of politics in its
relationship with morality.

For Machiavelli the end of politics is power's conquest and maintenance—which is a work of art to be performed. On the contrary,
according to the nature of things, the end of politics is the common
good of a united people; which end is essentially something concretely human, therefore something ethical. This common good consists of the good life—that is, a life conformable to the essential
exigencies and the essential dignity of human nature, a life both
morally straight and happy—of the social whole as such, of the
gathered multitude, in such a way that the increasing treasure and
heritage of communicable good things involved in this good life
of the whole be in some way spilled over and redistributed to each
individual part of the community. This common good is at once
material, intellectual and moral, and principally moral, as man
himself is; it is a common good of human persons.* Therefore, it
is not only something useful, an ensemble of advantages and profits,
it is essentially something good in itself—what the Ancients termed
bonum honestum. Justice and civic friendship are its cement. Bad
faith, perfidy, lying, cruelty, assassination, and all other procedures
of this kind which may occasionally appear *useful* to the power of
the ruling clique or to the prosperity of the state, are in themselves

*See our little book, *The Person and the Common Good,* 1947.

—insofar as they are political deeds, that is, deeds involving in some degree the common conduct—injurious to the common good and tend by themselves toward its corruption. Finally, because good life on earth is not the absolute ultimate end of man, and because the human person has a destiny superior to time, political common good involves an intrinsic though indirect reference to the absolutely ultimate end of the human members of society, which is eternal life, in such a way that the political community should temporally, and from below, help each human person in his human task of conquering his final freedom and fulfilling his destiny.

Such is the basic political concept which Machiavellianism broke down and destroyed. If the aim of politics is the common good, peace —a constructive peace struggling through time toward man's emancipation from any form of enslavement—is the health of the state; and the organs of justice, above all of distributive justice, are the chief power in the state. If the aim of politics is power, war is the health of the state, as Machiavelli put it, and military strength is the chief power in the state. If the aim of politics is the common good, the ruler, having to take care of the temporal end of a community of human persons, and having to avoid in this task any lack of clearsightedness and any slip of will, must learn to be, as St. Thomas taught, a man good in every respect, *bonus vir simpliciter*. If the aim of politics is power, the ruler must learn not to be good, as Machiavelli said.

The great rulers of modern times have well understood and conscientiously learned this lesson. Lord Acton was right in stating that "the authentic interpreter of Machiavelli is the whole of later history." We have to distinguish, however, two kinds of common Machiavellianism. There was a kind of more or less attenuated, dignified, conservative Machiavellianism, using injustice within "reasonable" limits, if I may put it so; in the minds of its followers, what is called Realpolitik was obfuscated and more or less paralyzed, either by a personal pattern of moral scruples and moral rules, which they owed to the common heritage of our civilization, or by traditions of diplomatic good form and respectability, or even, in certain instances, by lack of imagination, of boldness, and of inclination to take risks. If I try to characterize more precisely these moderate Machiavellianists, I should say that they preserved in some way, or believed they preserved, regarding the *end* of politics, the concept of common good—they were unfaithful to their master in this regard; and that they frankly used Machiavellianism regarding the *means* of procuring this common good. Such an unnatural split and disproportion between means and ends was, moreover, inevitably to lead to a perversion of the idea of common good itself, which became more and more a set of material advantages and profits for the state, or territorial conquests, or prestige and glory. The greatest representative of moderate Machiavellianism was, in my opinion, Richelieu. Bismarck was a transition from this first form of Machiavellianism to the second one.

This second form of Machiavellianism is absolute Machiavellianism. It was intellectually prepared, during the nineteenth century, by the Positivist trend of mind, which considered politics to be, not a mere art, but a mere natural science, like astronomy or chemistry, and a mere application of so-called "scientific laws" to the struggle for life of human societies—a concept much less intelligent and still more inhuman than that of Machiavelli himself. Absolute Machiavellianism was also and principally prepared by the Romanticist German philosophy of Fichte and Hegel. It is well known that the author of the *Address to the German Nation* wrote a *Character of Machiavelli*. As to the Hegelian cult of the state, it is a metaphysical sublimation of Machiavelli's principles. Now the turn has been completed, ethics itself has been swallowed up into the political denial of ethics, power and success have become supreme moral criteria, "the course of world history stands apart from virtue, blame and justice," as Hegel put it, and at the same time "human history," he also said, "is God's judgment." Machiavellianism is no longer politics, it is metaphysics, it is a religion, a prophetic and mystical enthusiasm.

It sufficed for such an enthusiasm to enter into some desperados who were empty, as it were, of the usual characters of rational personality, but open to the great collective forces of instinct, resentment and tellurian inspiration; it sufficed for such leaders to give a full practical significance to the old infernal discovery of the endless reserves of evil when thoroughly accepted and utilized, and of the seemingly infinite power of that which negates, of the dissolving forces and of the corruption of human consciences—in order for absolute Machiavellianism to arise in the world, and in order for the unmasking Centaur to be unmasked in its turn.* Here we are

*"Hitler told me he had read and reread the *Prince* of the Great Florentine. To his mind, this book is indispensable to every political man. For a long time it did not leave Hitler's side. The reading of these unequalled pages, he said, was like a cleansing of the mind. It had disencumbered him from plenty of false ideas and prejudices. It is only after having read the *Prince* that Hitler understood what politics truly is." Hermann Rauschning, *Hitler m'a dit.* (*The Voice of Destruction*, 1940.)

confronted with that impetuous, irrational, revolutionary, wild, and
demoniacal Machiavellianism, for which *boundless* injustice, *bound-*
less violence, *boundless* lying and immorality, are normal political
means, and which draws from this very boundlessness of evil an
abominable strength. And we may experience what kind of common
good a power which knows perfectly how not to be good, and whose
hypocrisy is a conscious and happy, ostentatious and gloriously
promulgated hypocrisy, and whose cruelty wants to destroy souls
as well as bodies, and whose lying is a thorough perversion of the
very function of language—what kind of common good such a
power is able to bring to mankind. Absolute Machiavellianism
causes politics to be the art of bringing about the misfortune of
men.

That's how it is. But absolute Machiavellianism *succeeds,* does it
not? At least it has succeeded for many years. How could it not
succeed, when everything has been sacrificed to the aim of success?
Here is the ordeal and the scandal of contemporary conscience.
Moreover it would be astonishing if a timid and limited Machiavellianism were not overcome and thrown away by a boundless and
cynical Machiavelianism, stopping at nothing. If there is an answer
to the deadly question which we are asked by the Sphinx of history,
it can only lie in a thorough reversal of a century-old political
thought. In the meantime, the peoples which stand against absolute Machiavellianism will be able to stop its triumphs and to overcome its standard-bearers only in risking in this struggle their blood
and their wealth and their dearest treasures of peaceful civilization,
and in threatening this Machiavellianism with its own material
weapons, material techniques and gigantic means of destruction.
But will they be obliged, in order to conquer it and to maintain
themselves, to adopt not only its material weapons, but also its own
spirit and philosophy? Will they yield to the temptation of losing
for the sake of life their very reason for living and existing?

VII.   THE GREAT PROBLEM

Here we arrive at the crucial conflict.

Confronted with any temptation of Machiavellianism, that is, of
gaining success and power by means of evil, moral conscience answers and cannot keep from answering, just as when it is tempted
by any profitable fault: It is never allowed to do evil for any good
whatsoever. And Christian conscience in this case is strengthened

by the very word of the Gospel. When the devil tempted Jesus by showing Him all the kingdoms of the world, and the glory of them, and telling Him: "All these things, will I give thee, if thou wilt fall down and worship me."—"Get thee hence, Satan," Jesus answered. "For it is written, Thou shalt worship the Lord thy God, and Him only shalt thou serve."

Such is the answer that the human Person, looking up to his own destiny as a person, to his immortal soul, his ultimate end and ever-lasting life, to his God, gives to Politics when Politics offers him the kingdom of the world at the price of his soul. This answer, and the personage to whom it was given, show us the root significance of Politics making itself absolutely autonomous, and claiming to be man's absolutely ultimate end. It shows us the transcendent mean-ing of the Pagan Empire, and of any paganized Empire, and of any self-styled Holy Empire if its Caesar—be he a Christian Emperor or a Socialist Dictator, or any kind of Grand Inquisitor in the sense of Dostoievsky's famous legend—wills to settle and manage on earth the final kingdom of God or the final kingdom of Man, which they see as the same final kingdom. "Get thee hence, Satan," answers Christ. State and politics, when truly separated from ethics, are the realm of those demoniacal principalities of which St. Paul spoke; the Pagan Empire is the Empire of Man making himself God: the diametrical opposite of the kingdom of Redemptive Incarnation.

Yet the answer we are considering does not solve our conflict; on the contrary, it increases this conflict, it widens the tear to the infinite, it clamps down on the Machiavellian temptation without appeasing the anguish and scandal of our intellect. For it is an answer given by Personal Ethics to a question asked by Political Ethics; it transcends the question, as the Person, with regard to his eternal destiny, transcends the state; it cuts short the question, it does not resolve it. Obviously no assertion of the individual Ethics of the Person, absolutely true, absolutely decisive as it may be, can constitute a sufficiently adequate and relevant answer to a problem stated by the Ethics of the Body Politic. Exactly because it is a transcendent answer, it is not a proper one. Machiavellianism suc-ceeds, does it not? Absolute Machiavellianism triumphs on earth, as our eyes have seen for years. Is Morality willing, is Christianity willing, is God willing that, of necessity, all our freedoms be con-quered, our civilization destroyed, the very hope annihilated of see-ing a little justice and brotherly amity raise our earthly life—are they willing that, of necessity, our lives be enslaved, our temples and in-

stitutions broken down, our brethren persecuted and crushed, our
children corrupted, our very souls and intelligences delivered over
to perversion by the great imperial standard-bearers of Machiavellianism—because of the very fact that we adhere to justice and refuse the devil, while they dare to use injustice and evil and accede
to the devil up to the end?

It is the true goal of the *Person* which is eternal, not that of the
Body Politic. If a man suffers martyrdom and enters paradise, his
own soul enjoys bliss; but suppose all the citizens of a state satellite
to some Nero suffer martyrdom and enter paradise, it is not the
soul of this state-which will enjoy bliss; moreover, this state no
longer exists. The Body Politic has no immortal soul, nor has a
nation, unless perhaps as concerns a merely spiritual survival of its
common moral heritage in the memory of men or in the virtues of
the immortal souls which animated its members long ago, at the time
when it existed. During the Second World War it was grim nonsense to console Frenchmen in asking them to accept destruction or
enslavement of their country while speaking to them of La France
éternelle. The soul of a nation is not immortal. The direct and
specifying end, the common good of a nation is something temporal
and terrestrial, something which can and should be superelevated
by Gospel virtues in its own order, but whose own order is natural,
not supernatural, and belongs to the realm of time. Therefore the
very existence, temporal and terrestrial, the very improvement, temporal and terrestrial, the very prosperity of a nation, and that
amount of happiness and glory which arises from the crises themselves and from the ordeals of history, really and essentially pertain
to the common good of this nation.

No doubt—to imagine a thoroughly extreme example—a nation
or a state could and should accept destruction, as did the legion of
Mauritius, if its citizens were summoned to choose between martyrdom and apostasy; but such a case would not be a political case,
it would be a case of sacrifice of political life itself to divine life,
and a witnessing, in some way miraculous, of the superiority of the
order of grace over the order of nature. But in political life itself,
in the order of nature, in the framework of the temporal laws of
human existence, is it not impossible that the first of the normal
means of providing the common good of a body politic, that is,
justice and political morality, should lead to the ruin and disaster
of this body politic? Is it not impossible that the first of the means
of corrupting the common good of a body politic, that is, injustice

and political treachery, should lead to the triumph and prosperity
of this body politic?

Yes, this is impossible.

Yet Machiavellianism succeeds in political history? Evil succeeds?
What is then the answer?

VII.   MACHIAVELLIANISM DOES NOT SUCCEED

The answer is that evil *does not* succeed. In reality Machiavellianism does not succeed. To destroy is not to succeed. Machiavellianism succeeds in bringing about the misfortune of men, which
is the exact opposite of any genuinely political end. More or less
bad Machiavellianists have succeeded for centuries against other
more or less bad Machiavellianists: this is mere exchange of counterfeit coin. Absolute Machiavellianism succeeds against moderate or
weak Machiavellianism: this also is normal. But if absolute Machiavellianism were to succeed absolutely and definitely in the world,
this would simply mean that political life would have disappeared
from the face of the earth, giving place to an entanglement and
commixture of the life of the animals and the slaves, and of the
life of the saints.

But in saying that evil and injustice do not succeed in politics,
I mean a more profound philosophical truth. The endless reserves
of evil, the seemingly infinite power of evil of which I spoke a
moment ago, are only, in reality, the power of corruption—the
squandering and dissipation of the substance and energy of Being
and of Good. Such a power destroys itself by destroying that good
which is its subject. The inner dialectic of the successes of evil con-
demn them not to be lasting. The true philosophical answer consists,
therefore, in taking into account the dimension of time, the duration proper to the historical turns of nations and states, which considerably exceeds the duration of a man's life. According to this
political duration, to the duration required by political reality to
mature and fructify, I do not say that a just politics will, even in
a distant future, always actually succeed, nor that Machiavellianism
will, even in a distant future, always actually fail. For, with nations
and states and civilizations we are in the order of nature, where
mortality is natural and where life and death depend on physical
as well as moral causes. I say that justice works through its own
causality toward welfare and success in the future, as a healthy
sap works toward the perfect fruit, and that Machiavellianism

works through its own causality for ruin and bankruptcy, as poison in the sap works for the illness and death of the tree.

Now, what is the illusion proper to Machiavellianism? It is the illusion of *immediate success*. The duration of the life of a man, or rather the duration of the activity of the prince, of the political man, circumscribes the maximum length of time required by what I call *immediate success*, for immediate success is a success that our eyes may see. And what we are speaking of, what Machiavelli is speaking of, in saying that evil and injustice succeed in politics, is in reality *immediate success*, as I have defined it. Yet immediate success is success for a man, it is not success for a state or a nation; it may be—it is, in the case of Machiavellian successes considered as to their inner causal law, a disaster according to the duration proper to state-vicissitudes and nation-vicissitudes. It is with regard to immediate success that evil and injustice enjoy a seemingly infinite power, a power which can be met and overcome only by a heroic tension of the antagonistic powers. But the more dreadful in intensity such a power of evil appears, the weaker in historic duration are the internal improvements, and the vigor of life, which have been gained by a state using this power.*

As I have already put it in other studies,† the good in which the state's justice bears fruit, the misfortune in which the state's injustice bears fruit, have nothing to do with the immediate and visible results; historic *duration* must be taken into account; the temporal good in which the state's justice bears fruit, the temporal evil in which its iniquity bears fruit, may be and are in fact quite different from the immediate results which the human mind might have expected and which the human eyes contemplate. It is as easy to disentangle these remote causations as to tell at a river's mouth which waters come from which glaciers and which tributaries. The achievements of the great Machiavellianists seem durable to us, because our scale of duration-measurements is an exceedingly small one, with regard to the time proper to nations and human communities. We do not understand the fair play of God, Who gives those who have freely chosen injustice the time to exhaust the benefits of it and the fullness of its energies. When disaster comes to

*Three years after these pages were written (they were first drafted in 1941, for a symposium on "The Place of Ethics in Social Science" held at the University of Chicago) the world contemplated the inglorious fall of Mr. Benito Mussolini. The triumphs of this wretched disciple of absolute Machiavellianism (he wrote a Preface to an edition of the *Prince*) lasted twenty years.

Hitlerist Machiavellianism had a similar fate. Sooner or later Communist Machiavellianism will have a similar fate.

†*Humanisme Intégral*, pp. 229–230 (English edit. *True Humanism*, pp. 219–220).

these victors the eyes of the righteous who cried against them to God will have long putrefied under the earth, and men will not know the distant source of the catastrophe.

Thus it is true that politics being something intrinsically moral, the first political condition of good politics is that it be just. And it is true at the same time that justice and virtue do not, as a rule, lead us to success in this world. But the antinomy is solved, because on the one hand success in politics is not material power nor material wealth nor world-domination, but the achievement of the common good, with the conditions of material prosperity which it involves. And because, on the other hand, these very conditions of material prosperity, terrible as the ordeals may be which the requirements of justice impose on a people, are not and cannot be put in jeopardy or destroyed by the use of justice itself, if historical duration is taken into account and if the specific effect of this use of justice is considered in itself, apart from the effect of the other factors at play.

I do not mean that God recompenses the just peoples by the blessings of military triumphs, territorial aggrandizements, accumulation of wealth, or infinite profit in business; such values are but secondary, sometimes even injurious to the political common good. Moreover, if it is true that the political life of peoples may be permeated in its own order by Christian influences, it may be that a Christian nation has to undergo in a measure the very law of evangelic trials, and to pay for a certain abundance of spiritual or cultural improvements at the price of certain weaknesses and infirmities in worldly values; such was the case of Italy in the Middle Ages and the Renaissance; never did Italy know a more splendid civilization than in those times when the power of the Popes brought her, as Machiavelli takes pleasure in pointing out, weakness and pain regarding her political unity. Nor do I mean that a body politic using political justice is by this fact alone protected against ruin or destruction. What I mean is that in such a misfortune the very cause of ruin or destruction is never the use of justice. What I mean is that the very order of nature and of natural laws in moral matters, which is the natural justice of God, makes justice and political righteousness work towards bearing fruit, in the long run, as regards their own law of action, in the form of improvement in the true common good and the real values of civilization. Such was the case for the policy of St. Louis, although he was beaten in all his crusading enterprises. Political injustices, on

the other hand, political treacheries, political greed, selfishness or
cowardice, exploitation of the poor and the weak, intoxication with
power or glory or self-interest—or that kind of political cleverness
which consists, as a professor in international politics told me can-
didly some years ago, in using flattery and leniency toward our
enemy, because he is an enemy, and therefore is to be feared, and
in forsaking our friend, because he is a friend, and therefore is not
to be feared—or that kind of political firmness which consists in
denouncing some predatory state which is attacking a weak nation,
and in selling weapons and supplies to the same aggressor, because
business must keep going—all this is always dearly paid for in the
end. Wars, even just wars which must be waged against iniquitous
aggressors, are often the payment thus exacted from a civilization.*
Then war must be waged with unshaken resolution. But victory will
be fruitful only on the condition of casting away the wrongdoings
of the past, and of decidedly converting oneself toward justice and
political righteousness.

The more I think of these things, the more I am convinced that
the observations I proposed a moment ago on the dimension of
time are the core of the question. To be lasting is an essential characteristic of the common good. A forester who would seek immediate visible success in planting plenty of big old trees in his forest,
instead of preparing young saplings, would use a foolish forest
policy. Machiavelli's prince is a bad political man, he perverts
politics, because his chief aim is his own personal power and the
satisfaction of his own personal ambition. But, in a much more
profound and radical sense, the ruler who sacrifices everything to
the desire of his own eyes to see the triumph of his policy is a bad
ruler and perverts politics, even if he lacks personal ambition and
loves his country disinterestedly, because he measures the time of
maturation of the political good according to the short years of his
own personal time of activity.

*What Sir Norman Angell said in Boston in April, 1941, is true for all contemporary
democracies. "If we applied," he said with great force, "ten years ago resolutely the
policy of aiding the victim of aggression to defend himself, we should not now be at
war at all.

"It is a simple truth to say that because we in Britain were deaf to the cries rising
from the homes of China smashed by the invader, we now have to witness the ruthless
destruction by invaders of ancient English shrines.

"Because we would not listen to the cries of Chinese children massacred by the invader we have now, overnight, to listen to the cries of English children, victims of that
same invader's ally.

"Because we were indifferent when Italian submarines sank the ships of republican
Spain we must now listen to the cries of children from the torpedoed refugee ship going
down in the tempest 600 miles from land."

But the remote responsibilities thus alluded to by Sir Norman Angell go back much
further than ten years. Western civilization is now paying a bill prepared by the faults
of all modern history.

As regards the great representatives of contemporary Machiavellianism—either Fascist and Nazi (they have been dealt with) or Communist (they are still threatening the world)—nothing is more instructive in this connection than the ferocious impatience of their general policy. They apply the law of war, which requires a series of immediate striking successes, but which is a supreme and abnormal crisis in the life of human societies, to the very development of the normal life of the state. In so doing, they appear, not as Empire-builders, but as mere squanderers of the heritage of their nations.

Yet a fructification which will come into existence in a distant future but which we do not see, is for us as immaterial as a fructification which would never exist on earth. To act with justice, without picking any fruit of justice, but only fruits of bitterness and sorrow and defeat, is difficult for a man. It is still more difficult for a man of politics, even for a just and wise one, who works at an earthly work that is the most arduous and the highest among temporal works—the common good of the multitude—and whose failures are the failures of an entire people and of a dear country. He must live on hope. Is it possible to live on hope without living on faith? Is it possible to rely on the unseen without relying on faith?

I do not believe that in politics men can escape the temptation of Machiavellianism, if they do not believe that there exists a supreme government of the universe, which is, properly speaking, divine, for God—the head of the cosmos—is also the head of this particular order which is that of ethics. Nor is escape from this temptation possible if they do not entrust the providence of God with the care of all that supra-empirical, dark and mysterious disentanglement of the fructifications of good and evil which no human eye can perceive—thus closing their eyes, by faith, as regards the factual achievements in the distant future, while they open their eyes and display, by knowledge and prudence, more watchfulness than any fox or lion, as regards the preparations of these achievements and the seeds to be right now put into the earth.

A merely natural political morality is not enough to provide us with the means of putting its own rules into practice. Moral conscience does not suffice, if it is not at the same time religious conscience. What is able to face Machiavellianism, moderate Machiavellianism and absolute Machiavellianism, is not, a just politics appealing only to the natural forces of man, it is Christian politics.

For, in the existential context of the life of mankind, politics, because it belongs by its very essence to the ethical realm, demands consequently to be helped and strengthened, in order not to deviate and in order to attain a sufficiently perfect point of maturity, by everything man receives, in his social life itself, from religious belief and from the word of God working within him. This is what the authors of the Declaration of Independence and of the Constitution of this country understood and expressed in a form adapted to the philosophy of their time, and what makes their accomplishment so outstanding to the mind of everyone who believes Christianity to be efficatious not only for heaven but also for earth.

Christian politics is neither theocratic nor clerical, nor yet a politics of pseudo-evangelical weakness and non-resistance to evil, but a genuinely political politics, ever aware that it is situated in the order of nature and must put into practice natural virtues; that it must be armed with real and concrete justice, with force, perspicacity and prudence; a politics which would hold the sword that is the attribute of the state, but which would also realize that peace is the work not only of justice but of love, and that love is also an essential part of political virtue. For it is never excess of love that fools political men, but without love and generosity there is regularly blindness and miscalculation. Such a politics would be mindful of the eternal destiny of man and of the truths of the Gospel, knowing in its proper order—in a measure adapted to its temporal ends—something of the spirit, and of love, and of forgiveness.

VIII.   THE SPECIFIC STRUCTURE OF POLITICAL ETHICS

We arrive now at the third consideration I indicated at the beginning, in which I should like to make clearer certain particular points concerning the relationship between Politics and Morality.

As I have previously pointed out, political reality, though principally moral, is by essence both moral and physical, as man himself, but in a different manner from man, because it does not have any substantial immortal soul. Societies are like ever-growing organisms, immense and long-living trees, or coral-flowers, which would lead at the same time a moral and human life. And in the order to which they belong, which is that of Time and Becoming, death is natural; human communities, nations, states and civilizations naturally die, and die for all time, as would these morally-living coral-flowers of which I just spoke. Their birth, growth and decay, their health, their diseases, their death, depend on basic

physical conditions, in which the specific qualities of moral behavior
are intermingled and play an essential part, but which are more
primitive than these qualities. Similarly, imprudence or intemper-
ance may hasten the death of a man, self-control may defer this
death, yet in any case this man will die.

Justice and moral virtues do not prevent the natural laws of
senescence of human societies. They do not prevent physical catastrophes from destroying them. In what sense are they the chief
forces of the preservation and duration of societies? In the sense
that they compose the very soul of society, its internal and spiritual
force of life. Such a force does not secure immortality to the society,
no more than my immortal soul protects me from death. Such a
force is not an immortal entelechy, because it is not substantial;
yet, insofar as it is spiritual, it is by itself indestructible. Corrupt
this force, and an internal principle of death is introduced into the
core of the society. Maintain and improve this force, and the internal principle of life is strengthened in the society. Suppose a
human community is hammered, crushed, overwhelmed by some
natural calamity or some powerful enemy: as long as it still exists
—if it preserves within itself justice and civic friendship and faith,
there is within it actual hope of resurging, there is a force within it
which tends by itself to make it live and get the upper hand and
avail itself of disaster, because no hammer can destroy this immaterial force. If a human community loses these virtues, its internal
principle of life is invaded by death.

What therefore must be said is that justice and righteousness
tend by themselves to the preservation of states, and to that real
success at long range of which I spoke a moment ago. And that
injustice and evil *tend by themselves* to the destruction of states,
and to that real *failure* at long range of which I also spoke.

Such is the law of the fructification of human actions which is
inscribed in the nature of things and which is but the natural justice of God in human history.

But if the normal fruit of success and prosperity called for by
political justice and wisdom does not come into actual existence
because the tree is too old or because some storm has broken its
branches; or if the normal fruit of failure and destruction, called
for by political wickedness and madness, does not come into actual
existence because the physical conditions in the sap or in the environment have counterbalanced the internal principle of death—
such an accident does not suppress that regularity inherent in the

law which I emphasized in the previous part of this essay, and only
bears witness to the fact that nations and civilizations are naturally
mortal. As I previously observed, justice may sometimes, even in a
distant future, not actually succeed in preserving a state from ruin
and destruction. But justice tends by itself to this preservation; and
it is not by virtue of justice, it is by virtue of physical conditions
counterbalancing from without the very effects of justice that misfortune will then occur. Machiavellianism and political perversion
may sometimes, even in a distant future, not actually break, they
may triumph decisively over weak and innocent peoples. But they
tend by themselves to self-destruction; and it is not by virtue of
Machiavellianism and political perversion, it is by virtue of other
conditions counterbalancing from without the very effects of these,
that success will then occur.

If a weak state is surrounded and threatened by Machiavellian
enemies, it must desperately increase its physical power, but also its
moral virtues. Suppose it delivers its own soul to Machiavellianism
—then it only adds a principle of death to its already existing weaknesses. If a civilization grown old and naturally bound to die, as
the Roman Empire was at the time of St. Augustine, if a political
state artificially and violently built up, and naturally bound to fail,
as was the German Reich of Bismarck and Wilhelm, wished none
the less to escape either death or failure by letting loose evil and
perversion, then it would only poison centuries and prepare for itself
a historical hell worse than death.

It seems not irrelevant to add the two following observations.
First: innumerable are, in the history of mankind, the cases where
the strong have triumphed over the weak; yet this was not always
a triumph of strength over right, for most often right's sanctity was
as immaterial to the conquered weak as it was to the conquering
strong. Greece was conquered by Rome (and was to conquer intellectually Roman civilization). At that time Greece had lost its political soul.

Second: As to the lasting or seemingly lasting triumphs of political injustice over innocent people, they also are not rare, at least
at first glance. They concern most often, however, the enslavement,
sometimes the destruction, of populations or human groups not yet
arrived at a truly political status by nations enjoying this very status
—of such a fact the most striking instance is to be found in the history of modern colonization. But it seems that in proportion as
peoples arrive at a truly political status, and really constitute a

civitas, a political house and community, in this proportion the immaterial internal force which abides in them and is made up of long-lived justice and love and moral energies, and of deep-rooted memories, and of a specific spiritual heritage, becomes a more and more *formed* and cohesive soul; and in this very proportion this soul takes precedence over the merely physical conditions of existence and tends to render such peoples unconquerable. If they are conquered and oppressed, they remain alive and keep on struggling under oppression. Then an instinct of prophecy develops among them, as in Poland at the time of Mickiewicz, and their hopes naturally lift up toward the supernatural example of any historical duration in the midst of oppression, the example of the house of Israel, whose internal immaterial force and principle of communion is of a supra-political and supra-temporal order.

IX.   JUSTICE AND NATURE IN HUMAN HISTORY

Yet a final question arises now, which is of a rather metaphysical nature. I have said that the natural laws, according to which political justice fructifies by itself into the good and the preservation of a given human community, evil and political injustice into its destruction, are to be identified with the natural justice of God in human history. But is not an essential *tendency* only connoted here? Did I not emphasize the fact that even at long range such normal fructifications may fail, that the fruit of evil for the unjust state, the fruit of good for the just one, may be marred, because of the physical factors and particularly because of the physical laws of senescence and death which interfere here with the moral factors? If this is the case, where is the natural justice of God? Justice does not deal with tendencies, essential as they may be, whose factual result may fail to appear, it deals with sanctions which never fail.

The question we are confronting here transcends the field of moral philosophy and historical experience, and deals with the knowledge we are able to stammer of the divine government of created things. The first answer which comes to the mind of a Christian metaphysician consists in affirming a priori that the natural fructification of good and evil never fail, the fruit of justice and the fruit of injustice are never marred—which seems self-evident, since the justice of God cannot be deceived. Because states and nations have no immortal destiny, not only must the sanctions deserved by their deeds reach men within time and upon the earth, but they must do so in an absolutely infallible manner.

In considering the problem more carefully, I believe, however, that this answer results from a kind of undue reverberation of considerations pertaining to theology upon metaphysical matters, which causes things which belong to time and history to be endowed with that absolute firmness which is proper to things relating to eternity.

It is perfectly true that God's justice cannot fail as regards the immortal destiny of each human person, which is accomplished in fact, according to Christianity's teachings, in the supernatural order. Yet it would be too hasty a procedure simply to conceive the divine justice which rules the historical fate of human societies, according to the pattern of that divine justice which rules the supra-historical destiny of the human person. In these two cases justice applies to its subject-matter in an analogical fashion. The supra-historical justice cannot fail, because it reaches moral agents—the human persons—who attain their final state above time. But the historical justice, dealing with human societies, reaches moral agents who do not attain any final state. There is no final sanction for them, sanctions are spread out for them all along time, and intermingled at each moment with their continuing and changing activity; often the fruit of ancient injustice starts up into existence at the very moment when a revival of justice occurs in a given society. Moreover, and by the same token, it appears that these sanctions *in the making* do not enjoy that absolute necessity which is linked with the immutability of some ultimate, eternal accomplishment. What seemed to us, a moment ago, to be self-evident, is not self-evident. It is possible that in the case of human societies the natural fructifications of good and evil are sometimes marred. The sanctions deserved by the deeds of nations and states must reach men within time and upon the earth, yet it is not necessary that they do so in a manner absolutely infallible and always realized.

Consider the civilization of the peoples which lived on legendary Atlantis. The good and bad political deeds of these peoples tended by themselves to bear fruit and to engender their natural sanctions. Yes, but when Atlantis was engulfed by the Ocean, all these fruits to come were cancelled from being as well as the peoples and the civilization from which they were to spring forth. The natural justice of God, as regards human societies, that is, moral agents immersed in time, may fail just as nature may fail in its physical fructifications: because this natural historical justice of God is nothing else than nature itself in its not physical, but moral fructifications. God's justice is at work in time and history, it reigns only in

heaven and in hell. The concept of perfect and infallible retribu-
tion for human deeds, with its absolute adamantine strength, is a
religious concept relating to the eternal destiny of human Persons;
it is not the ethico-philosophical concept which has to be shaped
relating to the destiny of human communities in time and history.

Such is the answer which appears to me the true answer to the
question we are considering. But we must immediately add that
these failures of historical justice are to occur in the fewest number
of cases, just as do the failures of nature in the physical order,
because they are accidents, in which the very laws of essences do
not reach their own effect. I do not ignore the fact that there is in
nature an immense squandering of seeds in order that a few may
have the chance of springing up, and still fewer the chance of bearing fruit. But even if the failures of natural historical justice were
abnormities as regards individual accomplishment, as frequent as
the failures of so many wasted seeds, the truth that I am pointing
out throughout this chapter would none the less remain unshaken:
namely, that justice tends by itself toward the welfare and survival
of the community, injustice toward its damage and dissolution, and
that any long-range success of Machiavellianism is never due to
Machiavellianism itself, but to other historical factors at play. Yet
the abnormities which really occur *ut in paucioribus* in physical
nature are *abnormities as regards specific accomplishment*—as in
the production of something deviating from the very essence of the
species, the production of "freaks." And it is with such physical
abnormities as regards specific accomplishment that the failures of
the natural fructification of good and evil, the failures in the accomplishment of the specific laws of moral essences, must rather be
compared. We must therefore emphasize more strongly than ever
the fact—which I have already stressed in a previous section—that
the sanctions of historical justice fail much more rarely than our
short-sighted experience might induce us to believe.

Here a new observation seems to me particularly noticeable.
These sanctions, which have been deserved by the deeds of the
social or political whole, must not necessarily reverberate on this
political whole as such, on the nation itself in its existence and power,
they may concern the common cultural condition of men considered
apart from the actual framework of this whole, yet in some kind
of solidarity with the latter—because the political whole is not a
substantial or personal subject, but a community of human persons,
and a community related to other communities through vital ex-

changes. Thus, during the life of a nation the fruit of its just or of its perverted deeds may appear only either in some particular improvement or in some particular plague of part or all of its internal strata. Still more, when a state, a nation, a civilization dies, it is normal that the fructifications of good and evil which its deeds had prepared pass over—in the cultural order and as regards such or such a feature of the common social or cultural status—to its remnants, to the scattered human elements which had been contained in its unity and to their descendants, or to the human communities which are its successors and inheritors.

Then a state or a civilization dissolves, but its good or bad works continue to bear fruit, not strictly political (for the word political connotes the common life of a given self-sufficient society), yet political in a broader and still genuine sense, which relates to the cultural life and to the common cultural heritage of mankind. For there exists a genuine temporal community of mankind—a deep intersolidarity, from generation to generation, linking together the peoples of the earth—a common heritage and a common fate, which do not concern the building of a particular *civil society*, but of the *civilization*, not the prince, but the culture, not the perfect *civitas* in the Aristotelian sense, but that kind of *civitas*, in the Augustinian sense, which is imperfect and incomplete, made up of a fluid network of human communications, and more existential than formally organized, but all the more real and living and basically important. To ignore this non-political *civitas humani generis* is to break up the basis of political reality, to fail in the very roots of political philosophy, as well as to disregard the progressive trend which naturally tends toward a more organic and unified international structure of peoples.

Thus another fundamental consideration must be added to that of *historic duration*, which I previously emphasized, namely the consideration of the *human extension*, down through generations, of the fructifications of political deeds. Then we see in a complete manner the law which binds Machiavellianism to failure, as a rule and as regards the essential tendencies inscribed in nature. If, even at long range, political justice and political injustice do not ever fructify into the political success or disaster of the state itself which has practiced them, they may still produce their fruit according to the laws of human solidarity. By the same stroke we perceive Machiavellianism's mischievousness, weakness and absurdity in their full implications. It is not only for particular states that it prepares misfortune and scourges—first the victims of Machiavellian states, then the Machiavellian states themselves—it is also for the human race in general. It burdens mankind with an ever-growing burden of evil, unhappiness and disaster. By its own weight and its own internal law it brings about failure, not only with reference to given nations, but with reference to our common kind, with reference to the root community of nations. Like every other sort of selfishness, this divinized selfishness is essentially blind.

X.   HYPERMORALISM AND MACHIAVELLIANISM

To sum up all that I have stated, I would say:

First: It suffices to be just in order to gain eternal life; this does not suffice in order to gain battles or immediate political successes.

Second: In order to gain battles or immediate political successes, it is not necessary to be just, it may occasionally be more advantageous to be unjust.

Third: It is necessary, although it is not sufficient, to be just, in order to secure and further the political common good, and the lasting welfare of earthly communities.

The considerations I have developed in this chapter are founded on the basic fact that Politics is a branch of Ethics but a branch specifically distinct from the other branches of the same generic stock. One decisive sign of this specificity of Political Ethics in contradistinction to Personal Ethics is that earthly communities are mortal as regards their very being and belong entirely to time. Another sign is that political virtues tend to a relatively ultimate end which is the earthly common good, and are only indirectly related to the absolutely ultimate end of man. Hence the authentic moral character, and at the same time the genuinely realist quality of many features of Political Ethics. Many rules of political life, which the pessimists of Machiavellianism usurp to the benefit of immorality, are in reality ethically grounded—say, for instance, the political toleration of certain evils and the recognition of the *fait accompli* (the so-called "statute of limitations") which permits the retention of long ago illgotten gains, because new human ties and vital relationships have infused them with new-born rights. In the last analysis Political Ethics is able to absorb and digest all the elements of truth contained in Machiavelli, I mean to say, to the extent that power and immediate success are actually part of politics—but a subordinate, not the principal, part.

May I repeat that a certain hypermoralism, causing Political Ethics to be something impracticable and merely ideal, is as contrary to this very Ethics as Machiavellianism is, and finally plays the game of Machiavellianism, as conscientious objectors play the game of the conquerors. The purity of means consists in not using means morally bad in themselves; it does not consist in refusing pharisaically any exterior contact with the mud of human life, and it does not consist in waiting for a morally aseptic world before consenting to work in the world, nor does it consist in waiting, before saving one's neighbor, who is drowning, to become a saint, so as to escape any risk of false pride in such a generous act.

If this were the time to present a complete analysis of the particular causes of lasting success and welfare in politics, I should add two observations here. First: While political justice—which is destroyed both by the dismissal of Ethics, that is, by Machiavellianism, and by its senseless exaltation, that is, by Hypermoralism—is the prime *spiritual* condition of lasting success and welfare for a nation as well as for a civilization, the prime *material* condition of this lasting success and welfare is on the one hand that heritage of accepted and unquestionable structures, fixed customs and deep-rooted common feelings which bring into social life itself something of the determined physical data of nature,* and of the vital unconscious strength proper to vegetative organisms; and on the other hand that common inherited experience and that set of moral and intellectual instincts which constitute a kind of empirical practical wisdom, much deeper and denser and much nearer the hidden complex dynamism of human life than any artificial construction of reason. And both this somewhat physical heritage and this inherited practical wisdom are intrinsically and essentially bound to, and dependent upon, moral and religious beliefs. As regards Political Ethics and political common good, the preservation of these common structures of life and of this common moral dynamism is more fundamental than any particular action of the prince, however serious and decisive this may be in itself. And the workings of such a vast, deep-seated physico-moral energy are more basic and more important to the life of human societies than particular political good or bad calculations; they are for states the prime cause of historic success and welfare. The Roman Empire did not succeed by virtue of the stains, injustices and cruelties, which tainted its policy, but by virtue of this internal physico-moral strength.

*Cf. "The Political Ideas of Pascal," in *Ransoming the Time*, 1941.

Now, and this is my second observation: What is in itself, even in the order of material causality, primarily and basically destructive of lasting historic success and welfare for a nation as well as for a civilization, is that which is destructive of the common stock and heritage I just described, that is, Machiavellianism on the one hand and Hypermoralism on the other. Both destroy, like gnawing worms, the inner social and ethical living substance upon which depends any lasting success and welfare of the commonwealth, as they also destroy that political justice which constitutes the moral righteousness, the basic moral virtue and the spiritual strength of human societies.

Thus the split, the deadly division created between Ethics and Politics both by Machiavellianists and by Hypermoralists is overcome. Because Politics is essentially ethical, and because Ethics is essentially realistic, not in the sense of any *Realpolitik,* but in the sense of the full human reality of the common good.

I am aware that if this antinomy which has been the scourge of modern history, is to be practically, not only theoretically, overcome, it will be only on condition that a kind of revolution take place in our conscience. Machiavelli has made us conscious of what is in fact the average behavior of politics in mankind. In this he was right. There is, here, a natural slope that the man who endeavors to overcome dissociation, the man of unity will have to climb up again. But slopes are made to be climbed. As Bergson pointed out, a genuine democracy, by the very fact that it proceeds from an evangelic motive power, works against the grain of nature and therefore needs some heroic inspiration.

With whatever deficiencies human weakness may encumber the practical issue, the fact remains, in any case, that such an effort must be made, and that the knowledge of what is true in these matters is of first and foremost importance. To keep Machiavelli's awareness, with reference to the factual conduct of most of the princes, and to know that this conduct is bad politics, and to clear our conscience of Machiavelli's rules, precepts and philosophy—in this consists the very end of Machiavellianism.

Here I emphasize anew what I pointed out at the beginning of this chapter. Machiavellianism does not consist of this unhappy lot of particular evil and unjust political deeds which are taking place in fact by virtue of human weakness or wickedness. Machiavellianism is a philosophy of politics, stating that by rights good politics is supra-moral or immoral politics and by essence must make use of evil. What I have discussed is this political philosophy. There will be no end to the occurrence of misdeeds and mistakes as long as humanity endures. To Machiavellianism there can and must be an end.

XI. ABSOLUTE MACHIAVELLIANISM AND MODERATE MACHIAVELLIANISM

Let us conclude. Machiavellianism is an illusion, because it rests upon the power of evil, and because, from the metaphysical point of view, evil as such has no power as a cause of being; from the practical point of view, evil has no power as a cause of any lasting achievement. As to moral entities like peoples, states, and nations, which do not have any supratemporal destiny, it is within time that their deeds are sanctioned; it is upon earth that the entire charge of failure and nothingness, with which is charged every evil action committed by the whole or by its heads, will normally be exhausted. This is a natural, a somewhat physical law in the moral order (though it is thwarted in some cases by the interference of the manifold other factors at play in human history). As a rule Machiavellianism and political injustice, if they gain immediate success, lead states and nations to misfortune or catastrophe in the long run; in cases where they seem to succeed even in the long run, this is not by virtue of evil and political injustice, but by virtue of some inner principle of misfortune already binding their victim to submission, even if the latter did not have to face such iniquitous enemies. Either the victims of power politics are primitive tribes which had been in a state of non-existence as to political life and therefore as to political justice, and their unjustly-suffered misfortune, which cries out against heaven and makes God's justice more implacable with regard to the personal destiny of their executioners, does not reverberate upon the unjustly conquering state unless in the form of some hidden and insidious, not openly political, self-poisoning process. Or else the victims of power politics are states and nations which were already condemned to death or enslavement by the natural laws of senescence of human societies or by their own internal corruption. And here also the very effect of the injustice which has been used against them is to introduce a hidden principle of self-destruction into the inner substance of their conquerors.

When the victims of power politics are mature and vital people, who keep struggling against oppression, they can be subjugated for a time, but the very order of nature promises that a day will come when they will reassert themselves over the oppressor's ruins.

In truth the dialectic of injustice is unconquerable. Machiavellianism devours itself. Common Machiavellianism has devoured and annihilated Machiavelli's Machiavellianism; absolute Machiavellianism devours and annihilates moderate Machiavellianism. Weak or attenuated Machiavellianism is inevitably destined to be vanquished by absolute and virulent Machiavellianism.

If some day absolute Machiavellianism triumphs over mankind, this will only be because all kinds of accepted iniquity, moral weakness and consent to evil, operating within a degenerating civilization, will previously have corrupted it, and prepared ready-made slaves for the lawless man. But if absolute Machiavellianism is ever to be crushed, and I hope so, it will only be because what remains of Christian civilization will have been able to oppose it with the principle of political justice integrally recognized.

In his introduction to Machiavelli, Mr. Max Lerner emphasizes the dilemma with which democracies are now confronted. This dilemma seems to me perfectly clear: either to perish by continuing to accept, more or less willingly, the principle of Machiavellianism, or to regenerate by consciously and decidedly rejecting this principle. For what we call democracy or the commonwealth of free men is by definition a political regime of men the spiritual basis of which is uniquely and exclusively law and right. Such a regime is by essence opposed to Machiavellianism and incompatible with it. Totalitarianism lives by Machiavellianism, freedom dies by it. The only Machiavellianism of which any democracy as such is capable is attenuated and weak Machiavellianism. Facing absolute Machiavellianism, either the democratic states, inheritors of the *Ancien Régime* and of its old Machiavellian policy, will keep on using weak Machiavellianism, and they will be destroyed from without, or they will decide to have recourse to absolute Machiavellianism, which is only possible with totalitarian rule and totalitarian spirit; and thus they will destroy themselves from within. They will survive and take the upper hand only on condition that they break with Machiavellianism in any of the forms in which it may appear.

CHAPTER TWELVE

THE PLURALIST PRINCIPLE

IN DEMOCRACY

I.   A QUALIFIED AGREEMENT

IN an article published under the title *The Dilemma of T. S. Eliot,** Mr. Sidney Hook reaches by means of questionable theoretical arguments a practical solution which for quite different reasons seems to me to be on the right track. Even if we are in agreement—in qualified agreement—on this practical solution, there are important particulars in which we disagree. These I should like to try to elucidate. Since I have endeavored for many years and in many books to discuss the matters involved, I shall take the liberty of summing up my position here.

1. In the "sacral" era of the Middle Ages a great attempt was made to build the life of the earthly community and civilization on the foundation of the unity of theological faith and religious creed. This attempt succeeded for a certain number of centuries but failed in the course of time, after the Reformation and the Renaissance; and a return to the medieval "sacral"† pattern is in no way conceivable. In proportion as the civil community has become more perfectly distinguished from the spiritual realm of the Church—a process which was in itself but a development of the Gospel distinction between the things that are Caesar's and the things that are God's—civil society has come to be based on a common good and a common task which are of an earthly, "temporal," or "secular" order, and in which citizens belonging to diverse spiritual groups or "families" equally share. Religious division

---

*The Nation, January 20, 1945.
†On the notion of "sacral" (or "consecrational") civilization, see *True Humanism*, pp. 137 ff., and *Man and the State*, pp. 157 ff.—See also Charles Journet, *L'Eglise du Verbe Incarné*, Desclée De Brouwer, Paris, 1941, p. 243.

among men is in itself a misfortune. But it is a fact that we must recognize, whether we wish to or not.

2. In modern times an attempt was made to base the life of civilization and the earthly community on the foundation of mere reason—reason separated from religion and from the Gospel. This attempt fostered immense hopes in the last two centuries, and rapidly failed. Pure reason appeared more incapable than faith of insuring the spiritual unity of mankind, and the dream of a "scientific" creed uniting men in peace, and in common convictions about the aims and basic principles of human life and society, vanished in contemporary catastrophes. In proportion as the tragic events of the last decades have given the lie to the optimistic rationalism of the eighteenth and nineteenth centuries, we have been confronted with the fact that religion and metaphysics are an essential part of human culture, primary and indispensable incentives in the very life of society.

3. As concerns, therefore, the revitalized democracy we are hoping for, the only solution is of the *pluralistic* type. Men belonging to very different philosophical or religious creeds and lineages could and should co-operate in the common task and for the common welfare of the earthly community, provided they similarly assent to the charter and basic tenets of a society of free men.

For a society of free men implies an essential charter and basic tenets which are at the core of its very existence, and which it has the duty of defending and promoting. One of the errors of individualist optimism was to believe that in a free society "truth," as to the foundations of civil life, as well as the decisions and modes of behavior befitting human dignity and freedom, would automatically emerge from the conflicts of individual forces and opinions supposedly immune from any irrational trends and disintegrating pressures; the error lay in conceiving of free society as a perfectly *neutral* boxing-ring in which all possible ideas about society and the bases of social life meet and battle it out, without the Body Politic's being concerned with the maintenance of any common conditions and inspiration. Thus democratic society, in its concrete behavior, had no *concept* of itself, and freedom, disarmed and paralyzed, lay exposed to the undertakings of those who hated it, and who tried by all means to foster in men a vicious desire to become free from freedom.*

*Cf. Augusto J. Duvelli, *Libération de la Liberté*, L'Arbre, Montréal, 1944.

If it is to conquer totalitarian trends and to be true to its own mission, a renewed democracy will have its own concept of man and society, and its own philosophy, its own faith, enabling it to educate people for freedom and to defend itself against those who would use democratic liberties to destroy freedom and human rights. No society can live without a basic common inspiration and a basic common faith.

But the all-important point to be noted here is that this faith and inspiration, this philosophy and the concept of itself which democracy needs, all these do not belong in themselves to the order of religious creed and eternal life but to the temporal or secular order of earthly life, of culture and civilization. Even more, they are matters of *practical* rather than theoretical or dogmatic agreement: I mean that they deal with practical convictions which the human mind can try to justify—rightly or wrongly—from quite different, even conflicting philosophical outlooks; probably because they depend basically on simple, "natural" apperceptions, of which the human heart becomes capable with the progress of moral conscience. Thus it is that men possessing quite different, even opposite, metaphysical or religious outlooks, can converge, not by virtue of any identity of doctrine, but by virtue of an analogical similitude in practical principles, toward the same practical conclusions, and can share in the same practical democratic faith, provided that they similarly revere, perhaps for quite diverse reasons, truth and intelligence, human dignity, freedom, brotherly love, and the absolute value of moral good. As Mr. Hook puts it, "the underlying premises, whether theological, metaphysical, or naturalistic, from which different groups justify their common democratic beliefs and practices must not be subject to integration"—let us say to socially or politically enforced integration. "It is enough, so to speak, that human beings live in accordance with democratic laws"—and, let us add, share in the common—human, earthly, temporal—democratic faith and inspiration. "It is foolish intolerance to make only one justification of laws legal."

Here, if we want to be thorough in our thought and do not fear words, we should point out that where faith is—divine or human—there are also heretics who threaten the unity of the community, either religious or civil. In the "sacral" society the heretic was the breaker of religious unity. In a lay society of free men the heretic is the breaker of "the common democratic beliefs and practices," the totalitarian, the one who denies freedom—his neighbor's freedom—and the dignity of the human person, and the moral power of law. We do not wish him to be burned, or expelled from the city, or outlawed, or put in a concentration camp. But the democratic community should defend itself against him, by keeping him out of its leadership, through the power of a strong and informed public opinion, and even by handing him over to justice when his activity endangers the security of the state—and over and above all by strengthening everywhere a philosophy of life, intellectual convictions, and constructive work which would make his influence powerless.

On the other hand, a serious task of intellectual re-examination should be undertaken regarding the essentials of democratic philosophy. And it would be especially desirable to develop the understanding of the pluralistic principle and the techniques of pluralistic co-operation. It seems to me that the free traditions and the historical set-up of this country would provide special opportunities for such a development.

II.   POINTS OF DISAGREEMENT

4. Now what about certain statements offered to us by Sidney Hook in connection with the preceding considerations, and which he seems to regard as self-evident? Are we ready to believe that in the type of society which we are discussing, the "world-wide common faith" implied would find in *scientific method* its highest source of authority? That an "intelligent social planning" would be sufficient to insure the "integration" of culture? And that, in the democratic culture of the future—if it has a future—it will be "the teacher dedicated to the scientific spirit," "and not the priest," "who will bear the chief responsibility for nurturing, strengthening, and enriching a common faith"?

Here are the main points on which I should like to express disagreement with Mr. Sidney Hook's views. I am afraid he has been inspired in these passages by that rationalistic bias whose illusory character I pointed out above (Paragraph 2).

The very expression "common faith" which Mr. Hook uses should make us realize that democratic inspiration cannot find in "scientific method" its highest source of authority. This "faith" is "of a secular not supernatural character"; yet even a secular faith implies the commitment of the whole man and his innermost spiritual energies, and draws its strength, therefore, from beliefs which go far beyond scientific method, being rooted in the depths of each one's individual options and personality. In other words, *the justification of the practical conclusions which make such a "common faith," common to all, is in each one, and in the perspective peculiar to each one, an integral part of this very faith.* As for social planning, even supposedly intelligent, it is hard to imagine a *culture* organized and unified by social planning alone. Planned and plain as it might be, such a cultural paradise would offer, I am afraid, little chance for the creative powers of human personality as well as for the enthusiasm and happiness of the people.

The scientific spirit is of invaluable help for culture in so far as it develops in human minds, in a general way, respect and love for truth and the habits of intellectual accuracy. (This is why, let us observe parenthetically, the scientific spirit of the thirteenth-century Schoolmen played so basic a part in the rise of Western culture.) Yet neither culture nor democracy lives on science alone. Science, especially modern science, deals with the means, especially with the material means, of human life. Wisdom, which deals with the ends, is also—and above all—necessary. And the fact remains that democratic faith—implying as it does faith in justice, in freedom, in brotherly love, in the dignity of the human person, in his rights as well as in his responsibilities, in that power of binding men in conscience which appertains to just laws, in the deep-rooted aspirations which call for political and social coming of age of the people —cannot be justified, nurtured, strengthened, and enriched without philosophical or religious convictions—"whether theological, metaphysical, or naturalistic"—which deal with the very substance and meaning of human life. Here appears the truth of T. S. Eliot's emphasis on the organic character of culture, as well as the injustice of reproaching him with suggesting proposals which, if enforced, would result in some kind of "ecclesiastical fascism." For we can be sure it is not to the compulsory power of any ecclesiastical agency but rather to the persuasive power of truth that he makes the effort toward the integration of culture appendant. The effort toward integration must not only be brought about on the level of personality and private life; it is essential to culture itself and the life of the community as a whole, on the condition that it tends toward real *cultural* integration, that is, toward an integration which does not depend on legal enforcement but on spiritual and freely accepted inspiration.

As a result, it is but normal that in a democratic culture and society the diverse philosophical or religious schools of thought which in their practical conclusions agree with regard to democratic tenets, and which claim to justify them, come into free competition. Let each school freely and fully assert its belief! But let no one try to impose it by force upon the others! The mutual tension which ensues will enrich rather than harm the common task.

5. As for myself, who believe that the idea of man propounded by the metaphysics of Aristotle and Thomas Aquinas is the rational foundation of democratic philosophy, and that the Gospel inspiration is its true living soul, I am confident that, in the free competition of which I just spoke, the Christian leaven would play an ever-growing part. In any case the responsibility for nurturing, strengthening, and enriching a common democratic faith would belong no less to the priest, dedicated to the preaching of the Gospel, than to the teacher, dedicated to the scientific spirit, if both of them came to a clear awareness of the needs of our times. Moreover, since it is a question of a secular faith dealing with the temporal order, its maintenance and progress in the community depend primarily on lay apostles and genuine political leaders, who are indebted to the scientific teacher for knowledge of the factual conditioning of human life, but much more, certainly, to the priest for knowledge of its meaning, its ends and its ethical standards.

Finally, if I affirm that without genuine and vital reconciliation between democratic inspiration and evangelical inspiration our hopes for the democratic culture of the future will be frustrated, I do not appeal to police force to obtain such reconciliation; I only state what I hold to be true. It would be foolish intolerance to label as intolerance any affirmation of truth which is not watered down with doubt, even if it does not please some of our democratic fellow-citizens. I insist as forcefully as T. S. Eliot that the Christian leaven is necessary to the life and integration of our culture. From the religious point of view, I would wish all men to believe in the integrity of Christian truth. From the social-temporal point of view, I would be satisfied if the Christian energies at work in the community were radiant with the fulness of supernatural faith in a number of men, and retained at least a sufficient degree of moral and rational efficacy in those in whom these energies still exist, but in a more or less incomplete—or secularized—form.

It is true, moreover, that supernatural faith does not provide us with any particular social or political system. In such matters supernatural faith must be complemented by sound practical philosophy, historical information, and social and political experience. Yet supernatural faith, if it is truly lived—in other words, if Christians know "of what spirit they are"—provides them with basic inspiration and vital truths which permeate their social and political systems and work for human dignity, against any kind of totalitarian oppression.

Allow me to add that to consider the religious faith of a poet like T. S. Eliot as "the object of a deliberate will-to-believe enjoying an uneasy triumph over the scruples of intelligence" is perhaps the only way in which an unbeliever can explain to himself such a strange phenomenon, but is, I venture to think, a sure proof of those lofty intellectual scruples and large capacities for explanation fostered by unbelief. It is not more relevant to pretend that the neo-Thomists regard as "disorder" "the spirit of inquiry and innovation"—I don't mean skepticism—and "the advance of liberty of thought and behavior," if this liberty is inspired by a love for what is true and good.

I should like to conclude by saying that I am sincerely pleased in finding myself this once in agreement, even qualified, with Sidney Hook—except for the points to which I have just referred, which are of no little importance. Such an agreement on practical conclusions between philosophers whose basic theoretical outlooks are widely separated is, to my mind, an illustration of the pluralistic co-operation of which I spoke.

CHAPTER THIRTEEN

THE POSSIBILITIES
FOR CO-OPERATION
IN A DIVIDED WORLD:

INAUGURAL ADDRESS TO THE SECOND
INTERNATIONAL CONFERENCE OF UNESCO*

PREAMBLE

IN addressing the Second International Conference of Unesco I should like first to make reference to two remarks made by President Léon Blum on November 1, 1945, when he spoke at the Conference which established the Organization. At that time Mr. Léon Blum recalled that, as early as 1944, in San Francisco, the French delegation had caused a motion to be adopted the first clause of which stated that "peace among nations, if it is to be just and enduring, must be based upon mutual understanding and knowledge." He added: "What all of us want (not only those of us here present, but also those whose temporary absence we regret) is to contribute to international security and peace, as well as to the welfare of the peoples of the world, as the blue-print of the Conference of ministers states in its first sentence."

Speaking of the French delegation's request to have the head-quarters of the Preparatory Commission established in Paris, Mr. Blum also said: "We beg you not to interpret our request as something which France would consider its due because of some intellectual or spiritual prerogative. France's qualifications are more ancient than those of other nations; they are not more glorious. If we did have an advantage, it would stem from the fact that

*United Nations Educational, Scientific and Cultural Organization. This conference was held in Mexico; November 6, 1947.

French culture has always tended towards universality, and that there is in France an age-old tradition of generosity and liberality with respect to the things of the mind which are in keeping with the spirit of the future organization. It would also stem from the fact that in France, all branches or forms of human civilization— the sciences, general culture, literature, the arts, and technology in so far as it borders upon art—have always developed side by side and in reciprocal connection."

In my opinion these lines accurately characterize the contribution which the French spirit may be expected to make to the common work of an organization in which all cultures and civilizations must play their part, each being animated by its own particular spirit, whether it springs from the Latin or from the English-speaking world, or from the Eastern or the Far-eastern world, and in which patient experimental inquiry and search after guiding rational principles must complement one another. Mr. Blum's general remarks are also of great value to a philosopher, as I am, whose calling demands that he examine things in their universal aspects, and that he endeavor to bring out from reality the principles of an intelligible synthesis. So I feel encouraged to call to your attention certain general problems which seem to me of crucial importance.

Our Conference meets at a particularly serious moment in the history of the world, a moment when faced with growing international tension and antagonisms the dangers of which cannot be ignored, vast portions of public opinion risk becoming obsessed by the spectre of catastrophe, and surrendering to the idea of war's inevitability. The anguish of peoples breaks like a mighty surf on every shore. In this world prostrated by post-war grief, and by the leaden mantle of rival economic, political and ideological interests, shall not those who are dedicated to the works of the mind and who feel the responsibility of such a mission give voice to the primitive instinct for preservation, to the immense longing for peace and freedom, to the repudiation of death and misfortune which, despite a strange apparent passivity more closely resembling despair than strength of soul, is stirring within the deepest recesses of men's consciousness? Shall they not proclaim that resignation to disaster is the worst of follies; that fear and fear-engendered reflexes, if one yield to them, attract the very dangers one most apprehends; that the more dramatic the plight of the people becomes, and the more clear-sighted firmness it demands of statesmen, the more vigorously the idea of the inevitability of war must be denounced as a fatal surrender on the part of human intelligence and human dignity? Shall they not, if only for the honor of our race and for the resources of the future, appeal to that conscience of men, which must be awakened and upon which depends the whole outcome of the struggle against collective suicide and for the actual building of peace? I am well aware that such declarations are neither within the province of Unesco nor of this Conference. At least I may say that the present conjuncture reminds us forcefully that the mission of Unesco is to contribute effectively—as Mr. Léon Blum said in the speech I have quoted—to international security and peace. I also may say, as Mr. Archibald MacLeish pointed out at the second session of the Executive Council, that Unesco was not created to look after the theoretical progress of Education, Science and Culture, but to make use of it in the concrete and positive work of peace to be established among peoples.

It is this practical goal of our organization that I wish to emphasize. At the same time I shall try to analyse its implications.

I.   THREE PROBLEMS

Before coming to Unesco's specific work, I shall take the liberty of making a few remarks concerning problems which inevitably arise in conjunction with the practical goal just mentioned, and which are of consequence for the personal conscience of each one of us. For it is not through *ideas* alone nor through *facts and figures* alone that the preliminary task which conditions and prepares the work of peace can be brought about both in the world and in human consciousness; it is through an effort of man's spiritual powers to bring to light the basic difficulties, and to reach decisions concerning them; and such an effort can only result from a personal meditation in which each individual commits himself.

The first questions which present themselves to one who meditates seriously on the conditions for a just and enduring peace are obviously those called forth by the idea of a supranational organization of the peoples of the world. Everyone is aware of the obstacles to carrying such an idea into effect; they are even greater today than immediately after victory. At the present time, a truly supranational world organization is beyond the realm of possibility. A philosopher, however, would fail in his duty if he did not add that this very thing which is today impossible, is nevertheless necessary, and that without it the creation of a just and enduring peace cannot be conceived. Hence it follows that the first obligation incumbent upon the men of today is that they work with all their forces to make possible what is thus necessary.

If you speak to specialists in international law of the ideas set forth by Mr. Emery Reves in his *Anatomy of Peace,* if you tell them that the advent of a state of permanent peace necessarily presupposes the abandonment of the concept of absolute national sovereignty, and demands that relations between nations be regulated no longer by treaties but by law, they will answer that these ideas are not new to them; they have known all this for a long time. What they also know full well is that, in the present structure of the world, as history has formed it, and precisely because it is based on the absolute sovereignty of states, all the paths by which the states and the governments, even if they so desired, could move toward such a transformation, are blocked by insuperable obstacles. What are we to conclude except that this transformation, if it is ever attained, will be attained along other paths? I mean through an impetus arising from human conscience and from the will of the peoples, and so vast and powerful that it will command the assent of states and governments, even of those least disposed to give free rein to spontaneous movements of opinion. If there exists an effort toward creative transformation in support of which men of good will may call upon the peoples of the earth, (and even should some irrational currents join in, as usually happens in such cases) it is precisely this effort toward a supra-national community founded upon law and directed, within the limits of its well-defined powers, by men whose functions invest them with a citizenship which is itself supra-national.

Is the world capable of making such an effort? What crises will still be needed to convince men that it is a necessity? All we can say, without being unduly optimistic, is that a few preliminary signs are to be seen. It is not without significance that under the authority of Doctor Robert M. Hutchins a *Committee* of intellectuals and educators *to Frame a World Constitution* was formed in the United States in 1945, deriving its inspiration from the initiative taken by *the Federalist* at the time of the struggle for the Constitution of the United States of America.* It is not without significance (and it is a privilege for me to have the honor of calling it to mind at this time), that one of the paragraphs in the preamble to the Constitution of

---

*Dr. Hutchins, who is now one of the Directors of the Ford Foundation, was then President of the University of Chicago. The "Preliminary Draft" for a world constitution was printed in the March, 1948, issue of the monthly *Common Cause* (University of Chicago), edited by Mr. G. A. Borghese.

the Fourth French Republic is drafted in the following terms: "On condition of reciprocity, France consents to those limitations of sovereignty necessary to the organization and defence of peace."

Now may I be permitted to dwell for a moment on an observation which, however commonplace, commands, I believe, the attention of every one of us: namely that in human history the spirit's achievement always lags behind matter and factual event. It is all too clear today that the spirit has failed in a certain number of essential tasks which the world expected of it, and whose non-fulfillment may well prove costly. Our intellectual atmosphere will remain poisoned as long as a few crucial problems are not clearly posed, and a solution to them proposed to men, at least as concerns the intrinsic truth of the matter. Among these problems, I shall cite three, each of a very different nature.

The first is the problem of Machiavellianism and *Realpolitik*. The rehabilitation of the post-war world imperiously required that (if not, alas, in the behavior of states, then at least in the consciousness of the peoples, and in common intelligence) it be clearly understood that the maxim according to which politics must not be concerned with moral good and evil is a homicidal error. We had to understand that Machiavellianism, although it may afford immediate success, by its very nature leads to ruin in the long run; that absolute Machiavellianism inevitably devours moderate Machiavellianism, and that the principle and virtue of Machiavellianism, whether absolute or moderate, can only be conquered by the principle and virtue of genuinely political justice, in a spiritual climate fit for the development of some heroic determination.

The second problem concerns the collective moral transgression into which a people may fall, and the collective moral recovery to which they may be bound in conscience. For speculative thought as well as for practical judgment, there is no more difficult, no more perilous problem. But that is no reason for evading it. Ever since we were confronted with the crimes committed against humanity by Nazi Germany, this problem has had us by the throat. It is not good for men to remain in the dark about it.

It is doubtless true that no nation is blameless; in the distant origins of the conflicts which have taken place in the course of history, every nation may have more or less cause for self-accusation. But that is not the point. Nor is it the point that the faults committed by a state and by its leaders entail historical sanctions which the nation must accept, not only as inevitable, but as justified. The true question concerns a people's awareness or lack of awareness of the evil by which they allowed themselves to be contaminated, and of which the members of a community (even those who remained personally immune, even those who fought against that evil) recognize or do not recognize that the community was guilty.

It is not good for a people to humiliate itself before others. But it is not good for a people to settle into stiff-necked pride. There is a way of beating the breast and accepting abjection which destroys the dignity of a nation. But there is also a way of refusing to beat the breast, while deceiving one's conscience and nurturing hatred, which destroys this dignity just as unmercifully. Is there no way out of this dilemma? Is there not a way of acknowledging, with sorrow and strength of soul, the faults of the community to which one belongs, and of desiring at all cost that the community atone for them and free itself of them—a way which, for a people determined to rehabilitate itself morally, is at the same time an evidence and a safeguard of its dignity? After having wished to enslave the world and trusted in a Fuehrer of perdition for the sake of national interest placed above any other consideration, the German people underwent an unprecedented defeat. Today they are suffering grievously, and it is our duty as human beings to have compassion on them in their pain. But the worst tragedy which could befall them would be if such suffering proved vain and failed to awaken an awareness of their responsibilities, and, at the same time a horror of the evil committed and the will to give worthy service to the human community in a purified moral atmosphere. It is up to the nations to help the German people against despair. It is up to those who are solicitous of the spiritual rehabilitation of the German people, particularly those who, within Germany itself, are in charge of moral and religious interests, also and first of all to tell them the truth, not in order to humiliate them or to overwhelm them, but in order to give them what they have a right to expect in their misfortune, and what is the primary condition of their moral rebirth. At this point it is necessary more than ever to reaffirm the primacy of the spiritual. If, in the depths of the German conscience, repentance and hope—a virile repentance and a righteous hope—are not awakened at one and the same time, then the German problem will continue to be fraught with misery for the German people themselves and for the peace of the world.

The third problem, the urgency of which each one of us realizes, is the problem of the human value and human use of science and technology. The coming of the atomic age has suddenly exposed to the world the terrible countenance of this problem. Man no longer believes that science and technical skills can by themselves ensure the progress and happiness of the race. Rather he is filled with terror at the sight of the destruction and calamities science and technical skills can bring about. Men of science are examining themselves; and it is with profound respect and in a sincere attempt to discern the bearing of the drama involved, that we must consider the anguish of a scientist of genius like Albert Einstein.

It is not enough to draw the attention of the peoples to the world-destroying catastrophes which the discoveries of modern physics may well lead to, if another armed conflict should occur. Fear is not enough to make men wise. And it is not enough to tell them that these same discoveries, if used for purposes of peace, can open unprecedented vistas of prosperity and freedom to the human race. A possibility is not enough to create happiness. What is required of human intelligence is an awareness of the fact that we have entered a crucial age in our history, a period when, under pain of death, the gigantic implements of power obtained by the scientific mastery of matter must be made subject to reason, in overcoming the irrational temptations to which human beings are liable, especially in their collective existence. It is also necessary to understand that there is an inner hierarchy and a vital inter-connection among the virtues of the human soul, so that, whereas the province of science deals with the *means,* the realm of *ends* pertains to something which is not science, and is not commensurable with it, and is called wisdom. We can be assured of neither peace, nor liberty, nor dignity in the world of tomorrow so long as, in the structures of civilization and in the consciousness of men (and of the scientists themselves) science and wisdom are not reconciled, and the practical applications of science are not rigorously submitted to right ethical will and to the true ends of human life. There was a time when we expected science to solve or do away with problems of ethics, metaphysics and religion, then we counted on the scientists to constitute one day the spiritual authority which would lead mankind toward the green pastures of necessary progress. Today we have to defend science against those who, after asking of it more than it could give, now accuse it, just as unreasonably, of being bankrupt. And, on the other hand, we see men of science engaged in a serious internal examination, in which is questioned the relationship between their conscience as men and the possible use of their work as scientists. We even see them in danger of being treated by the states as mere industrial ore made particularly valuable by its output in terms of discoveries. Thus it is the very dignity of science and of the scientist which is at stake; and it is to maintain and preserve this dignity, as well as to direct the applications of science toward the welfare of the world and not toward its destruction, that mankind stands in need of a powerful renewal of the disciplines of wisdom, and of a re-integration of ethical, metaphysical and religious truths into its culture, and of that reconciliation of science and wisdom which I have mentioned above.

II. CAN INTELLECTUALLY DIVIDED MEN CO-OPERATE IN PRACTICAL MATTERS?

I have spoken of a few problems which concern all of us because they relate to certain spiritual and cultural conditions dealing with that to which Unesco aims to contribute, namely the building of peace. My final remarks will bear upon another type of problem, which refers to the proper work of Unesco and to the kind of agreement in the midst of diversity which is required by that work.

At first glance there is something paradoxical in Unesco's task: it implies intellectual agreement among men whose conceptions of the world, of culture, of knowledge itself are different or even mutually opposed. In my opinion it behooves us to face this paradox, which is but an expression of the great distress in which the human spirit finds itself today.

Modern thought has been labeled with *Babelism,* and not without reason. Never indeed have men's minds been so deeply and cruelly divided. As human thought is pigeon-holed into more and more specialized compartments, it becomes more difficult to bring to consciousness the implicit philosophies to which each of us, willy nilly, is committed in actual fact. Doctrines and faiths, spiritual traditions and schools of thought come into conflict without it being possible for the one even to understand the signs which the others use to express themselves. Every man's voice is but noise to his fellow-men. However deep we may dig, there is no longer any common foundation for speculative thought. There is no common language for it.

How then, under these circumstances, is an agreement conceivable among men assembled for the purpose of jointly accomplishing a task dealing with the future of the mind, who come from the four corners of the earth and who belong not only to different cultures and civilizations, but to different spiritual lineages and antagonistic schools of thought? Should an agency like Unesco throw up the game, give up any assertion of common views and common principles, and be satisfied only in compiling documents, surveys, factual data and statistics? Or should it, on the contrary, endeavor to establish some artificial conformity of minds, and to define some doctrinal common denominator—which would be likely, in the course of discussion, to be reduced to the vanishing point?

I believe that the solution must be sought in another direction; precisely because, as I pointed out at the beginning, Unesco's goal is a practical one, agreement among its members can be spontaneously achieved, not on common speculative notions, but on common practical notions; not on the affirmation of the same conception of the world, man and knowledge, but on the affirmation of the same set of convictions concerning action. This is doubtless very little; it is the last refuge of intellectual agreement among men. It is, however, enough to undertake a great work, and it would mean a great deal to become aware of this body of common practical convictions.

I should like to note here that the word *ideology* and the word *principle* can be understood in two very different ways. I have just said that the present state of intellectual division among men does not permit agreement on a common *speculative* ideology, nor on common *explanatory* principles. However, when it concerns, on the contrary, the basic *practical* ideology and the basic principles of *action* implicitly recognized today, in a vital if not a formulated manner, by the consciousness of free peoples, this happens to constitute *grosso modo* a sort of common residue, a sort of unwritten common law, at the point of practical convergence of extremely different theoretical ideologies and spiritual traditions. To understand that, it is sufficient to distinguish properly between the rational justifications, inseparable from the spiritual dynamism of a philosophical doctrine or a religious faith, and the practical conclusions which, separately justified for each, are, for all, analogically common principles of action. I am fully convinced that my way of justifying the belief in the rights of man and the ideal of liberty, equality, fraternity, is the only one which is solidly based on truth. That does not prevent me from agreeing on these practical tenets with those who are convinced that their way of justifying them, entirely different from mine, or even opposed to mine in its theoretical dynamism, is likewise the only one that is based on truth. Assuming they both believe in the democratic charter, a Christian and a rationalist will, nevertheless, give justifications that are incompatible with each other, to which their souls, their minds and their blood are committed, and about these justifications they will fight. And God keep me from saying that it is not important to know which of the two is right! That is essentially important. They remain, however, in agreement on the practical affirmation of that charter, and they can formulate together common principles of action.

Thus, in my opinion, can the paradox I pointed out earlier be solved. The ideological agreement which is necessary between those who work toward making science, culture and education contribute to the establishment of a true peace, is restricted to a certain body of practical points and of principles of action. But within these limits there is, and there must be, an ideological agreement which, for all its merely practical nature, is none the less of major importance. In the justification he offers for that body of practical principles, everyone commits himself fully, with all of his philosophical and religious convictions—how could he speak with faith, if not in the light of the speculative convictions which quicken his thought? But he is not entitled to demand that others subscribe to his own justification of the practical principles on which all agree. And the practical principles in question form a sort of charter which is indispensable for any effective common action, and the formulation of which would matter to the good itself and the success of the peace-making work to which their common endeavors are dedicated.

That is why it is fitting to stress the crucial importance—but limited to the merely practical order—of the common ideology to which Unesco has appealed from the time of its foundation. I am thinking especially of the declaration of principles, in the Preamble drafted at the London Conference, in which it is stated, among other things, "that the great and terrible war which has just ended was made possible by the denial of the democratic ideal of dignity, equality and respect for the human person, and by the will to substitute for that ideal—in making capital out of ignorance and prejudice—the dogma of the inequality of races and of men"; and "that, since the dignity of man requires that culture and education be made available to all in view of fostering justice, freedom and peace, all nations have in this regard sacred obligations to fulfil in a spirit of mutual assistance." That is why I believe that one of the most important tasks undertaken by the United Nations is the new declaration of the rights of man, which Unesco is helping to draft.*

More generally speaking, if it is true not only that the end of Unesco's task is a practical end, but also that on this practical end depend both the harmony of the minds within the organization and the effectiveness of its action, then is it not obvious that the Organization of the United Nations for Education, Science and Culture can best carry out the difficult work assigned to it, and fulfil the expectations of the peoples, by concentrating primarily on a small number of far-reaching accomplishments? This view has already been supported by the representatives of France on previous occasions.

I should like to add another recommendation: that we should not give to human sciences less interest and favor than to the physical ones. Do we not believe that the knowledge of man and the development of a new humanism are, in the order of science and culture, what matters most for the preparation of a peace lastingly established? Our knowledge of man, moreover, is much more difficult and much less advanced than our knowledge of the physical world; it needs all the more to be helped and encouraged. In this connection one is surprised to see that up to now, in the budget of Unesco, not only are the credits set aside for administrative expenses considerably larger than those destined to creative undertakings, but that even within this latter category, the amounts allocated to human sciences—to that science of human relations whose importance President Roosevelt rightly stressed—have been much smaller than those ear-marked for the sciences concerned with material nature.

I should like to add that to make science, culture and education serve the tasks of peace does not mean separating the organization of scientific work from action for peace in such a way that on the one hand we would concentrate on purely theoretical and supposedly exhaustive, analysis and planning and, on the other hand, we would confine our practical activity for peace to a mere effort to spread Unesco's ideals by means of the techniques of mass-communication. Our specific task consists rather in organizing the scientific work itself, as well as the cultural and educational work,

---

*This new declaration was adopted and proclaimed by the United Nations on December 10, 1948.

with a view to the task of peace to be promoted. It is from the very beginning that the organization should aim at that practical goal, so that by serving science itself in its very search for truth, by furthering international co-operation between scholars and scientists, and by urging them to join forces in enlightening common consciousness, we may succeed in interesting the world of science and culture, as well as peoples themselves in the work of peace pursued by Unesco.

In any case, what I have tried to set forth in the latter part of this address is the practical nature of the goal toward which we are working together, and the necessity that our task be based on practical convictions and practical principles held in common. The goal of Unesco is to contribute to the peace of the world, to international security and to the lasting welfare of peoples, through the instrumentality of Education, Science, and Culture. We all know that there is no peace without justice. We all know that, in the words of the Preamble I referred to a moment ago, "since wars are born in the minds of men, it is within the minds of men that the defences of peace must be erected." And we all know that if the work of peace is to be prepared in the thought of men and in the consciousness of nations, it is on the condition that minds come to be deeply convinced of principles like the following: Good politics is first and foremost a politics that is just;—every people should strive to understand the psychology, the development and traditions, the material and moral needs, the proper dignity and historic calling of the other peoples, because every people should look out not only for its own advantages but for the common good of the assembly of nations;—this awakening of mutual understanding and of the sense of the civilized community, though it supposes (given the age-old habits of human history) a sort of spiritual revolution, nevertheless answers requirements of public emergency in a world which, from now on, is one world for life or for death, while it remains disastrously divided as to political passions and interests;— to place national interest above everything is a sure means of losing everything;—a community of free men is only conceivable if it recognizes that truth is the expression of what *is*, and right the expression of what is *just*, and not of what is most expedient at a given time for the interest of the human group;—it is not permissible to take the life of an innocent man because he has become a useless and costly burden to the nation, or because he impedes the successful undertakings of any group whatsoever;—the human person is endowed with a dignity which the very good of the community presupposes and must, for its own sake, respect, and is also endowed, whether as a civic, or as a social or working person, with certain fundamental rights and fundamental obligations;—the common good comes before private interests;—the world of labor has a right to the social transformations required by its coming of age in human history, and the masses have a right to participate in the common treasure of culture and of the spirit;—the domain of consciences is inviolable;—men of various beliefs and spiritual lineages must recognize each other's rights as fellow-citizens in the civilized community;—it is the duty of the state, for the very sake of the common good, to respect religious freedom as well as freedom of research;—the basic equality of men makes prejudices of race, class or caste, and racial discrimination, offences against human nature and the dignity of the person as well as a deep-seated threat to peace.

If a state of peace worthy of the name, firm and enduring, is to be established one day among the peoples of the world, this will depend not only upon the economic, political and financial arrangements reached by diplomats and statesmen, nor will it depend solely upon the juridical building up of a truly supra-national co-ordinating organism endowed with efficient means of action; it will depend also upon the deep adherence of men's consciousness to practical principles like those I have recalled. And, to state things as they are, it will depend also upon that *bigger soul* which, according to Bergson, our world, become technically greater, needs, and upon a victorious outpouring of that supreme and free energy which comes to us from on high, and whose name we know—whatever may be our religious denomination or school of thought—to be brotherly love, a name which has been pronounced in such a manner by the Gospels that it has stirred the conscience of man for all time.

CHAPTER FOURTEEN

CHRISTIAN HUMANISM

I. THE SECULARIZATION OF THE CHRISTIAN IMAGE OF MAN

EVERY great period of civilization is dominated by a certain peculiar idea that man fashions of man. Our behavior depends on this image as much as on our very nature—an image which appears with striking brilliance in the minds of some particularly representative thinkers, and which, more or less unconscious in the human mass, is none the less strong enough to mold after its own pattern the social and political formations that are characteristic of a given cultural epoch.

In broad outline, the image of man which reigned over medieval Christendom depended upon St. Paul and St. Augustine. This image was to disintegrate from the time of the Renaissance and the Reformation—torn between an utter Christian pessimism which despaired of human nature and an utter Christian optimism which counted on human endeavor more than on divine grace. The image of man which reigned over modern times depended upon Descartes, John Locke, the Enlightenment, and Jean-Jacques Rousseau.

Here we are confronted with the process of secularization of the Christian man which took place from the sixteenth century on. Let's not be deceived by the merely philosophical appearance of such a process. In reality the man of Cartesian Rationalism was a pure mind conceived after an angelistic pattern. The man of Natural Religion was a Christian gentleman who did not need grace, miracle, or revelation, and was made virtuous and just by his own good nature. The man of Jean-Jacques Rousseau was, in a much more profound and significant manner, the very man of St. Paul transferred to the plane of pure nature—innocent as Adam before the fall, longing for a state of divine freedom and bliss, corrupted by social life and civilization as the sons of Adam by the original sin. He was to be redeemed and set free, not by Christ, but by the essential goodness of human nature, which must be restored by means of an education without constraint and must reveal itself in the City of Man of coming centuries, in that form of state in which "everyone obeying all, will nevertheless continue to obey only himself."

This process was not at all a merely rational process. It was a process of secularization of something consecrated, elevated above nature by God, called to a divine perfection, and living a divine life in a fragile and wounded vessel—the man of Christianity, the man of the Incarnation. All that meant simply bringing back this man into the realm of man himself ("anthropocentric humanism"), keeping a Christian façade while replacing the Gospel by human Reason or human Goodness, and expecting from Human Nature what had been expected from the virtue of God giving Himself to His creatures. Enormous promises, divine promises were made to man at the dawn of modern times. Science, it was believed, would liberate man and make him master and possessor of all nature. An automatic and necessary progress would lead him to the earthly realm of peace, to that blessed Jerusalem which our hands would build by transforming social and political life, and which would be the Kingdom of Man, and in which we would become the supreme rulers of our own history, and whose radiance has awakened the hope and energy of the great modern revolutionaries.

II. THE MODERN MAN

If I were to try now to disentangle the ultimate results of this vast process of secularization, I should have to describe the progressive loss, in modern ideology, of all the certitudes, coming either from metaphysical insight or from religious faith, which had given foundation and granted reality to the image of Man in the Christian system. The historical misfortune has been the failure of philosophic Reason which, while taking charge of the old theological heritage in order to appropriate it, found itself unable even to maintain its own metaphysical pretense, its own justification of its secularized Christian man, and was obliged to decline toward a positivist denial of this very justification. Human Reason lost its grasp of Being, and became available only for the mathematical reading of sensory phenomena, and for the building up of corresponding material techniques—a field in which any absolute reality, any absolute truth, and any absolute value is of course forbidden.

Let us therefore say as briefly as possible: As regards man himself, modern man (I mean that man who seemed himself to be modern, and who starts now entering into the past) modern man knew truths—without *the* Truth; he was capable of the relative and changing truths of science, incapable and afraid of any supra-temporal truth reached by Reason's metaphysical effort or of the divine Truth given by the Word of God. Modern man claimed human rights and dignity—without God, for his ideology grounded human rights and human dignity on a godlike, infinite autonomy of human will, which any rule or measurement received from Another would offend and destroy. Modern man trusted in peace and fraternity—without Christ, for he did not need a Redeemer, he was to save himself by himself alone, and his love for mankind did not need to be founded in divine charity. Modern man constantly progressed toward good and toward the possession of the earth—without having to face evil on earth, for he did not believe in the existence of evil; evil was only an imperfected stage in evolution, which a further stage was naturally and necessarily to transcend. Modern man enjoyed human life and worshipped human life as having an infinite value—without possessing a soul or knowing the gift of oneself, for the soul was an unscientific concept, inherited from the dreams of primitive men. And if a man does not give his soul to the one he loves, what can he give? He can give money, not himself.

As concerns civilization, modern man had in the bourgeois state a social and political life, a life in common without common good or common work, for the aim of common life consisted only of preserving everyone's freedom to enjoy private ownership, acquire wealth, and seek his own pleasure. Modern man believed in liberty—without the mastery of self or moral responsibility, for free will was incompatible with scientific determinism; and he believed in equality—without justice, for justice too was a metaphysical idea that lost any rational foundation and lacked any criterion in our modern biological and sociological outlook. Modern man placed his hope in machinism, in technique, and in mechanical or industrial civilization—without wisdom to dominate them and put them at the service of human good and freedom; for he expected freedom from the development of external techniques themselves, not from any ascetic effort toward the internal possession of self. And how can one who does not possess the standards of human life, which are metaphysical, apply them to our use of the machine? The law of the machine, which is the law of matter, will apply itself to him, and enslave him.

As regards, lastly, the internal dynamism of human life, modern

man looked for happiness—without any final end to be aimed at,
or any rational pattern to which to adhere; the most natural concept and motive power, that of happiness, was thus warped by the
loss of the concept and the sense of purpose or finality (for finality
is but one with desirability, and desirability but one with happiness). Happiness became the movement itself toward happiness, a
movement at once limitless and increasingly lower, more and more
stagnant. And modern man looked for democracy—without any
heroic task of justice to be performed and without brotherly love
from which to get inspiration. The most significant political improvement of modern times, the concept of, and the devotion to, the
rights of the human person and the rights of the people, was thus
warped by the same loss of the concept and the sense of purpose
or finality, and by the repudiation of the evangelical ferment acting
in human history; democracy tended to become an embodiment of
the sovereign will of the people in the machinery of a bureaucratic
state more and more irresponsible and more and more asleep.

III.   THE CRISIS OF OUR CIVILIZATION

I have spoken just now of the infinite promises made to man at
the dawn of modern times. The great undertaking of secularized
Christian man has achieved splendid results for everyone but man
himself; in what concerns man himself things have turned out
badly—and this is not surprising.

The process of secularization of the Christian man concerns
above all the idea of man and the philosophy of life which developed in the modern age. In the concrete reality of human history,
a process of growth occurred at the same time, great human conquests were achieved, owing to the natural movement of civilization
and to the primitive impulse, the evangelical one, toward the democratic ideal. At least the civilization of the nineteenth century remained Christian in its real though forgotten or disregarded principles, in the secularized remnants involved in its very idea of man
and civilization; in the religious freedom—thwarted as this may
have been at certain moments and in certain countries—that it willingly or unwillingly preserved; even in the very emphasis on reason
and human grandeur which its freethinkers used as a weapon
against Christianity; and finally in the secularized feeling which
inspired, despite a wrong ideology, its social and political improvements, and its great hopes.

But the split had progressively increased between the real be-

havior of this secularized Christian world and the moral and spiritual
principles which had given it its meaning and its internal consistency, and which it came to ignore. Thus this world seemed emptied
of its own principles; it tended to become a universe of words, a
nominalistic universe, a dough without leaven. It lived and endured
by habit and by force acquired from the past, not by its own power;
it was pushed forward by a *vis a tergo*, not by an internal dynamism.
It was utilitarian, its supreme rule was utility. Yet utility which is
not a means toward a goal is of no use at all. It was capitalistic
(in the nineteenth-century sense of this word, which is the genuine
and unmitigated sense), and capitalist civilization enabled the initiatives of the individual to achieve tremendous conquests over material nature. Yet, as Werner Sombart observed, the man of this age
was neither "ontologic" nor "erotic"; that is to say, he had lost the
sense of Being because he lived in signs and by signs, and he had
lost the sense of Love because he did not enjoy the life of a person
dealing with other persons, but he underwent the hard labor of
enrichment for the sake of enrichment.

Despite the wrong ideology I have just described, and the disfigured image of man which is linked to it, our civilization bears
in its very substance the sacred heritage of human and divine values
which depends on the struggle of our forefathers for freedom, on
Judaeo-Christian tradition, and on classical antiquity, and which
has been sadly weakened in its efficiency but not at all destroyed
in its potential reserves.

The most alarming symptom in the present crisis is that, while
engaged in a death struggle for the defense of these values, we
have too often lost faith and confidence in the principles on which
what we are defending is founded, because we have more often than
not forgotten the true and authentic principles and because, at the
same time, we feel more or less consciously the weakness of the
insubstantial ideology which has prayed upon them like a parasite.

IV. MARXIST AND RACIST DELUSIONS

The great revolutionary movements which reacted against our
secularized Christian world were to aggravate the evil and bring it
to a peak. For they developed toward a definitive break with Christian values. Here it is a question both of a doctrinal opposition to
Christianity and of an existential opposition to the presence and
action of Christ at the core of human history.

A first development continued and climaxed the trend of secu-

larized reason, the "anthropocentric humanism," in the direction
which it followed from its origin, in the direction of rationalistic
hopes, now no longer constituted solely as philosophical ideology
but as a lived religion. This development arises from the unfolding
of all the consequences of the principle that man alone, and through
himself alone, works out his salvation.

The purest case of this tendency is that of Marxism. No matter
how strong some of the pessimistic aspects of Marxism may be, it
remains attached to this postulate. Marxist materialism remained
rationalistic, so much so that for it the movement proper to matter
is a *dialectical* movement.

If man alone and through himself alone works out his salvation,
then this salvation is purely and exclusively temporal, and must be
accomplished without God, and even against God—I mean against
whatever in man and the human world bears the likeness of God,
that is to say, from the Marxist point of view, the likeness of "alienation" and enslavement; this salvation demands the giving up of
personality, and the organization of collective man into one single
body whose supreme destiny is to gain dominion over matter and
human history. What becomes then of the image of man? Man is
no longer the creature and image of God, a personality which implies free will and is responsible for an eternal destiny, a being
which possesses rights and is called to the conquest of freedom and
to a self-achievement consisting of love and charity. He is a particle
of the social whole and lives on the collective consciousness of the
whole, and his happiness and liberty lie in serving the work of the
whole. This whole itself is an economic and industrial whole, its
essential and primordial work consists of the industrial domination
of nature, for the sake of the very whole which alone presents absolute value, and has nothing above itself. There is here a thirst for
communion, but communion is sought in economic activity, in pure
productivity, which, being regarded as the paradise and only genuine goal of human endeavor, is but the world of a beheaded reason,
no longer cut out for truth, but engulfed in a demiurgic task of
fabrication and domination over things. The human person is sacrificed to industry's titanism, which is the god of the merely industrial community.

Rationalistic reason winds up in intoxication with matter. By the
same token it enters a process of self-degradation. Thus it is that
in the vision of the world offered by Marxist materialism, rationalistic
overoptimism comes to coincide, in many respects, with another

development, depending upon a quite opposite trend of mind, which may be described as an utter reaction against any kind of rationalism and humanism. The roots of this other development are pessimistic, it corresponds to a process of animalization of the image of man, in which a formless metaphysics avails itself of every misconception of scientific or sociological data to satisfy a hidden resentment against Reason and human dignity. According to this trend of mind the human species is only a branch which sprouted by chance on the genealogical tree of the monkeys; all our systems of ideas and values are only an epiphenomenon of the social evolution of the primitive clan; or an ideological superstructure determined by, and masking the struggle for life of class interests and imperialistic ambitions. All our seemingly rational and free behavior is only an illusory appearance, emerging from the inferno of our unconscious and of instinct. All our seemingly spiritual feelings and activities, poetic creation, human pity and devotion, religious faith, contemplative love, are only the sublimation of sexual libido or an outgrowth of matter. Man is unmasked, the countenance of the beast appears. The human specificity, which rationalism had caused to vanish into pure spirit, now vanishes in animality.

Yet the development of which I am speaking has its real sources in something much more profound, which began to reveal itself from the second half of the last century on: anguish and despair, as exemplified in Dostoevski's *Possessed*. A deeper abyss than animality appears in the unmasking of man. Having given up God so as to be self-sufficient, man has lost track of his soul. He looks in vain for himself; he turns the universe upside down trying to find himself; he finds masks and, behind the masks, death.

Then was to be witnessed the spectacle of a tidal wave of irrationality, of hatred of intelligence, the awakening of a tragic opposition between life and spirit. To overcome despair, Nietzsche proclaimed the advent of the superman of the will to power, the death of truth, the death of God. More terrific voices, the voices of a base multitude whose baseness itself appears as an apocalyptic sign, cry out: We have had enough of lying optimism and illusory morality, enough of freedom and personal dignity and justice and peace and faithfulness and goodness which made us mad with distress. Let us give ground to the infinite promises of evil, and of swarming death, and of blessed enslavement, and of triumphant despair!

The purest case of this tendency was Nazi racism. It was

grounded not in an idolatry of reason ending in the hate of every transcendent value, but in a mysticism of instinct and life ending in the hatred of reason. Intelligence for it was of use only to develop techniques of destruction and to pervert the function of language. Its demonic religiosity tried to pervert the very nature of God, to make of God Himself an idol. It invoked God, but as a spirit protector attached to the glory of a people or a state, or as a demon of the race. A god who will end by being identified with an invincible force at work in the blood was set up against the God of Sinai and against the God of Calvary, against the One Whose law rules nature and human conscience, against the Word Which was at the beginning, against the God of Whom it is said that He is Love.

Here, too, man is no longer the creature and image of God; a person animated by a spiritual soul and endowed with free will, and responsible for an eternal destiny, who possesses rights and is called to the conquest of freedom and to a self-achievement consisting of love and charity. And now this disfigured image of man is rooted in a warring pessimism. Man is a particle of the political whole, and lives by the *Volksgeist*, yet for this collective whole there is even no longer any decoy of happiness and liberty and of universal emancipation, but only power and self-realization through violence. Communion is sought in the glorification of the race and in a common hatred of some enemy, in animal blood, which, separated from the spirit, is no more than a biological inferno. The human person is sacrificed to the demon of the blood, which is the god of the community of blood.

There is nothing but human despair to be expected either from Communism or Racism. On the one hand, Racism, on its irrational and biological basis, rejects all universalism and breaks even the natural unity of the human race, so as to impose the hegemony of a so-called higher racial essence. On the other hand, if it is true that in the dialectic of culture, Communism is the final state of anthropocentric rationalism, it follows that by virtue of the universality inherent in reason—even in reason gone mad—Communism dreams of an all-embracing emancipation and pretends to substitute for the universalism of Christianity its own earthly universalism—the universalism of the good tidings of Deception and Terror, and of the immolation of man to the blind god of History.

V. THE IDEA OF A NEW CHRISTIAN CIVILIZATION

If the description which I outlined above is accurate, it appears that the only way of regeneration for the human community is a rediscovery of the true image of man and a definite attempt toward a new Christian civilization, a new Christendom. Modern times have sought many good things along wrong tracks. The question now is to seek these good things along right tracks, and to save the human values and achievements aimed at by our forefathers and endangered by the false philosophy of life of the last century, and to have for that purpose the courage and audacity of proposing to ourselves the biggest task of renewal, of internal and external transformation. A coward flees backward, away from new things. The man of courage flees forward, in the midst of new things.

Christians find themselves today, in the order of temporal civilization, facing problems similar to those which their forefathers met in the sixteenth and seventeenth centuries. At that time modern physics and astronomy in the making were at one with the philosophical systems set up against Christian tradition. The defenders of the latter did not know how to make the necessary distinction; they took a stand both against that which was to become modern science and against the philosophical errors which at the outset preyed upon this science as parasites. Three centuries were needed to get away from this misunderstanding, if it be true that a better philosophical outlook has actually caused us to get away from it. It would be disastrous to fall once again into similar errors today in the field of the philosophy of civilization. The true substance of the nineteenth century's aspirations, as well as the human gains it achieved, must be saved, from its own errors and from the aggression of totalitarian barbarism. A world of genuine humanism and Christian inspiration must be built.

In the eyes of the observer of historical evolution, a new Christian civilization is going to be quite different from medieval civilization, though in both cases Christianity is at the root. For the historical climate of the Middle Ages and that of modern times are utterly diverse. Briefly, medieval civilization, whose historical ideal was the Holy Empire, constituted a "sacral" Christian civilization, in which temporal things, philosophical and scientific reason, and the reigning powers, were subservient organs or instruments of spiritual things, of religious faith, and of the Church. In the course of the following centuries temporal things gained a position of autonomy, and this was in itself a normal process. The misfortune has been that this process became warped, and instead of being a process of distinction for a better form of union, progressively severed earthly civilization from evangelical inspiration.

A new age of Christendom, if it is to come, will be an age of reconciliation of that which was disjoined, the age of a "secular" Christian civilization, in which temporal things, philosophical and scientific reason, and civil society, will enjoy their autonomy and at the same time recognize the quickening and inspiring role that spiritual things, religious faith, and the Church play from their higher plane. Then a Christian philosophy of life would guide a community vitally, not decoratively Christian, a community of human rights and of the dignity of the human person, in which men belonging to diverse racial stocks and to diverse spiritual lineages would work at a temporal common task which was truly human and progressive.

In the last analysis, I would say that from the end of the Middle Ages—a moment at which the human creature, while awakening to itself, felt itself oppressed and crushed in its loneliness—modern times have longed for a rehabilitation of the human creature. They sought this rehabilitation in a separation from God. It was to be sought in God. The human creature claims the right to be loved; it can be really and efficaciously loved only in God. It must be respected in its very connection with God and because it receives everything—and its very dignity—from Him. After the great disillusionment of "anthropocentric humanism" and the atrocious experience of the anti-humanism of our day, what the world needs is a new humanism, a "theocentric" or integral humanism which would consider man in all his natural grandeur and weakness, in the entirety of his wounded being inhabited by God, in the full reality of nature, sin, and sainthood. Such a humanism would recognize all that is irrational in man, in order to tame it to reason, and all that is supra-rational, in order to have reason vivified by it and to open man to the descent of the divine into him. Its main work would be to cause the Gospel leaven and inspiration to penetrate the secular structures of life—a work of sanctification of the temporal order.

This "humanism of the Incarnation" would care for the masses, for their right to a temporal condition worthy of man and to spiritual life, and for the movement which carries labor toward the social responsibility of its coming of age. It would tend to substitute for materialistic-individualistic civilization, and for an economic system based on the fecundity of money, not a collectivistic economy but a "Christian-personalistic" democracy. This task is joined to today's crucial effort to preserve freedom from totalitarian aggression, and to a simultaneous work of reconstruction which requires no less vigor. It is also joined to a thorough awakening of the religious conscience. One of the worst diseases of the modern world, as I pointed out in an earlier essay,* is its dualism, the dissociation between the things of God and the things of the world. The latter, the things of the social, economic, and political life, have been abandoned to their own carnal law, removed from the exigencies of the Gospel. The result is that it has become more and more impossible to live with them. At the same time, Christian ethics, not really permeating the social life of people, became in this connection—I do not mean in itself or in the Church, I mean in the world, in the general cultural behavior—a universe of formulas and words; and this universe of formulas and words was in effect made subservient in practical cultural behavior to the real energies of this same temporal world existentially detached from Christ.

In addition, modern civilization, which pays dearly today for the past, seems as if it were pushed by the self-contradiction and blind compulsions suffered by it, toward contrasting forms of misery and intensified materialism. To rise above these blind compulsions we need an awakening of liberty and of its creative forces, of which man does not become capable by the grace of the state or any party pedagogy, but by that love which fixes the center of his life infinitely above the world and temporal history. In particular, the general paganization of our civilization has resulted in man's placing his hope in force alone and in the efficacy of hate, whereas in the eyes of an integral humanism a political ideal of justice and civic friendship, requiring political strength and technical equipment, but inspired by love, is alone able to direct the work of social regeneration.

VI. THE TRUE IMAGE OF MAN

The image of man involved in integral humanism is that of a being made of matter and spirit, whose body may have emerged from the historical evolution of animal forms, but whose immortal soul directly proceeds from divine creation. He is made for truth, capable of knowing God as the Cause of Being, by his reason, and of knowing Him in His intimate life, by the gift of faith. Man's dignity is that of an image of God, his rights derive as well as his duties from natural law, whose requirements express in the creature

*Scholasticism and Politics, 1940, Chapter I, page 22.

the eternal plan of creative Wisdom. Wounded by sin and death
from the first sin of his race, whose burden weighs upon all of us,
he is caused by Christ to become of the race and lineage of God,
living by divine life, and called upon to enter by suffering and love
into Christ's very work of redemption. Called upon by his nature,
on the other hand, to unfold historically his internal potentialities
by achieving little by little reason's domination over his own animality and the material universe, his progress on earth is not automatic or merely natural, but accomplished in step with freedom
and together with the inner help of God, and constantly thwarted
by the power of evil, which is the power of created spirits to inject
nothingness into being, and which unceasingly tends to degrade
human history, while unceasingly and with greater force the creative energies of reason and love revitalize and raise up this same
history.

Our natural love for God and for the human being is fragile;
charity alone received from God as a participation in His own life,
makes man efficaciously love God above everything, and each human person in God. Thus brotherly love brings to earth, through
the heart of man, the fire of eternal life, which is the true peace-
maker, and it must vitalize from within that natural virtue of
friendship, disregarded by so many fools, which is the very soul of
social communities. Man's blood is at once of infinite value and
must be shed all along mankind's roads "to redeem the blood of
man." On the one hand, nothing in the world is more precious
than one single human person. On the other hand, man exposes
nothing more willingly than his own being to all kinds of danger
and waste—and this condition is normal. The meaning of that
paradox is that man knows very well that death is not an end, but
a beginning. If I think of the perishable life of man, it is something
naturally sacred, yet many things are still more precious: Man can
be required to sacrifice it by devotion to his neighbor or by his duty
to his country. Moreover a single word is more precious than human
life if in uttering this word a man braves a tyrant for the sake of
truth or liberty. If I think of the imperishable life of man, of that
life which makes him "a god by participation" and, beginning here
below, will consist in seeing God face to face, nothing in the world
is more precious than human life. And the more a man gives himself, the more he makes this life intense within him. Every self-
sacrifice, every gift of oneself involves, be it in the smallest way,
a dying for the one we love. The man who knows that "after all,

death is only an episode," is ready to give himself with humility, and nothing is more human and more divine than the gift of oneself, for "it is more blessed to give than to receive."

As concerns civilization, the man of Christian humanism knows that political life aims at a common good which is superior to a mere collection of the individual's goods and yet must flow back upon human persons. He knows that the common work must tend above all toward the improvement of human life itself, enabling everyone to exist on earth as a free man and to enjoy the fruits of culture and the spirit. He knows that the authority of those who are in charge of the common good, and who are, in a community of free men, designated by the people, and accountable to the people, originates in the Author of Nature and is therefore binding in conscience, and is binding in conscience on condition that it be just. The man of Christian humanism cherishes freedom as something he must be worthy of; he realizes his essential equality with other men in terms of respect and fellowship, and sees in justice the force of preservation of the political community and the prerequisite which, "bringing unequals to equality," enables civic friendship to spring forth. He is aware both of the tremendous ordeal which the advent of machinism imposes on human history, and of the marvelous power of liberation it offers to man, if the brute instinct of domination does not avail itself of the techniques of machinism, and of science itself, in order to enslave mankind; and if reason and wisdom are strong enough to turn them to the service of truly human aims and apply to them the standards of human life. The man of Christian humanism does not look for a merely industrial civilization, but for a civilization integrally human (industrial as it may be as to its material conditions) and of evangelical inspiration.

VII. THE VERTICAL MOVEMENT AND THE HORIZONTAL MOVEMENT IN MAN'S LIFE

As regards, finally, the internal dynamism of human life, the man of Christian humanism has an ultimate end, God to be seen and possessed—and he tends toward self-perfection, which is the chief element of that imperfect happiness which is accessible to him in earthly existence. Thus life has meaning and a direction for him, and he is able to grow up on the way, without turning and wavering and without remaining spiritually a child. This perfection toward which he tends is not perfection of some stoic athleticism wherein a man would make himself impeccable, but rather the per-

fection of love, of love toward Another whom he loves more than
himself, and whom he craves above all to join and love even more,
even though in the process he carries with him imperfections and
weaknessses. In such an evangelical perfection lies perfect freedom,
which is to be conquered by ascetic effort but which is finally given
by the very One Who is loved, and Who was the first to love us.

But this vertical movement toward divine union and self-perfection is not the only movement involved in the internal dynamism
of human life. The second one, the horizontal movement, concerns
the evolution of mankind and progressively reveals the substance
and creative forces of man in history. The horizontal movement of
civilization, when directed toward its authentic temporal aims,
helps the vertical movement of souls. And without the movement
of souls toward their eternal aim, the movement of civilization
would lose the charge of spiritual energy, human pressure, and
creative radiance which animates it toward its temporal accomplishment. For the man of Christian humanism history has a meaning
and a direction. The progressive integration of humanity is also a
progressive emancipation from human servitude and misery as well
as from the constraints of material nature. The supreme ideal which
the political and social work in mankind has to aim at is thus the
inauguration of a brotherly city, which does not imply the hope
that all men will someday be perfect on earth and love each other
fraternally, but the hope that the existential *state* of human life
and the structures of civilization will draw nearer to their perfection, the standard of which is justice and friendship—and what aim,
if not perfection, is to be aimed at? This supreme ideal is the very
one of a genuine democracy, of the new democracy we are expecting. It requires not only the development of powerful technical
equipment and of a firm and rational politico-social organization
in human communities, but also a heroic philosophy of life, and
the quickening inner ferment of evangelical inspiration. It is in
order to advance toward such an ideal that the community must
be strong. The inauguration of a common life which responds to
the truth of our nature, freedom to be achieved, and friendship to
be set up at the core of a civilization vitalized by virtues higher
than civic virtues, all these define the historical ideal for which
men can be asked to work, fight, and die. Against the deceptive
myths raised by the powers of illusion, a vaster and greater hope
must rise up, a bolder promise must be made to the human race.
The truth of God's image, as it is naturally impressed upon us,

freedom, and fraternity are not dead. If our civilization struggles with death, the reason is not that it dares too much, and that it proposes too much to men. It is that it does not dare enough or propose enough to them. It shall revive, a new civilization shall come to life, on condition that it hope for, and will, and love truly and heroically truth, freedom, and fraternity.

CHAPTER FIFTEEN

A FAITH TO LIVE BY

A FAITH to live by? That is the topic of an inquiry I was requested to answer some years ago. I wonder whether these words satisfactorily present the question. What is necessary? What do we desperately need? A faith to live by? Or a faith to live for, a faith to live and die for? Just because our very life is at stake we are compelled to rediscover a faith to live and die for.

In the conception of many of our contemporaries faith, a faith to live by, far from being defined by any intrinsic and incontrovertible truth superior to man and human life, is merely something measured by human feeling or human needs, and destined to comfort human life's intellectual and social order, man's security in gaining possession of the earth and mastery over nature. From the time of Descartes and John Locke to the present, faith in God progressively became, for a great number of men, such a faith to live by. Finally, the religious feeling shifted to the cult of man. Our forebears undertook and pursued, with infinite hopefulness, a courageous, stubborn, and bright search for a faith to live by, which was a faith in man. This faith, during some decades, seemed allpowerful and produced splendid, though brittle achievements. The blunt fact is that we have lost faith in man.

What is called today atheistic existentialism is the clearest symptom of this fact. Kirkegaard's existentialism was the anguish of faith searching for incomprehensible and unspeakable reality. Even Heidegger's existentialism searches for the mystery of being through the heartrending experience of nothingness. But atheistic existentialism, such as has been heralded in recent years by writers who are but submissive mirrors of their time, does not reflect the anguish of man confronting nothingness; it reflects and declares the longing of man for nothingness. It expresses the temptation and desire not to be any longer. Yet this is impossible. Longing for nothingness and condemned to be, man abandons himself.

Communism, which is the ultimate vicissitude of anthropocentric rationalism, declares indeed its faith in man and offers itself as the last hope of optimism. Its optimism, however, is the optimism of the titanic and coercive energies of matter and technique; its man is totally subservient to the fate of history embodied in a social group. Faith in man, yes, but in what kind of man? In a collective man who deprives the individual of the liberties of the mind and makes himself into a spurious God emerging from the evolution of matter and the antinomies of history. The real man, the human person, is sacrificed to a devouring idol of the greatness of man.

Well, does despair, then, have the last word? Are we hemmed in by a tragedy?

As a matter of fact, reason demands that we have faith in man. Let us turn from the present world of man and look at the world of nature—I mean with an unsophisticated gaze. We see that, despite the all-pervading law of struggle and conflict, nature in its depths is permeated with an abysmal, supra-individual, and inescapable peace, which is the root goodness and the universal strength of being. And man, as part of nature, has an essence which is good in itself. We see that the evolution of the cosmos is a persevering, though constantly thwarted, movement toward higher forms of life and consciousness, which achieves a final victory in the human species and is taken over, within the limits of the latter, by human liberty, and that from the age of the cave man, the slow and painful progress of mankind testifies to energies in man which make any contempt of the human race childish and presumptuous. Consider with a little love any individual whatever in the anonymous common mass of poor humanity. The better you know him, the more you discover in him hidden resources of goodness that evil has been unable to destroy. Man's difficult condition comes from the fact that he is not only a creature of nature but also one of reason and freedom—elements which are weak in him and yet are his indestructible fortitude and tokens of his abiding dignity. No failures or stains can efface his original greatness.

Yes, we see that we must have faith in man. But we cannot. Our experience keeps reason in check. The present world of man has been for us a revelation of evil; it has shattered our confidence. We have seen too many crimes for which no just revenge can compensate, too many deaths in desperation, too sordid a debasement of human nature. Our vision of man has been covered over by the unforgettable image of the bloody ghosts in extermination camps.

Totalitarian craving for power, either Nazi or Communist, feeding on our moral weaknesses, has let devils loose everywhere. Everything we loved seems to have been poisoned; everything in which we trusted seems to have failed. Science and progress are turned to our own destruction. Our very being is threatened by mental and moral atomization. Our very language has been perverted: our words have become ambiguous and seem only able to convey deception. We live in Kafka's world. Where is our faith to live by?

Perhaps we have chosen the wrong road. Perhaps we would have done better to cling to a faith to live and die for, instead of seeking a faith to live by only. Ancient pagan wisdom knew that man's noblest, happiest, and most human aspect is appendant to what is supra-human, and that he can only live by what he lives for and is ready to die for, and what is better than himself. If our humanism has failed, it is perhaps because it was centered in man alone, and was utilitarian, not heroic; because it tried to relegate death and evil to oblivion, instead of facing them and overcoming them by an ascent of the soul into eternal life; because it trusted in techniques instead of in love, I mean in Gospel love.

St. Paul says that faith is the substance of things hoped for and goes on to say that it is a conviction of things not seen. Faith is an adherence to superhuman truth, an entrance into the realm of invisible and divine things; faith makes our whole life appendant to a living Whole which is infinitely better and more lovable than our own life; faith is a meeting with a Person Who is Truth itself and Love itself, and to Whom the giving of oneself results in supreme freedom, and in Whom dying results in indestructible life.

Then we live for truth, and that truth for which we live is stronger than the world. Then we live for love, and that love for which we live has made the world and will finally renew and transfigure it. Then we are free, and nothing in the world can break our faith.

And this God Who is Truth and Love has made man in His image. He has destined man to share in His own life. His Son died to save man. Despite all the catastrophies that man's failures and refusals cause, He leads man's history toward godlike fulfilment and transfiguration. Such is the greatness of man. Here is the rock of our faith in him.

Thus faith in man revives if it is rooted in the supra-human. Faith in man is saved by faith in God.

Human history moves in a definite direction. It depends on both natural and spiritual energies, and among all kinds of conflicts it tends to the natural fulfilment of mankind—namely, the progressive manifestation of the essence and potentialities of man, the progressive development of the structures of his knowledge, his moral conscience, and his social life, mankind's progressive conquest of unity and freedom. And it tends also to a spiritual fulfilment which is supra-temporal and transcends history, and which the Christian considers to be the kingdom of God and the revelation of the sons of God. Though inseparably intermingled, these two trends of history relate to two thoroughly distinct orders, and often the weakness of man opposes the one while furthering the other. And contrary to them, evil also develops in history; so that a downward movement causes losses to increase at the same time as an upward movement causes the sap of the world to produce better fruits. In the happiest periods of history evil is at work obscurely in the bloom of our precarious gardens. In the darkest eras the good is invisibly preparing unforeseeable conquests. And good is stronger than evil. Finally the saying of the Scriptures will be fulfilled: Tell the righteous that all is well. In old Jewish apocalyptic writings it was stated that the age of the sufferings of the Messiah would be the age of his greatest victories.

In presenting his book, *On the Threshold of the Apocalypse,* to one of his readers some thirty years ago, Léon Bloy wrote on the first page: "Cher ami donnez-vous la peine d'entrer" ("Dear friend, pray walk in"). It seems that, as a matter of fact, we did walk in. Our age appears as an apocalyptic age, a liquidation of several centuries of history. We are picking the grapes of wrath. We have not finished suffering. But at the end of the crisis a new world will emerge.

Bearing these thoughts in mind, experience—that very experience which jeopardized our faith in man—is transfigured. It assumes a meaning. It is not the revelation of the absurdity of existence but of the pangs and travail of history, not the revelation of the root baseness and contemptibleness of man but of his distress laid bare when he falls from his pride, and of the trials and catastrophes through which the abiding greatness of his destiny asserts itself.

A historical reckoning such as the one we are undergoing does not take place in one day. Time is necessary to make reason able to control the formidable material means which industrial and technological revolution has put in our frail hands. Time is necessary to stir up, from the depths of human bewilderment, the moral and

spiritual revolution that is incomparably more needed than any
other revolution. For nothing less is required than a terrestrial triumph of Gospel inspiration in the social behavior of mankind. We
do not lose hope. The renewal of civilization that we hope for, the
age of integral humanism, the time when science and wisdom are
to be reconciled, the advent of a fraternal commonwealth and of
true human emancipation—all this we do not await on the morrow.
But we await them on the day after the morrow, on that day which
St. Paul announced will be, after the worst darkness, like a spring-
time of splendor and renovation for the world.*

Every effort made in this direction will finally bear fruit. I refer
not only to the spiritual struggle of those who have heard, as Henri
Bergson put it, the call of the hero, and who awaken men to
evangelic love, but also to the temporal struggle of all those—scientists, poets, pioneers of social justice—who give themselves to the
improvement and illumination of their brothers' lives; I refer to the
daily exertion of those who can know no rest as long as their
brothers are in enslavement and misery. Even if the general state
of the world and our stock of accumulated errors prevent such efforts from overcoming at present the evils which are streaming in
from everywhere, they are preparing an era, under God, of greater
dignity for man and of expanding love.

Yet even that will be but a moment in the history of a small and
perishable planet. And hope goes beyond time. For finally we are
waiting for the resurrection of the dead, and life eternal. Such is
the faith we live for, and, because we live for it, the faith we
live by.

*Cf. St. Paul, Rom., 11:12, 15.

CHAPTER SIXTEEN

THE WAYS OF FAITH*

I. THE WONDERS OF FAITH

I AM only a philosopher—not even one of those theologians whom the Cartesian Minerva ironically described as supermen. In order to tell you something of the virtues of faith, I shall let someone speak for me who stands above philosophers and theologians—the Apostle Paul himself.

In the Epistle to the Hebrews which, if it was not drafted word for word by him, nevertheless conveys to us faithfully his doctrine and his thought, Saint Paul, speaking of Faith (Hebrews 11, 1–39), says: "Faith is the substance of things to be hoped for . . . By faith Abraham, when he was tried, offered Isaac . . . By faith also of things to come, Isaac blessed Jacob and Esau . . . By faith Moses, when he was born, was hid three months by his parents . . . By faith he left Egypt, not fearing the fierceness of the king . . . By faith they [the Israelites] passed through the Red Sea, as by dry land . . . By faith the walls of Jericho fell down . . . By faith [the heroes of God and the prophets] conquered kingdoms, wrought justice, obtained promises, stopped the mouths of lions, quenched the violence of fire, escaped the edge of the sword . . . put to flight the armies of foreigners. Women received their dead raised to life again. . ."

One would like to be able to draw a picture in our times of comparable wonders. This we cannot do. Is it because we are men of little faith? Is it because the present day is for faith itself a time of anguish and of purifying night? It is as though, while awaiting a new Enoch, a new Elijah, the signs and wonders have become so rare among us that, in order to have them keep on being present and bearing testimony, the Queen of Heaven feels compelled to move and intervene herself, from time to time, and write upon the

*Inaugural address to the *Semaine des Intellectuels Catholiques*, Paris, May 8, 1949.

ground of this planet letters of fire proffered to the inattention of
human beings.

II.   THE AVERAGE FUNCTIONING OF INTELLIGENCE IN OUR TIME:
THE CRYSTALLIZATION IN THE SIGN

Faith is itself a mystery. It is a gift from heaven, but a gift received within ourselves. One may observe first of all, it seems to
me, that the very way of functioning which characterizes as a rule
the state of the intellect in a period such as ours tends of itself, if
we are not careful, to react unconsciously upon the manner in
which faith is received within us, upon the paths faith follows
within us. Preceding the formulation of any atheistic philosophy,
sometimes even in philosophies which pride themselves on making
room for religion, even indeed on protecting it, there is a *way of
functioning* of the intellect which in itself is atheistic, because instead of longing for and cherishing being, it eliminates being and
nullifies it. Perhaps this is why Kierkegaard, faced with an intelligence functioning in such manner, and, moreover, fully aware of
the rights of reason, thought that faith exacted an anguished division of the soul and must always propose a perpetual challenge to
reason.

But the remarks I would like to make are of a less general nature:
They concern two typical aspects of the average functioning of
intelligence in our times. I am not speaking of philosophical theories
of knowledge, for in that case I would call the two aspects in question idealism and empiricism. I am speaking of the practical way
in which a large number of thinking individuals are led by the
tendency of the day to make use of their intellect—a way which
perhaps the philosophical theories of knowledge do no more than
reflect. This practical way of putting intelligence to use seems to
me revealed in two symptomatic tendencies, one of which I shall
take the liberty of calling *mental productivism* and the other the
primacy of verification over truth.

The productivism in question deals with concepts and conceptual
statements, signs and symbols. Judging by the intellectual behavior
of many of our contemporaries, one can say that we neglect as
much as possible and disregard the moment of passive receptivity
in which we *listen* before we *speak,* in which reality, grasped by
sense and experience, engraves itself upon the intelligence before
being brought, in a concept or an idea, to the level of intelligibility
in act. We concern ourselves only with the productive aspect of the

activity of intelligence, with the manufacture of concepts and ideas. The result is that what interests us above all are the signs thus manufactured, and not the real being which is made manifest by them. We go to meet reality with a gust of formulas. Ceaselessly, we launch prefabricated concepts. At the slightest contact with things a new concept is formed of which we make use in order to take advantage of being, while protecting ourselves from it and avoiding having to submit to it. We do not try to see, our intellect does not *see*. We content ourselves with signs, formulas, expression of conclusions. We seize upon some information about reality which can be of use to us, and that is all we want. But there is no question of using the information as a means of obtaining a view of reality itself. I read today's temperature on the thermometer: I shall, or shall not wear my overcoat; to try to learn what is heat itself is all the more out of the question because the quality of heat is such that we can get no intelligible grasp of it. In the same sense, I learn that one of my friends has lost his father; I shall write him a few words of sympathy; there will be no question of my seeing *into* his grief.

This way of functioning of the intellect—let us call it "crystallization in the sign"—is all very well for the physico-mathematical sciences, for these ask nothing of reality except that it furnish a base for the *entia rationis* on which they are working. But it does not suffice philosophy. It does not suffice faith. In both, the way the intelligence works is not through "crystallization in the sign" but through a "transition to the reality signified,"—as when knowing that my friend has lost his father I truly see into his grief, I truly understand that my friend is in sorrow. "Faith," says Saint Thomas,* "does not stop at statements, at conceptual signs; its object is nothing less than reality itself attained by means of these signs"—in other words, the actual mystery of the Godhead communicating Himself to us.

Well, it is this very thing that we are actually disregarding when we allow our faith to become contaminated by the mental productivism of which I have just spoken and follow the road taken by the modern intellect. For when we do this our faith crystallizes in the sign, it does not progress beyond, or as little beyond as possible, into the reality signified. It thus wrongs and offends the formulas of dogma, those infinitely precious conceptual signs whereby the living God tells of Himself in our language, and whose sacred virtue

*Sum. theol. II-II, 1, 2, ad 2.

and dignity lie precisely in the fact that they are the vehicles of
divine reality. There have always been Christians for whom to
know that Christ redeemed the sins of the world is a piece of purely
intellectual information of the same caliber as the information that
the temperature this morning was 54 degrees Fahrenheit. For them,
stating the fact is enough, just as the reading of the thermometer
is enough. They have every intention of using the information to
get to heaven; but they have never been face to face with the reality
of the mystery of the Redemption, with the reality of the sufferings
of the Savior. They have never experienced the shock of recognition of faith, the scales have not fallen from their eyes. What I
mean is that the way the modern intelligence functions risks making
this manner of living our faith appear normal whereas it tends indeed to empty faith of its content.

III.   THE PRIMACY OF VERIFICATION OVER TRUTH

The second typical aspect of the way of functioning of the contemporary intellect arises naturally from the first: I called it the
primacy of verification over truth. We take more interest in verify-
ing the validity of the signs and symbols we have manufactured
than in nourishing ourselves with the truth they reveal. Has not the
word truth itself become suspect to many contemporary philosophers? In fact our intelligence cares very little for the delights
and enchantments of the truth, any more than for those of being;
rather, our intelligence fears both; it stops at the level of verification, just as it stops at the symbol.

What are the consequences entailed by this attitude of mind with
regard to belief? Belief is based on testimony. Well, for us, belief
will not be that we are sure of a thing *as though we had seen it,*
on the oath of a trustworthy witness. Belief, for us, will be only that
we have verified the fact that a trustworthy witness tells us something *the entire responsibility for which we leave to him,* and which
we accept, of course, but without vouching personally for its truth.
That is all very well for history. But it will not do for faith. For
when it comes to faith I myself vouch for the veracity of what has
been told me. I am more certain of it than of my own existence,
since the Prime Truth itself has told me through the intermediary
of the Church, who here is but an instrumental cause, an instrument for the transmission of the revealed and is herself an object of faith: "id *quod* et *quo* creditur." "There are three things,"

writes Saint Thomas, "which lead us to the faith of Christ: natural reason, the testimony of the Law and the Prophets, the preaching of the Apostles and their successors. But when a man has thus been led as it were by the hand to the Faith, then he can say that he believes for none of the preceding motives; not because of natural reason, nor the witness of the Law, nor because of the preaching of men, but only because of the First Truth itself. . . It is from the light which God infuses that faith derives its certitude."*

Thus it is that he who receives the grace of faith hears in his heart the voice of the Father, and is supernaturally enlightened by the *lumen fidei*. In one single impulse he adheres to the objective truths presented by the Church, entrusts himself wholly to God, Prime Truth, in an ineffable relation of person to person, and clings to Christ the Savior.

There are believers, however, whose faith consists merely in accepting what the Church teaches them, while leaving the responsibility to the Church, and without risking themselves in this adventure. If they inquire as to what the Church holds to be the truth, it is in order to be advised as to the properly authenticated formulas which they are asked to accept, not in order to learn the realities which are given them to know. God said certain things to His Church; in turn the Church said them to me; it is the priests' business, not mine; I subscribe to what I am told, and the less I think about it the happier I am. I have a deaf and merely mechanical faith (or, as Frenchmen say, *la foi du charbonnier*), and I am proud of it. A faith of this kind if it were put to the extreme would be no longer a matter of knowledge at all, but merely one of obedience, as Spinoza saw it. And in that conception of faith I do not believe because of the testimony of the Prime Truth teaching me from within, by means of the truths universally presented by the Church. I believe because of the testimony of the Church *as a separate agent*, because of the testimony of the apostles taken apart from the testimony of the Prime Truth which they heard, but which means nothing to me; I believe because of the testimony of men. But then where is the theological virtue of faith? Here again the way in which intelligence functions within faith leads, practically speaking, to emptying faith of its content. Here again we have to do with an intellect which in its general way of functioning has given up seeing, and thus warps the conditions of exercise required by faith. For faith, which believes, and does not see, dwells—de-

*Comment on *Joann.* IV, lect. 5, a. 2.

pendent on the will moved by grace—in the intellect, the law of which is to see. From this it follows that it is essential for faith not to be quiet, to suffer a tension, an anxiety, a movement, which beatific vision alone shall end. *Credo ut intelligam.* Essentially, faith is an élan toward vision. That is why it wants to flower here below in contemplation, to come to be *fides oculata* through love and gifts of the Spirit to enter into the very experience of that which it knows through riddles and "in a glass, darkly."* Actually, faith's eyes are never closed. It opens its eyes in the sacred night, and if it does not see, it is because the light which fills this night is too pure for sight which is not yet one with God.

Precisely because faith is a supernatural virtue infused in the intellect, it is not surprising that the fortuitous ways in which the intellect functions at this or that moment in the evolution of humanity should tend to affect faith itself as to the conditions in which it is exercised. It is for evil rather than for good, as I have just pointed out, that faith is affected by the manner of functioning of our contemporary intelligence. A priest, a friend of mine, told me that according to his experience in hearing confessions, he thought that a number of cases of doubt and vacillations in faith, having nothing to do with the authentic trials of faith, depended on the mental habits of modern intelligence which I tried to describe a moment ago. He often asked himself whether the souls of whom he was speaking had ever truly had faith. In any case, it is clear that today the spirit of faith must climb back up the slopes of an intelligence no longer accustomed to the knowledge of being. And it is doubtless possible that a heroic faith is all the more pure and sublime, the more it dwells in an intelligence the general tenor of which is alien to it. Nevertheless, the fact is that faith itself, in order to find normal conditions for its exercise, needs to dwell in an intelligence which has itself regained its normal climate. An intellect patterned exclusively on the mental habits of technology and the natural sciences is not a normal climate for faith. Natural intelligence, the kind which is to be found in common sense, is spontaneously focused on being, as philosophy is in a systematic and premeditated way. Never have men had a greater need for the intellectual climate of philosophy, metaphysics and speculative theology; probably this is why they appear so fearful of them, and why such great care is taken not to frighten men with them. Yet they are the one and only way of restoring the intellect to its most

*St. Paul, I Cor., 13, 12.

natural and deep-rooted functioning, and thus to bring back the paths of intelligence into the main highway of faith itself.

IV. FAITH AND UNITY OF INSPIRATION

Faith is an obscure communion with the infinitely luminous knowledge which the divine Abyss has of itself. Faith instructs us in the depths of God. Faith stands above any human system, no matter how valid; it is concerned with the revealed data, with that very glory which cannot be named by any human name, yet has desired to make itself known to us in words which all may understand. The transcendence of faith entails a strange paradox: Faith in its own domain—in the things which are *of faith*—unites minds absolutely and upon certainties absolutely essential to human life; it alone can create such a unity of minds. But faith only creates unity of minds at the top; it does not create unity of doctrine or of behavior in any of the categories of our activities which touch only human affairs, affairs which are not *of faith*.

All the Catholic intellectuals before whom I am speaking are united in the Faith and in the discipline of the Church; for all other things, whether it be philosophy, theology, aesthetics, art, literature, or politics (although there are certain positions which none of them would hold since they are incompatible with Faith), they can and doubtless do hold the most various positions. The unity of faith is too lofty to impose itself upon human affairs, unless they have a necessary connection with faith. Faith itself wants reason to be free in human affairs and it guarantees this freedom. And intelligence is willing to be held captive, but by God alone, the Subsistent Truth.

Faith creates unity among men, but this unity is in itself a divine, not a human unity, a unity as transcendental as faith.

And yet is it not in the very nature of good that it should diffuse itself? Could it possibly be that from the peak of the eternal mountains divine unity does not come down into our plains, carrying with it continually its unifying virtue? Indeed, it does diffuse itself among us, it does communicate itself. Indeed, had we the spirit of faith; were our faith not anemic and ailing; were it to find in us those full conditions of exercise which it naturally demands; did that faith—informed by charity so as to become perfect virtue—inform in its turn all our intellectual and moral life,—then the transcendent unity of living faith would provide us with a unity at every level of our human activities: yet still in the mysterious and secret way, free and internal, and after the transcendent fashion

inherent in faith itself, not by any external conformity or regimen-
tation; not in a visible, formulated or tangible manner, but by the
wholly spiritual springs, the invisible breath of the workings of
grace. This would be a unity brought about by faith in the things
which are not of faith, in other words a unity of inspiration rather
than of objective doctrine or guidance. There exists no code or system capable of expressing such a unity; it arises at the wellsprings
of the soul like that peace which Jesus gives and which the world
cannot give.

Can we attempt to describe it still further? I would say that it
requires a certain attitude in regard to truth, to wisdom, to freedom, that faith alone can produce; I would also say that it depends
on the degree of depth to which the Gospels penetrate in us.

V.   A CERTAIN ATTITUDE IN REGARD TO TRUTH

The unity of which I speak requires a certain attitude toward
truth, a very simple attitude, evangelically simple, the attitude of
the simple in spirit. To have the artless integrity to prefer truth to
all intellectual opportunism and to all trickery, whether in philosophy, theology, art, or politics, to have such artlessness demands
a purification more radical than one might think. Every philosopher
loves truth, but with what admixtures? The super-ego of the philosopher is there to intrude into that love all sorts of monsters in
disguise. If you analyze the philosophical systems from that point
of view, you will find that a number of them embrace not only a
sincere search for the truth but at the same time a shrewd desire
to discover the most advantageous intellectual standpoints or to
connive with the times, or the passion to rule tyrannically over a
fictitious universe in order to compensate for various secret frus-
trations. If our love of the truth were purified by the flame of faith,
no doubt we would not all share in the same philosophy, but we
would be set free from an appreciable number of parasitical motives
that cause division among us.

I should like to point out, with regard to theology, another way
in which intellectual opportunism can commingle with the pursuit
of the truth. We know that theology, rooted in supernatural faith,
makes use of purely rational disciplines and of philosophy as an
instrument in order to acquire some understanding of the revealed
mysteries. For theology, philosophy is a *means;* therefore, theology
chooses to put to its service the philosophy most *useful* for its own
purposes. What philosophy, then, will be the most useful? The one,

more or less true, more or less false, which has the strongest hold
on our times, and is, therefore, most easily able to reach men's souls
and turn them to God? If that choice is made, then in the very
sphere of the highest knowledge you have opportunism taking the
place of truth. For the philosophy *the most useful* to theology can
only be the philosophy which is *the most true,* regardless of whether
or not it pleases our contemporaries. The instrument of knowing
placed at the service of theological truth cannot be other than
philosophic truth, as we attain it first of all in its proper order,
merely natural and rational. As disproportionate as it is before the
divine mystery, philosophy is raised up in its regard by the very
use which theology makes of it, as the instrumental cause is raised
above itself through being moved by the principal agent. But it is
philosophic truth, not philosophic error, which can be thus elevated.
In order to be a useful instrument, philosophy needs only to be true;
all that is asked of it is that it be true.

At this point I ask permission to say something parenthetical,
because I seem to hear some voices which are somewhat shocked.
"Ah, we see what you have been leading up to! You want us all to
be Thomists!" Would to God that, philosophers and theologians,
we were all Thomists; assuredly that is (as French pulpit orators
used to say), the grace that I wish for us. But I do not seek to
compel everyone to be a Thomist in the name of Faith! I do not
reproach theologians who are distrustful of Saint Thomas with a
lack of faith at all; surely not! only with a lack of intelligence.
They may be much more intelligent than I, that I do not doubt.
They are still not intelligent *enough.* Their faith is not in question.

My remarks on the subject of theology go no further than those
I proposed a while ago on the subject of philosophy. In both cases
I do not claim that the unity which comes down from faith will
produce a unity of system or of doctrine. But there is another sort
of unity, one that cannot be seen or formulated, that in the human
domain itself of theology and philosophy would be a unity of spirit,
a similar basic attitude of spirit. There is no doubt that it would diminish, but it would not suppress the diversity and opposition of
systems. We would not all be Thomists, but in the love of truth
which is in all of us there would be less mixed elements.

I want to say nothing unkind of anyone; it must be noted, however, that a certain firm resolution to have nothing to do with St.
Thomas hardly does honor to the perspicacity of certain intellectuals
who are intent on modern problems and modern consciousness. But

P

Thomism will always have two things against it: the teaching itself
which becomes commonplace in the schools with its text-books, its
stereotyped formulas, its inevitable simplifications and its routines;
and its proper technical perfection which frightens those minds who
consider themselves original and have not understood that the keys
prepared with so much care by St. Thomas are destined to open
doors, not to close them.

I have reached the end of my parenthesis. I would add that this
attitude toward truth which I have attempted to describe, and
which is induced in us by living faith, would be brought, were the
spirit of faith more widespread, not only into the domains of philosophy and theology, but also into the domain of art—a domain in
which truth is no longer the universal truth, but the truth of the
creative intuition of the artist, of his own individual treasure to
which he must be faithful at the cost of sacrificing all else. The
spirit of faith would also bring this attitude toward truth into the
domain of politics, a domain in which the name of the truth in
question is justice.

VI. A CERTAIN ATTITUDE IN REGARD TO WISDOM

I have spoken of the first attribute—the attitude toward the truth
—of the unity brought down in our midst by transcendent faith.
The second attribute of this unity is, it seems to me, a certain attitude toward wisdom. Wisdom is a savory science, *sapida scientia;*
it is fruition; and of the three wisdoms recognized by Saint Thomas,
metaphysical wisdom, theological wisdom and the wisdom of contemplation, this last, which operates in the superhuman way of the
Gift of Wisdom and is rooted in the living faith, preeminently de-
serves the name of wisdom. Well then, does not faith itself, as I
described it a while ago, tend inevitably toward contemplation,
toward the contemplative experience which faith alone however
does not suffice to procure, since this experience depends also upon
love and the gifts of the Holy Spirit? Had we more faith, we would
all reach out, each according to his own fashion, toward that experience of union with God which is the highest Wisdom; we would
understand that this alone makes action truly seminal. Moreover,
infused contemplation, since it is achieved by and in charity, tends
to superabound in action; but contemplation alone, with the trials
it imposes, truly dispossesses man of himself, truly makes of man an
instrument, a fellow-laborer with God. Even the most generous activity, if it is not mystically dispossessed, if it does not somehow

spring from the experience of contemplation—no matter how hidden, how disguised—runs the unavoidable risk of ending up in disillusion or in bitterness.

I believe that the spirit of contemplation is called upon to assume new forms, to make itself more pliable and bolder, to clothe itself in the love of one's neighbor in proportion as it spreads out into ordinary life. This means that action can be a disguise for mysticism, but it does not mean there can be a mysticism of action. There is no more a mysticism of action than there is one of inertia. Stop now, says the Lord, wait a minute, keep quiet a little; be still and learn that I am God.

Those of us who believe only in activity will doubtless have some surprises. We have all read Bergson's book on *The Two Sources of Morality and Religion*. We know the lesson taught by Aldous Huxley, who understands nothing of our dogma, but has grasped the supreme importance of spiritual experience for humanity. We know, in the activity of a Gandhi, how much was due to a certain mystical meditation, even though it could perhaps only belong to the natural order. Allow me to draw your attention to the fact that a book on the subject of contemplation written comparatively recently by a poet who became a Trappist sold tens of thousands of copies in the United States, as did also the book by the same author in which he tells of his conversion. This is only the most trifling indication, but it interests me particularly because I have the highest regard for Thomas Merton, and because for many years I have thought that the most active land in the world is obsessed with a latent desire for contemplation. Where will that desire lead? One thing is certain, and that is that all over the world, no matter where, wisdom and contemplation are daughters of God whom the human race cannot do without.

VII.   A CERTAIN ATTITUDE IN REGARD TO FREEDOM

The third attribute of the unity brought us by faith is, it seems to me, a certain attitude toward freedom. If it is true that grace makes us the adopted children of God, then the more profoundly faith works in us the more intensely it leads us to long for the liberty of those children, that freedom of autonomy which means independence with regard to creatures and dependence with regard to God. Then the theologian is free with respect to theology, the philosopher with respect to philosophy, the artist with respect to art, the politician with respect to politics. And this kind of freedom through which we transcend whatever makes each one of us most inflexibly committed is also a mysterious way, ironic and winged, of transcending our differences.

Then, too, we are free so far as the world is concerned. We give the invisible the upper hand over the visible. We put social and legal considerations in their true place which is doubtless important, but still secondary. It is to the forces at work in human souls that we give primary importance. We respect in them the liberty which we have become aware of in ourselves. We do not desire the conversion of heretics into ashes, but rather to the living God. We grasp the meaning of Saint Augustine when he said: "You think you hate your enemy, when it is your brother whom you hate." In the most arduous conflicts our awareness of the rights and dignity of our adversary is never obliterated. That internal freedom, when it is mutually recognized and respected, is the sign of a unity of the mind which touches the very heart of human relations and which in a certain way reflects in us the transcendent unity of supernatural faith.

VIII. THE DESCENT OF THE GOSPEL WITHIN US

Thus it is by relationship to the truth, to wisdom, to liberty that the unity we seek to define is characterized; it goes down to the heart of human things; but it is only concerned with an attitude of mind and is too subtle and tenuous to have an expression which can be formulated. Nevertheless, it is also of central importance and of overpowering significance: all this because it stems from a supernatural virtue which itself unites men through their adherence to divine truth, but through that adherence alone,—in other words because it is that transcendent unity as radiating beyond itself, and being poured into the fragile vessels that we are.

It is clear that this additional unity produced by faith, this spread-out unity, depends on how deeply the Gospel has penetrated in us. Each time one rereads the Gospel, one sees a new reflection of its demands and its freedom, as terrible and sweet as God Himself. Happy is he who loses himself forever in that forest of light, who is ensnared by the Absolute whose rays penetrate everything human. The greater our experience, the more inadequate we feel in the practice of the evangelical teachings, yet at the same time the more we are impressed with their mysterious truth, the more deeply we desire it. That is what may be called the descent of the Gospel within us. When we meditate upon the theological truths, it is we who do the meditating upon theological truths, but when we meditate upon the Gospels, it is the Gospels which are speaking to us; we need only give heed. And no doubt, when we are thus walking with Matthew, Mark, Luke and John, the One Whom the Gospel tells of draws near us, to make our mind a little more alert. *Mane nobiscum, Domine, quoniam advesperascit.* Abide with us, Oh, Lord, for the evening comes.

It seems to me that if a new Christendom is to come into being, it will be an age when men will read and meditate upon the Gospel more than ever before.

IX. ABOUT A NEW CHRISTENDOM

I have just alluded to the idea of a new Christendom. Actually, I have been alluding to it throughout this chapter: for what else are those roads that faith travels through the depths of human activities; what else is that unity brought down among us by faith which I referred to, if not one of the preliminary conditions for the coming of a new Christendom?

The dearer our hope, the more we must beware of illusions about it. The hope of the coming of a new Christian era in our civilization is to my mind a hope for a distant future, a very distant future. My opinion about this was already intimated in a book written many years ago.* The events which have occurred since that time have only served to confirm these surmises—which are pessimistic as to the present, optimistic as to the future. After the war it would have been impossible for the spirit to assume control over the forces unleashed in the sick world save by a kind of heroism which could not be demanded of the nations. Since human intelligence has thus inevitably failed in its task, one can only hope that for the immediate future things will somehow settle themselves, thanks to the natural resources of human mediocrity, in other words thanks to a kind of animal shrewdness adjusting itself to the natural pressures of history. But taking as a whole the phase of the world's history which we have reached, it has become a commonplace remark to say that we have crossed the threshold of the Apocalypse. The atomic bomb is a brilliant advertisement for Léon Bloy.

But does that imply that the end of the world is due tomorrow, and that after the great crises no new phase of world history is to begin? As for me, I believe that a new phase will begin, and it is to

Humanisme Intégral, Aubier, Paris, 1936. (English translation, *True Humanism,* 1938.)

that phase that I delegate my hopes for the coming of a new age of Christian civilization, more successful than the Middle Ages. But it will come *after* the general liquidation of which we have seen the beginnings, and especially after the major event prophesied by Saint Paul, the reintegration of Israel which, according to the Apostle, will be for the world like a resurrection from the dead. Let us admit that from now till then there are still too many poisons to eliminate. Let us also admit that things have come to such a pass that for Christianity again to take the lead in history the Gentiles could well afford to receive help from the ancient spirit of the prophets.

If the new Christendom that we await is only to come in the distant future, it is nevertheless from the present moment that we must prepare the way for it and with even greater energy. In this realm of the historic preparations for a new Christendom, may I say that obviously all Christian peoples have their special contribution to offer, and that in considering some of the apostolic initiatives which are now being taken in France we are helped to realize that the universality of the Church embraces virtually all of human kind, so that Catholics must have care not only for their own interests, their fellow Catholics, their works, their legal positions, but also for everything which touches upon the sacred interests of man, as well as upon the cause of justice, and the demands of natural law, or the sufferings of the persecuted and the abandoned, the injured and the humiliated of all the earth. We are also helped to realize that the best means of winning victories of the spirit is not to barricade oneself behind the walls of a fortress but to go out into the highways to conquer through love and the gift of self.

CHAPTER SEVENTEEN

BLESSED ARE THE PERSECUTED

"BLESSED are they that suffer persecution for justice's sake: for theirs is the kingdom of heaven." The eighth beatitude confirms all the others (*est firmitas quaedam omnium beatitudinum,* says Thomas Aquinas)* and corresponds to the first; the circle of the Gospel's happiness, which begins with the poor in spirit, is completed with the persecuted. They are placed under the same banner; theirs is the kingdom of heaven, *ipsorum est:* meaning not simply a possession to which they have a right, but something much more intimate, inward and personal—a thing which is within me as well as belonging to me, sweet to my heart more than is my very self. In the very manner in which Christ speaks to the poor and the persecuted, there is a tenderness which already consoles them. He, the Poor and Persecuted One above all the elect of poverty and persecution, is not He, Himself, also the Kingdom of heaven? He tells them that He is their treasure.

Those who suffer persecution for justice's sake. We know fairly well, or we believe we know, what persecution is. But "for justice's sake"—there we feel we are meeting the mystery. What is this justice for the sake of which they are persecuted?

The saints know what this justice is. They are persecuted for the sake of the justice which makes us adopted sons of God and participants in His life through grace; they are persecuted for the sake of the divine truth to which they bear witness and of that Word that was made flesh and came to dwell in the world and that "His own received not"; they are persecuted for the sake of Jesus Who is our justice. "Blessed are ye when they shall revile you and persecute you and speak all that is evil against you, untruly, for My sake: be glad and rejoice, for your reward is very great in heaven. For so they persecuted the prophets that were before you."

Blessed are the saints. They know wherefor they suffer. Not only do they suffer "because" of justice but "for" justice, which they

---

**Sum. theol.* I-II, 79, 4, ad 2; *cf.* 3, ad 5.

219

know and which they love and which they will. Throughout their worst sufferings and darkest nights they are well pleased to be persecuted, they know that persecution is good for them, they desire it as an earthly paradise, they are astonished and worried when deprived of it. But never are they without it long. Saint Paul reassures them, and tells them that all those who seek to live piously in Christ Jesus will suffer persecution. When they are persecuted they have that which they have wanted, they have that blessedness of the Gospel for which they have asked, they are well served.

And when they die abandoned and persecuted, the Holy Spirit, Who is called the Consoler, reminds them in the depths of their hearts of all the things which their Savior has told to those who are His, and this same Spirit places before the eyes of their souls the image of Him Who has opened the way for them and Who has loved them first, even unto giving His life for them upon that cross of redemption to the partaking of which He has now invited them.

The saints are not the only ones to be persecuted. And the inner justice of the soul is not the only justice for the sake of which men suffer persecution. All those who have sought justice within the earthly community and who have suffered for its sake imprisonment or exile or death, and who, moreover, have been looked upon as fools or bad citizens, have not been offered the promise of the eighth beatitude for such things. The immediate object of their thirst, the immediate cause of their sufferings is not to conform themselves to the Savior Who makes man just and holy in the eyes of God; it is rather the imperfect and obstructed labor whereby a little more human justice is introduced into the world. They have battled against the oppression or enslavement in which men have been held by men of another race, another nation, another caste or another class; they have battled with human means and for human ideas; they have very often had to have recourse to force against force, to appeal to the wrath of the humiliated and downtrodden. On occasion their passion for earthly justice has been fevered by hatred and violence, or else led astray by great illusions which made them dream of constructing without God the Jerusalem of peace, or else darkened by a despairing revolt against both Creator and creation. At times they have sought to be titans, at times "grand inquisitors" like the one in Dostoievsky's tale. Unhappy are those who seek for justice in this world and suffer persecution for its sake. To have done so is not sufficient to assure them of the promise of the kingdom of heaven. And the justice they seek and for the sake of which they suffer, they usually see rejected by men throughout the length of their struggle for it, and betrayed by men at the very moment when it succeeds in passing among men.

Nonetheless they also have that which they wanted. For they have labored in time and under the law of time, for a thing of the earth and an idea entrusted to history. Time will bring them their reward when they are no longer, their labor and their trouble will bear their own fruits on earth, under forms which they themselves had not foreseen, carried along as these were in the eddies of the vast stream of history. I do not mean to say that every effort on behalf of justice automatically succeeds in producing an effect in the history of mankind; I am not so optimistic. To my mind everything depends upon the depth at which the thirst after justice and the suffering on behalf of justice—however mixed these may be—have been brought into life within the secret substance of a heart and of a spirit. If a man's actions, before having been given outward manifestation, have thus been given birth in the very depths of the spirit, they will equally take their place in the depths of history, and there they will go their shadowy way until one day a few of the seeds they contain come to take root and bear fruit among men.

Having granted this, it is clear that if we look upon things in themselves, there is neither separateness nor conflict between thirst after the justice of God's kingdom and thirst after justice in this world. The one summons the other. The latter threatens to drive a man out of his mind unless it is accompanied by the former; the former requires and awakens and sanctifies the latter. How could men who daily ask that the will of the Father be done on earth as it is in heaven not thirst after justice on earth and within the human community? How could men who believe in the Gospel as far as eternal life is concerned not believe in it for life here below—how could they resign themselves to men's earthly hope in the Gospel being disappointed? So long as misery and slavery and injustice exist in the lives of men and in their perishable societies, there will be no rest for the Christian. He knows that his God suffers in the persons of all those who are suffering, all those who are spurned, all those who are persecuted throughout the world.

Hence blessed is he who suffers persecution for the sake of the justice of God's kingdom and for the sake of justice on earth. He suffers abuse for Christ's sake while he is abused for the sake of his

brethren. Blessed is he if he is doubly persecuted. The more unhappiness he bears in his temporal existence because of his desire
for justice in temporal society and because of his undertaking to
"ransom the evil of the days," the more utterly and the more surely
is he persecuted; and the more may he consequently hope, if he is
faithful, to have in life everlasting, which for the just begins even
here below, the blessedness of the persecuted; the more can he hope
that his is the kingdom of heaven.

* * *

In our own day we have seen monstrous persecutions: persecutions in which hangmen beyond number scientifically organized
cruelty and assassination, bending themselves to the task of debas-
ing man in his body and in his soul, not striking down persons condemned by reason of a faith to which at least they gave witness,
but masses of men and women guilty only of the fact of their existence and wiped out like rats. And we have been able to verify the
truth of the saying that next to the hangman what men detest most
is his victim. Confronted by these great herds of victims left to
their fate, the Christian questions his heart, and his faith.

He thinks of his Jewish brethren, of the ancient devastated olive
tree onto whose branches he has been grafted. Six million Jews have
been *liquidated* in Europe. Other masses of human beings have been
deliberately exterminated, also in millions, in Poland, in Russia—
either by the Soviet Government or by the Germans in the areas
they controlled for a time during the war—in a number of unhappy
countries which passed from one oppressor to another, and this in
the name of "living space" or through political vengeance. But the
Jews, they have been put to death because one hated them in their
very quality as a people and because one had the will to wipe their
race from the face of the earth. This animal hatred possessed supernatural eyes. In truth it was their very election, it was Moses and
the prophets who were harried in them, it was the Savior sprung
from them against whom the grudge was held. It was the dignity
of Israel, into which the Catholic Church prays God to have all
nations enter, which was buffeted in these despised wretches treated
like the vermin of the earth. It was our God Who was slapped and
scourged in His fleshly lineage, before being persecuted openly in
His Church. How strangely knowing a hatred, more aware than the
weak love of our own hearts: even before that day foretold by
Saint Paul, when Church and Synagogue would be reconciled, and

which would be for the world like life from the dead, both of these
have been reunited in this devilish hatred. Just as Christianity was
hated because of its Jewish origins, Israel was hated because of the
belief in original sin and redemption and because of Christian pity,
all of which had their source in Israel. As has been pointed out
with deep truth by the Jewish writer, Maurice Samuel,* it was not
because the Jews killed Christ but rather because they gave Christ
to the world that Hitlerian anti-Semitism in its rage dragged the
Jews along all the roads of Europe, through filth and blood, tore
from their mothers children thenceforth not even possessed of a
name, undertook to dedicate an entire race to despair.

Thus it happened that unwitting Israel has been pursued by the
same hatred which also and first of all pursued Jesus Christ. Its
Messiah shaped Israel to His own likeness in suffering and humiliation before shaping it, one day, to His likeness in the light. Such
are the bloody first-fruits of that fulness of Israel of which Christians, if they lay it to heart, can detect the precursory signs in the
sequence of abominable events whose memory will always burn in
us—and yet which are already sinking to oblivion in the hearts of
those who survive. Like strange companions, Jews and Christians
have together journeyed along the road to Calvary. The great mys-
sterious fact is that the sufferings of Israel have more and more
distinctly taken on the shape of the cross.

But could they have any knowledge of this, all these innocent
people struck down like the accursed? Blessed are they that suffer
persecution—these words were not for them, were not yet for them,
at least on our earth. They knew not that they suffered persecution
for the sake of the Just Man sprung from Jesse's tree and from a
daughter of Israel full of grace; they knew not of what "receiving,"
of what reintegration—wherein the kingdom of heaven would be
within reach of their people—the persecution they suffered was the
hidden tidings.

At least they did know that they were dying because of their
people's calling and because their people's passion for justice on
earth is hated by this world. At least those of them who cherished
in their hearts the spirit of prayer and the religion of the Scriptures
must have known that they were dying for the hope which is Israel's.

*   *   *

But the Christian thinks of other abandoned beings, whose lot

*Cf. Maurice Samuel, *The Great Hatred*, Knopf, New York, 1940.

awakens in the soul an unbearable anguish because of the unrelieved darkness of the night in which death struck them. I do not refer to those who throughout Europe lay in prisons and concentration camps, were shot down as hostages, perished under torture, because they had resolved not to bend their heads to the conqueror. Such men and women knew why they were suffering and why they were dying. They had chosen to fight and to resist, they gave their lives for freedom, for their countries, for human dignity. I am thinking rather of those poor human beings who had done nothing except their humble daily tasks, and upon whom in a flash death pounced like some wild beast. Immolated by the whims of war and of savagery—persecuted not for the sake of justice about which they were not even thinking, but for the sake of the innocent fact of their mere existence at an unlucky point in time and space. What are, moreover, their sufferings and their death except the likeness and brief summary wherein we may read the sufferings of millions of the poor and forsaken throughout the course of the centuries, ground down without defense by the great mill of pride and greed which is as old as humanity? The conquered who have been reduced to slavery, the untouchables, the classless, the slaves of all ages, the black men sold at auction by merchants of human flesh, women and children laboring in sweatshops, the proletarians of the industrial age, all those whom misery has stripped of their human condition, all the accursed of the worldly community.

Certain events which took place during the course of the Second World War serve as terrible illustrations of what I am attempting to say. Let us remember the slaughtered people of the village of Lidice, the women and children machine-gunned and burned alive at Oradour on Corpus Christi, those peasants of the Vercors whom the SS, seeking vengeance for the fighting achievements of the underground, suddenly seized in their peaceful homes and hung head downward, encouraging dogs to tear at their faces. Let us remember others who by every artifice were induced to die in despair, for instance by hanging them just a little above the level of the ground so that they would jump continuously until their strength failed them and the hangman's rope strangled mere shreds and tatters of a human being. Let us remember those Jews overwhelmed with weariness, who, after weeks of bloody journeying, upon arriving at Büchenwald, would lay themselves of their own accord upon the steps of the crematorium; let us remember the unfortunates who were starved to death in sealed railway carriages. Where lay the consolation of these persecuted innocents? And how many others died completely forsaken. They did not give their lives, their lives were taken from them, and under the shadow of horror. They suffered without having wanted to suffer. They did not know why they died. Those who know why they die are greatly privileged people.

It all seems to take place as though the death agony of Jesus—being so divinely vast—must be divided into its contrasting aspects in order that some image of it might pass into His members, and that men might completely participate in this great treasure of love and of blood. The saints of their own wills enter into Christ's passion, offering themselves along with Him, in knowing the secrets of the divine life, in living in their souls their union with Him, in putting into action, in the depths of their being, the gifts they have received. In any torture of the body or of the spirit, in the abysses of utter abandonment, they are still privileged people. The beatitude of the persecuted illumines their earthly existence. The more they are abandoned, the more can they say with John of the Cross: "Mine are the heavens and mine is the earth, mine are men, the just are mine and mine are the sinners; the angels are mine and the Mother of God and all things are mine; and God Himself is mine and for me. What then, O my soul, dost thou ask and dost thou seek? All this is thine and everything is for thee. . . ."*

But those wholly and completely forsaken, the victims of the night, those who die as though they were the outcasts of earthly existence, those who are hurled into Christ's death agony without knowing it and without wanting it—all these are making manifest another aspect of the same agony, and surely it is necessary that all be made manifest. Jesus gave His life because He willed it. But He likewise was "made sin for us";† He was "made a curse for us, for it is written: cursed is everyone that hangeth on a tree";‡ He was abandoned by God on His cross of misery, without protection against suffering, without help against those who persecuted Him.§ As a legacy left to His saints, He said: *Into Thy hands I commend My spirit.* And as a legacy left to His other flock, He said: *My God, My God, why hast Thou forsaken Me?* The great flock of the truly destitute, of those dead without consolation—would He not take care of those who bear this mark of His agony? How could it happen that their very forsaking itself would not

*St. John of the Cross, *Avisos y Sentencias,* Silv., IV, p. 235.
†II Cor., 5, 21.
‡Gal., 3, 13–14.
§*Sum. theol.* III, 47, 3.

serve as the signature of their belonging to the crucified Savior, and as a supreme title to His mercy? At the corner of death, in the moment when they pass to the other side of the veil, and the soul is on the verge of leaving a flesh for which the world had no use, is there not yet time enough to say to them: Thou shalt be with Me in paradise? For them there are no signs, for them hope is stripped as bare as they are themselves; for them, to the bitter end, nothing, even from the direction of God, has shone forth in men's eyes. It is in the invisible world, beyond everything earthly, that the kingdom of God is given to these persecuted ones, and that everything becomes theirs.

INDEX OF NAMES

JACQUES MARITAIN,

born in Paris in 1882, has long been recognised
as one of the most influential thinkers in contemporary philosophy. Since 1906, the year of
his conversion to Catholicism, he has been a
central figure in the Neo-Scholastic movement
of the Twentieth Century and has lectured on
the philosophy of St. Thomas Aquinas in uni-
versities all over the world.

His many books are famous. Since 1914,
when as Professor of Philosophy at the *Institut
Catholique de Paris* he published his critical
attack on the philosophy of his former master,
Henri Bergson, Maritain has written numerous
philosophical works propagating, reinterpre-
ting, re-applying the doctrines of St. Thomas
Aquinas, and in contact with modern metaphysical problems he has shown the inex-
haustible power of Thomist thought.

In addition to these academic works, Maritain has also dealt with present-day political
and social problems, and has written wisely
and independently on burning topics of recent
history, on racial intolerance, and on the principles of democracy.